Death of the Father

# Death of the Father

## An Anthropology of the End in Political Authority

*Edited by*

John Borneman

*Berghahn Books*

NEW YORK • OXFORD

Published in 2004 by

Berghahn Books

www.berghahnbooks.com

© 2004 John Borneman

Library of Congress Cataloging-in-Publication Data

Death of the father: an anthropology of the end in political authority / edited by
John Borneman.
   p. cm.
Includes bibliographical references and index.
ISBN 1-57181-111-7  (alk. paper)
1. Political anthropology. 2. Authority. 3. Patriarchy. I. Borneman, John.

GN492.25.D43 2003
306.2—dc21

2002043991


British Library Cataloguing in Publication Data

A catalogue record for this book is available from
the British Library.


Printed in the United States on acid-free paper

# Contents

# Preface

## Rupture, End, Death, Closure

Rupture, end, death, closure—different moments in the transformation of regimes. This volume seeks to theorize ruptures in political authority by examining the end of regimes and the mythologization of these ends. Its focus is restricted to a specific subset of regimes that collapsed around the end of World War II ("1945") and the end of the Cold War ("1989"). For shorthand, we refer to the end of "totalizing" and "patricentric" authority, of an authority that represents itself as the single source and locus of meaning, as the "Death of the Father."

Accompanied by a web site (http://cidc.library.cornell.edu/DOF/), this volume represents and analyzes the end of totalizing, patricentric regimes; the relation of the leaders' mode of death to this end; and attempts at regime closure following this death. It considers these moments in regime transformation through an analytics of changes in their symbolic forms and affect, which are particularly vital to the processes of democratization of successor regimes. Six anthropologists take up ruptures following the end in four state political forms: Fascist Italy (1943), Nazi Germany (1945), Imperial Japan (1945), and the State Socialist regimes of East Germany (1989), Romania (1989), the Soviet Union (1991), and Yugoslavia (1991). Changes in regime are considered in light of the death of the leader/fathers: Mussolini (1943), Hitler (1945), Hirohito (1989), Honecker (1989), Ceauşescu (1989), Lenin and Stalin (1924 and 1953), and Tito (1991). In all but two cases we begin with a temporal discrepancy between a physical death and a social death. In the case of Italy and Japan, the regime's death precedes that of its leader; in Germany and Romania, the deaths are coterminous; in the Soviet Union and Yugoslavia, the death of the leader(s) precedes that of the regime.

How does one know when a regime ends? In a sense, no regime ever really ends, since its traces can be found, or rediscovered and reinvigorated, centuries after its death. An end is not only always disputed but also must be retroactively claimed—and thereafter repeatedly proclaimed, in literature, film, historiography, and commemorative events. The twentieth century was characterized by a proliferation of regime ends, as dictatorial forms of rule—most often totalizing and patricen-tric—once eagerly embraced, were then later vigorously and abruptly rejected in Oedipal-like acts of parricide. As we enter a new century, we are witnessing a nearly universal embrace of democratic form, what Churchill called "the worst of all possible systems, the only problem [being] that none of the others is better." In this context, then, it might be useful to inquire into the kind of transformations out of which democra-tizing processes are expected to flourish. For this purpose, we have selected extreme cases: the transformations out of some of this century's most notorious, prototypical totalizing and patricentric regimes. Although we expect our insights to apply to a wide range of regimes in all conti-nents, for the sake of parsimony we have limited our comparisons to the ethnographic examples with which we have developed ethnographic competence as individuals.

Several aporias accompany any attempt to conceptualize regime change. First, although the end is not always coterminous with the death of the leader, a regime rarely ends before the leader dies. Frequently the much sought-after regime closure, a settling of accounts, occurs long after the physical death of the leader. Second, a regime might end without any acknowledgment or recognition of this fact by the participants, perhaps even accompanied by a denial that anything much has changed. Or, alter-natively, people might represent themselves as having effected a change in regime when in fact, from any external perspective, that change is difficult to recognize. Hence, self-representation of the end can never be sufficient proof of a change; yet it is an essential condition to take into account in an anthropological inquiry into the end. How do people come to represent themselves as having ended, or departed from, a specific regime of authority? How does this self-representation relate to the death of the leader? What does this self-representation mean for the successor regime?

Our selection of cases for comparison is drawn from two symbolic ruptures—"1945" and "1989"—and from the end of the two macropolit-ical regime types—"totalitarianisms" of left and right—that were responsible for much of the violence in the twentieth-century Western world. The immediate successor regimes of Fascist Italy and Nazi Ger-many represented themselves as having dramatically changed, as com-pletely repudiating forms of authority that characterized the prior regime, and they adopted democratic forms of government. The succes-sor to Imperial Japan, the third Axis power from World War II (and the one case we take up from outside of Europe), represented itself as both continuous in symbolic form (the emperor system) but also radically changed in its most essential institutional arrangements, which were democratized under American tutelage. What the three successors to former Axis powers had in common was a repudiation of both the death and reproductive cults that had been indispensable to the symbolic forms of the previous regime. In short, at the end they strove for imme-diate closure. Today this legacy is expressed in the peculiar significance of the elimination of war-making activities and the death penalty—as a social taboo on killing the other.

The other regimes we consider, the State Socialist type in East-Central Europe, dissolved from 1989 to 1991 in a series of domino effects. For comparative purposes, we have taken up East Germany, Romania, Yugoslavia, and the Soviet Union. The diversity of sociopolitical contexts here, and the short time that has elapsed since the changes, make for difficult comparison. None of these most recent changes (except for East Germany), moreover, have resulted in a total dissolution and repudiation of old structures of authority. Yet each successor regime informs us of a different lesson in the art of ending a regime and in the possibility of closure. Among these variants, the case most difficult to characterize as a rupture, end, or closure, is Yugoslavia. In 1991, there was certainly a rupture. Yugoslavia dissolved into a series of Slavic republics, a change that began with Tito's death in 1979 but also coincided with the collapse of the other socialist regimes in 1989. But the self-representations of what changed varies—as series of ends, new beginnings, regression into a prior fantasized pre-Tito form, or repetition compulsion—depending on the frame used by individuals in the different successor regimes. In short, while much has changed for all of the individuals in the former Yugoslavia, the direction and perceptions of change are not uniform. Only some ends seem to suggest change to a democratic future.

## Representing Symbolic Form and Affect

The performance of contemporary political authority includes both subjection to practices, norms, and rules, as well as the exercise of power over forms of subjection. One of our great debts to Foucault is in alerting us to the first part of this equation, to how power is exercised by subjects over themselves through submission to norms of selfhood. But Foucault's effort to move the study of politics away from its obsession with external coercion—"the repressive hypothesis"—has resulted in a relative analytical neglect of conscious attempts to exercise power over forms of subjection. We seek to bring these two aspects of authority together, and to examine how modern authority operates simultaneously on three interconnected levels—domestic, governmental, and transcendent—levels that draw upon both secular and sacred elements.

We also attend to the affective dimensions of political authority, to the efficacy of symbolic forms that are not easily put into textual form, in particular, the ubiquitous use of visual and aural stimuli. Written descriptions of image and sound can approximate visual and aural form, but this translation is partial. Textualization of form is always a re-presentation; it re-cognizes an experience that does not derive its primary efficacy from cognition. The efficacy of many images, especially when combined with sound, is based more on visceral and reactive effects than on rational understanding of them. Inattention to the efficacy of form, based on the assumption that all experience can be translated into written prose, tends to skew the study of affect toward those aspects that are assimilable to textual strategies. Yet the affective dimension of authority in image and sound, as modern political advertising has successfully demonstrated, may be able to circumvent logical thought or linguistic representation. In short, much as replicating a song melody in social science prose vitiates the melody of its affective force, submitting political imagery to textual operations of understanding (e.g., semiotic or hermeneutic) occludes the primary appeal of the image. That appeal is oriented less to an understanding of its object than to an emotional reaction.

Therefore, this project includes, via a web site, visual and aural components that *complement* the written essays in this volume. They cannot replace the written essays, and therefore they also do not seek to replicate the information provided in these pages. Rather, they seek to maintain the integrity of image and sound so as to comprehend the affective force of authority. By replicating and representing through collage and juxtaposition rather than translating into written discourse, aural and visual experiences elicit reactions to the symbolic forms of authority that better approximate affective force.

## History of the Project

The origins of this volume rest with a panel that I organized at the American Anthropological Association (AAA) Meetings in 1995. It was followed by an invited Team Residency of one week in 1996 at the Rockefeller Foundation's Bellagio Conference Center, and by a second Team Residency of ten days at Bellagio in 1997. The first residency involved work on analysis of individual cases and initial filming for the video; the second enabled us to construct a solid comparative framework for the individual cases and to do filming for a potential video, and made possible the construction of an interactive web site.

The outcome should be viewed as the product of an international dialogue between six anthropologists, a historian, an anthropologist/historian, a composer/media artist, and a digital/electronic archivist. Credit for most of the planning and implementation of the web site goes to Linda Fisher, with initial assistance from Noni Korf Vidal. Moreover, Linda Fisher has been the primary conduit of an international search for aural and visual archival materials. Tone Bringa, Maria Pia Di Bella, Kyung-Koo Han, John S. Schoeberlein, and I were at the initial AAA panel in 1995, as was Nicholas Dirks, who served as discussant. David A. Kideckel, Linda Fisher, and Baber Johansen (as discussant) joined us in 1996, as did Noni Korf Vidal the following year.

## On a Personal Note

I might say a few words about my own motivations for this project. Having grown up in the placid, peaceful Midwestern United States, my own experiences with authority are simple in comparison to those analyzed here. It is perhaps, above all, my confrontation with that difference, between the triviality of my own experience and the trauma of the other, that has spurred me on in this project. In retrospect, I could trace the origin of my interest back to the question of what changed in Germany after Hitler's death, after the end of Nazism. But that is too easy and too abstract.

Although the question of the relation between the political and personal and the authority of the Father surfaced continually during fieldwork in Germany in the 1980s, it beckoned to me again shortly after my own father's death in 1995, at which time I was trying to register two other events. One had to do with the major changes in State Socialist political regimes of 1989 (which I had been studying ethnographically since 1986). Here they were, all within a few months of each other, collapsing, disintegrating, transforming themselves out of existence. Were these quick turnabouts in regime, these sudden disappearances, real? How could I trust what I was seeing? Are there any telltale signs that signal the actuality of a change?

The other event was a visit in 1994 to two of my closest friends from my undergraduate days, that is, twenty years after we had completed our degrees together. What struck me was that they had not only changed very little, but also seemed to be reversing earlier changes and consciously repeating the lives of their own parents about whom they had been critical some twenty years prior. Marriage, children, private homes—they were following the sequence like a beaver builds a dam, as if preprogrammed into the American way. They seemed to have abandoned all the utopic interests, which at one point we had shared and to which I continued to cling—or rather, they exchanged these interests for a more mundane vision.

If I experienced the one event, continuity in the lives of my friends, as mere loss of utopia, I experienced the other event, the death of my own father, also as liberation. It did not just end something for me, for the rupture in our relationship was well over a decade old. But his death provided closure to these other losses for which he had somehow been the locus. And it enabled me to begin an examination of the "Death of the Father."

# Acknowledgments

I wish to thank, above all, the Rockefeller Foundation, and especially those in charge of its Bellagio Conference and Study Center—Susan Garfield, Gianna Celli, and Pasquale Pesce—for their encouragement and support for this project. In addition to the support for two short visits in 1996 and 1997 as a "team project" at the Center, we received a small grant for materials for collection and assemblage of visual material from the Rockefeller Foundation Innovation Fund in 1996, and a larger grant the following year.

We have also received support from Cornell University's Rose Goldsen Fund on Images in Society, and for travel and research by our various universities, including Cornell's Office of the Provost, Institute for European Studies, and Peace Studies Program. Cornell's Institute for Digital Collections, under the direction of Thomas Hickerson, kindly agreed to host our web site on their server. I thank them all. I am very grateful to Baber Johansen for his critical comments on all of the essays while at Bellagio.

The project also benefited from comments from various audiences who, over the last several years, have listened to me present versions of this project. They include the Graduate Center of the City University of New York; the University of Bremen, Germany; Harvard University; and the University of California at Berkeley. Finally, I thank the anonymous reviewer for Berghahn Books.

# Introduction:
# Theorizing Regime Ends

*John Borneman*

The death of authority figures such as fathers or leaders can be experienced as either liberation or loss. Liberation because relations to such figures constrain through the exercise of authority, loss because these relations bind through emotional ties. In the twentieth century, the authority of the father and of the leader became closely intertwined; constraints and affective attachments intensified in ways that had major effects on the organization of regimes of authority. Fathers and leaders sent their sons and followers to die in gruesome wars of mass destruction and lured them into internal purification campaigns in the name of the collective body. Indeed, as sovereigns, their exercise of power in everyday life was more intimate if not more invasive than ever in recorded history. In those cases where the exercise of sovereignty by fathers and the leader involved events such as arbitrary and widespread killing, torture, and repression, domestic authority and national political leadership have produced trauma—a temporally delayed and repeated suffering of these events that can only be grasped retrospectively. The defeat of imperial and fascist regimes in 1945, and the implosion of communist regimes in 1989, were critical moments of rupture, or potential rupture, in the production of national trauma. Most self-representations of these breaks reconstruct the dissolution of authority as both liberation and loss. I am calling this end "Death of the Father."

This comparative project takes up the end of an authority crisis, a crisis in symbolic identification, which had crystallized around four state political forms: Fascist Italy, Nazi Germany, Imperial Japan, and the Communist or State Socialist regimes of East Germany, Yugoslavia, Romania, and the Soviet Union. It explores the end of political forms characterized by national trauma. Variously called "fascist," "Nazi," "imperial," "cult of personality," "totalitarian," "patriarchal," "paternalistic," "communist," or "state socialist," these regimes resist reduction to a common name, and even after their end, the nature of their identifications retains for us mystical and mysterious qualities to which we—lay and academic publics—continue to return. This should come as no surprise: authority is always exercised *in someone's name* and through an *identification*—naming and identification being two of the key mechanisms necessary for the enchantment that authority generally deploys to legitimate itself. Our focus is less on the origin and operation of these forms, about which much has been written, than on their ends, and the reconstruction of those ends in memory: on the modes of death—hanging, suicide, execution, old age—and the sequence of events following the collapse of authority. How do people come to represent themselves as having ended, or departed from, a specific leader and regime of authority? And if symbolization of the leader's living body was central to tyrannical authority, is the public symbolization of his mode of death and the dead body now central to the successor regime? This is an inquiry into the anthropology of ends.

The initial scenes of death and their sequencing with respect to regime end varied. In Italy, Mussolini and his mistress, Claretta Petacci, were executed together, hung by their feet, and kicked and spit upon by the public—and a new regime of sons, based on a public repudiation of fascism, was established. In Germany, Hitler first married his longtime mistress, Eva Braun, before taking cyanide capsules with her. The remains of his body, burned following his orders, were secretly moved around by the Soviet occupiers, while the German public endured an enforced silence about the scene of death and the whereabouts of the corpse; and under the tutelage of occupiers, two German states, both of which repudiated nazism, were established. In Japan, Hirohito renounced his godliness, as a condition of retaining his authority, and became human, only to die a natural death and be buried in a proper state funeral four decades later.

In the Soviet Union, first Lenin and later Stalin died suddenly, were mummified, and were then put on public display to be symbolically resuscitated when needed—still there after the dissolution of the Soviet Union in 1991. In Romania, Nicolae Ceauşescu and his wife, Elena, were executed together following a summary trial (select parts of which were shown on television four months later), their bodies initially placed in unmarked graves, which were subsequently marked and now serve as sites for public debate. In Yugoslavia, Tito's funeral, which was staged with great pomp and elegance and attended by many presidents, kings, and world dignitaries, was followed by a fight for succession that, within eleven years of Tito's death, tore the country apart in a genocidal and separatist war—a war that reversed Tito's project of "brotherhood and unity." Hanging and humiliation, suicide and silence, desacralization and confident state funeral, suspect natural death and mummification, execution and "secretive" public burial, anxious state funeral and genocidal fight for succession—these are the public faces and initial effects of the death of the Father, the symbolic forms taken at the end.

The end of these regimes—the mode of death and the self-representation of that end over time—directly affected the successor forms of authority, both domestic and political, and the democratizing processes that followed. By analyzing a small but select group of regimes that spanned most of this century, 1917 to 1991, and that ruptured in two great symbolic ends, 1945 and 1989, we begin a comparative social anthropology of caesurae: the end of traumatic political regimes, of its symbolic forms, political consequences, and probable futures. All of the societies we examine are European except for the Japanese case, which we hope, through comparison, will clarify and delimit some of the claims we make for European authority. We suspect that our theoretical insights about authority and regime transformation in Europe apply in some part to the death of comparable regimes elsewhere, including those of China's Mao, Indonesia's Sukarno, Chile's Pinochet, Spain's Franco, Syria's Assad, to give but five infamous examples. But general theoretical insights can at best explain only some aspects of any specific ethnographic reality. It remains for other scholars to demonstrate their utility, or its lack, in other places.

## Death, Sovereignty, and Life

What is common to the forms and regimes of authority examined in these essays? Do they share any essential features pertaining to the exercise of sovereignty? For one, they shared historicity. Responding to the collapse of empires, they faced similar problems in the construction of viable political authority. But more important for our project, these regimes were *totalizing* in their claims on sovereignty and *patricentric* in their leadership. They sought to *totalize* authority in that they claimed an absolute and exclusive right to rule—to decide who was to be included and excluded, who was to be killed, and how to live—in the name of a posited prior or future Utopian wholeness. This totalizing claim to power appealed to a premodern and nondemocratic form of sovereignty, which these regimes then incorporated into their legitimation strategies. Simultaneously, in order to secure their rule, they carried to new extremes the emerging form of modern sovereignty, characterized by Foucault (1978: 139) as a "biopolitics of the population" and an "anatomo-politics of the human body," concerned foremost with the regulation and management of life. This meant employing the new population sciences in projects of national eugenics, political repression, terror, and, for some, systematic genocide.[1]

These regimes were *patricentric* in that they attempted to unify their subjects and create a modern subjectivity through identification with a leader who becomes the general equivalent of his subjects, the standard of all value, but who himself operates outside measurement (cf. Goux 1990). This leader appropriates for himself all forms of paternal authority; all authority is exercised in his name. And he demands subjective identification—one of the outstanding features that most separates totalizing regimes from both the monarchical or imperial forms of power that preceded them, and from the democratic-republican forms of the nation that were contemporaneous to them. Monarchical and republican forms require mere obedience, not identification. Among the most novel aspect of these regimes, then, is their reliance on both premodern and modern forms of sovereignty, on both death cults and biopolitics, as well as a demand for subjective identification with the father.[2]

Our use of the term "father" appeals both to its Indo-European etymological references to power and political authority—to leadership—and to its contemporary associations with familial sentiment or physical paternity. The original usage of "father" in Indo-European mythology (including Sanskrit, Armenian, Greek, Latin, Old Irish, Gothic, and Tokharian) excludes the relationship of physical parentage, referring instead to "a permanent qualification of the supreme God" (Benveniste 1973: 170). Father was solely a classificatory term that indexed a universal source of authority. Eventually the term was extended beyond its initial classificatory use and employed to describe kinship, indexing an individual relationship to a particular person. This linguistic shift has, in turn, affected political leadership. We wish to draw attention to the way in which the relationship with the leader in the twentieth century becomes fused with the significance of familial sentiments at the same time as the leader becomes a general equivalent. By investing the relation to political authority with paternal affect, that is, with emotional qualities such as love, honor, loyalty, and fear, this authority partakes in both the power and the fragility of an intimate bond. In modern Europe, the semantic term "father" denotes a relationship with kin related consanguineously, and it takes on meaning in relation to complementary terms—"child," "son," or "daughter." Or, alternately, "father" becomes the basis for analogy of authority generally, sharing a signifying space or drawing from terms such as "uncle," "brother," or "mother."[3] Uncle, as we shall see particularly with respect to Hirohito and Japan (see Han, this volume), and to Stalin and the USSR (see Schoeberlein, this volume), frequently occupies one important symbolic position of the father. With respect to social authority, however, "father" is most frequently paired with "son," and it is this relationship that has been the model for conceptualizing Western political authority.

In Western conceptualizations of sovereignty, the relationship between "father" and "son" has undergone three successive transformations, in each case redefining the right to kill.[4] I call these ancient, medieval, and modern models, and I employ them heuristically as ideal types. In the first, or ancient model, as initially explicated by Foucault (1978: 136, 135), the sovereign either killed or refrained from killing; his power was "in reality the right to take life or let live." This form derived from the ancient doctrine of *patria potestas* and "granted the father of the Roman family the absolute right to 'dispose' of the life of his children and slaves." Following this line of inquiry, Agamben (1998) argues that such forms of authority are defined by their ability to threaten people with the possibility of transforming their existence into "naked life"; they can reduce individuals to objects without intrinsic value, agency, or rights. This was in fact a defining characteristic of Nazi authority (see Borneman, chapter 2, this volume).

The ancient model corresponds to the conventional power of the despot, whose political authority had no reproductive component and who required no religious legitimation or personal identification. As it developed in Roman law, the model for the despot became the pater (father), he who could punish or kill his son with impunity. The premodern world offers countless examples of this structure of sovereignty, where the familial father-son relationship serves as the model for political authority. It of course predates the Romans: consider Saturn and Jupiter; Abraham and Isaac; David and Absalom; Claudius and Hamlet; Duncan and Macbeth. In this model, the relation of father to son is not conceptualized as a private domain, subordinate and totally separate from that of governance. In fact, the sacrilegious act of parricide posed the greatest threat to authority; it was the most heinous possible crime, the "unthinkable." Later, when the emperor arrived on the Roman scene, his authority became superordinate, though still linked, to the domestic pater.

During the Middle Ages, a second model of sovereignty evolved out of premodern practice and developed around kingships. Christians introduced the necessity of religious legitimation for the exercise of much authority, in particular for killing, and, in the fourteenth century, they began ritualizing the status of victims. They also developed the king's Two Bodies doctrine, later explicated by Kantorowicz (1957). If the king could be assumed to have two bodies, one mortal and human, the other eternal and representing the body politic, his physical death would not result in the death of the eternal secular power. This new attribution of continuity and immortality to the body politic contributed to a redefinition of the relation between political and domestic authority. Christian kings increasingly took upon themselves the function of protecting a putatively separate "familial order," ruled in turn by the patriarchal domestic father. By the sixteenth century, a new concentration of power was emerging in the form of states, justified either by a theological-jural idea of a natural authority coming from God or by a particular reason of state. For the new leaders, the right to take life was no longer absolute but contingent on the defense of the sovereign. Thereafter, the king, or the despot, still had the right to take the life of his subjects, much as the father had the right to take the life of his sons, but only in defense of his power and only when backed by religious authority. In practice, of course, there were regular challenges to the rights of kings and fathers, including uprisings of subjects that resulted in the death of the sovereign and murder by sons.

The American and French Revolutions at the end of the eighteenth century mark the advent of a third, or modern, form of sovereignty: a national form that assumed an inherent worth for each life and therefore forbade the taking of life without cause. This assumption also came to characterize the nondemocratic states of the time, exemplified by the Prussian state's 1794 reform of criminal law that shortened the list of capital crimes and secularized the execution ceremony. The attitude toward death in this modern form is fundamentally ambivalent; it still grants the father a limited right to kill, but it also institutionalizes the death of the father himself in the form of ritual elections. Modernist doctrine still justified killing, but only as a "rational" safeguard for the society, only in the name of the nation, the population, or the species. The nineteenth-century father, for example, could no longer take the life of his own children, yet he retained the right to have them arrested and held in state prisons (Perrot 1990: 169). The old "power of death," wrote Foucault (1978: 140), "was now carefully supplanted by the administration of bodies and the calculated management of life." Inspired by the successes of the Americans and the French, democratization movements in the extant dynastic empires of Europe contributed to a demystification and desacralization of the sovereign's power. Indeed, since the end of the eighteenth century, European reform movements have arrogated to themselves the right to take the life of sovereigns in the form of revolutions, assassinations, or coups d'etat, and they have represented themselves as breaking with both premodern and medieval forms of the exercise of sovereignty.

It is no coincidence that eighteenth-century democratization movements and the figuring of modern notions of sovereignty coincided with a marked shift in the symbolization of death, mortality, and life. In this transformative period, death, writes Ariès (1981: 36), no longer remains "tame," or "close, familiar … diminished, defused"; instead it "becomes a terror so powerful that we no more dare to pronounce its name." Initially, death became such a terror due to profound changes in the experience of death in the domestic sphere. Only later was death organized around the massive killing fields of war. With scientific and medical intervention in and clarification of dying and death, doctors could frequently arrest the very act of dying. Life expectancy increased, death lost its routinized everydayness and became an exceptional event in the lives of survivors. In short, death was made into a self-conscious "terror" precisely because it became less random, less mystical, and less familiar than before. Much as death became a new "terror" at this time, so the sovereign began to lose his mystical hold on terror through the taking of life. With growing demands for rights by women and children, and increased state intervention in private life, many of the father's legal prerogatives also slowly eroded.

In the twentieth century, the decline in the number of random deaths was offset by an increase in the number of planned deaths, and this on an unprecedented historical scale. Massive killing and self-sacrifice for the future of the nation, the *Volk*, fatherland, state, or home—perhaps initiated by Napoleon—became the focus of new political death cults. Because every life was now in principle equal and valuable, the individual was no longer to die in vain. Lives could not be publicly wasted. Each death required a memorialization; each life was to be remembered forever. In this fashion, a secular remystification of death—as eternal life in memory or memorial—took place at the same time as religious authorities were losing their monopoly on defining the good death. No longer was the power over death assigned to sovereign religious and political authority, yet death, if ordered and administered, was still to be justified in the name of the Father.

Under the terms of modern sovereignty, the new death cults required alternative forms of legitimation. Their justification, Koselleck (1994: 12) concludes, was no longer simply the defense of life over death, or the defense of the sovereign, but the special "honoring of a violent death" in the name of the population. Within one hundred years of the American and French Revolutions, societies and political regimes in much of the world became engulfed in what Hobsbawm (1990) dubbed "the First Wave of Nationalism." After political leaders deployed this nationalism to mobilize "the people" for the futile killings of World War I, the authority of the remaining Christian monarchs and the legitimate exercise of the established forms of sovereignty collapsed. In quick succession, the Russian tsar in 1917, the Austrian Kaiser in 1918, and the German Kaiser in 1919—figures who still pretended to represent Christian monarchs—were killed or deposed, and eventually replaced by totalizing, patricentric regimes. This first wave of nationalism was largely responsible for the two global hot wars in the first part of the twentieth century, where socialist and liberal-democratic regimes fought together against fascist, Nazi, and imperial ones.

The Cold War in the second half of the twentieth century, by contrast, pitted "actually existing" socialist regimes against liberal-democratic ones. Although both socialist and liberal regimes claimed to be democratic, their public disagreements about economic organization (communist or capitalist) and about the nature of change (stability or revolution) provided a context for the Second Wave of Nationalism, primarily manifested in wars of national liberation and decolonization in the Third World. From the beginning, these various nationalisms worked in odd and uneven complicity with the ancient, medieval, and modern forms of sovereignty. Differences notwithstanding, each new nationalism justified killing and the "calculated management of life" with similar, modern strategies of legitimation. Because each was responding in some way to popular demands for democratization and political identification, the father's exercise of power over his sons was both ideologically charged and limited. State regimes had to invent new forms of propaganda and means of indoctrination to mobilize, and new technologies of surveillance to control. The newly politicized masses, in turn, were frequently giddy with a sense of their own powers, for in the spirit of universalist democratic ideology they could—in theory—question the goals of the sovereign through elected representatives in national parliaments.

Our analyses include regimes caught up in both the first and second waves of nationalism. Although the two periods of nationalism are, of course, distinct and to be understood on their own terms, select comparisons are revealing. I have already indicated that what these two types of regime have in common is that they were totalizing in their claims on sovereignty and patricentric in their leadership. The most recent departure from these forms—which coincided with the end of World War II and the Cold War, respectively—has, in turn, been followed by radical restructuring of sovereignty claims in both political and domestic authority, and insofar as we can ascertain, renewed pressures for and experimentation with democratization. Here I would like to elaborate upon a distinction within the modern form of sovereignty, that between democratic regimes and totalizing, patricentric ones, which will clarify my second point above concerning the limitation placed on the power of the father over the sons in modern sovereignty.

Of the three models for conceptualizing political authority, only the modern form refuses the fundamental principle of the father's authority over his sons. But that refusal only pertains to democratic regimes with mechanisms to limit their own sovereignty. Modernist totalizing regimes, by contrast, quickly reinstated the ancient principle of reducing humans to *homo sacer*, what Arendt (1983: 455) in her classic study of totalitarianism had already pointed to as their defining characteristic: "the society of the dying established in the camps is the only form of society in which it is possible to dominate man entirely."

Democratic regimes are subject to populist pressures, which frequently leads to a form of legitimation through an egalitarian ideology oriented toward "growth and development," metaphorical domains that in Europe are traditionally maternal or feminine. This legitimation ideology effects a change in the semantic content of the terms "father" and "son." Political authority becomes open to degendering, with women and the entire set of practices associated with the household now fodder for the conceptualization and practical exercise of sovereignty. Today, for example, the father might require a local specification in the domestic mother instead of the domestic father, and the analogy of the relation between father and son is frequently replaced by a "co-dependent" relation between parent and child, mother and daughter, husband and wife, or between lovers generally. By co-dependence I mean a relationship based on care and mutual desire, need or abuse, or exchange rather than on status, descent, domination, or any a priori authority such as the father had over his sons. The populist possibility of co-dependence was of course always present in the conjugal couple of the triadic Oedipal complex, explicated by Freud. But there the "woman" and the power of the domestic sphere represented at most a supplement to the man and his power, if not a fundamental challenge to and violation of paternal authority. Today, instead, the idea of co-dependence is often promulgated as a positive performative principle for the exercise of democratic authority. Indeed, in the contemporary identification with money, co-dependence is built into the capitalist economic form.

Not only do democratizing regimes no longer grant the father any kind of automatic right to take the life of his sons, they in fact now ritually require the sons to take the life of the father. Modern sovereignty in its democratic variant institutionalizes the "killing" of the Father through ritualized elections in multi-party systems. These elections demand periodic change in the administration of state: the old ruling party or coalition moves into the opposition, an opposition party or coalition rules in turn. In contrast to the ancient and medieval sovereign father, democracy requires, as Luhmann (1990: 232) puts it, a "bifurcation of the top." Instead of a cephalic authority model of an unchallengeable, single head that characterizes kingships and tyrants, democratic regimes are bicephalic. Governments are recognized and "accepted as 'democratic,'" argues Luhmann (175, see 167–183), only when they are structured by the "binary code of government/opposition." Hence, in parliamentary democracies, for example, the government and opposition rarely rule simultaneously, for that would represent a forced consensus. Instead, they must exhibit the temporal possibility of switching places in the next election (see Borneman 2002a).

The continuous symbolic decapitation of the leader takes place not only in the form of displacement through elections but also through the generation of social movements, frequently youth-driven, that tend to challenge the consensus of ruling elites. This decapitation contains an important prohibition: that the deposed leader or party be kept alive. The winner in elections, for example, is normally obliged to avoid humiliating members of the opposition; instead one must honor them as worthy and necessary for the legitimation of one's own rule. With respect to the regimes included in our study, all reasserted premodern principles of sovereignty—the right to kill arbitrarily—and all embraced cephalism— one-party, if not one-man, rule. One yardstick, then, as to whether there has been an actual end and systemic transformation is the extent to which they have embraced the fundamental principle of "bifurcation at the top" integral to the democratic variant of modern sovereignty.

Analysis of the "effects" of the Death of the Father is subject to an infinite regress, for each "end" of a particular sovereign was preceded by other ends, each new form of authority embedded in other forms. Although there is often a primal death scene, there is no end to its symbolization and therefore no moment of virgin birth of new forms of authority. Each subsequent form is impure, containing within it traces of its past. But one can begin an analysis with local caesurae, moments of radical regime rupture following revolutions, coups, or leader's deaths, when people assume that they are about to break with the past. It is such moments of self-representation of national regime change with which we are concerned. Many excellent histories that seek to interpret "the past" through these transformative moments have already been or are being written. Our contribution in this volume is toward an analytics of the transformative moment of the end, to a fuller narrative description of the sequence of events and the mechanisms that might account for transformations from totalizing and patricentric rule.

Unlike historical accounts, such analytics cannot assert causal relationships between any particular "before" and "after" of these regime closures. As part of a succession of events, each sequential moment revolves around symbolizing the leader's death and making narrative links that order the events with reference to this break or departure from a prior regime. An ordering into a "before" and an "after" is, in these cases, especially difficult given the trauma attributed to the particular forms of national authority that are the subject of our analyses. The inability to grasp trauma at the time of the experience and the repeated, retrospective suffering of traumatic events make any sequencing of the end a fiction. To narrate the before and after of the regime, people must themselves create a story of transformation, which itself is a departure from trauma. Even though such self-representation alone is insufficient evidence to conclude that there has been a regime change, this narration and the memory work it entails are necessary preconditions for an efficacious death of the father. In other words, the experience of the mode of death—hanging, suicide, desacralization, old age, execution—and its emplotment in a sequence of events provide direct indices into assessing what kind of transformation is taking place.

## The Symbolic Forms of the Sovereign: Transcendent, National, and Familial Fathers

If one understands the father as a symbolic form, then two further analytical distinctions are necessary to understand the form the father takes within the practices of modern sovereignty. A first distinction, initially brought to our attention by Di Bella, is that between the pater and genitor, two functions assigned to the father in Roman law. The pater is the ecclesiastical or spiritual father, associated with authority and repression. The genitor, as the name implies, is the reproductive (by the nineteenth century, the biological) father. The relative efficacy of these totalizing regimes rested on peculiar kinds of fusing and splitting of the pater and genitor roles that differ from the democratic model, a point on which I will elaborate later.

The second distinction concerns forms of embodiment. The modern sovereign, in both his democratic and nondemocratic variant, relies on a father with minimally three symbolic embodiments: transcendent, national-territorial, and domestic. Loosely linked through the "name-of-the-father," these forms have conceptual equivalents in most languages as the divine or transcendent, the territorial or national, and the domestic or familial. Consider merely the linguistic relations between transcendent, national, and domestic in the cases of "1945." In German, the corresponding terms are *Gottvater, Landesvater* paired with *Vaterland,* and *Familienvater.* In Italian, the terms are *il Padre eterno* (god), *il Papa* (pope), *il prete/Padre* (priest), *il Padre della nazione* (national father), *mio padre* (my father), *papà/babbo* (daddy/father)—with usage dependent on who is addressing whom. In Japanese, loyalty to the emperor and filial piety were constituent virtues peculiar to the Japanese *kokutai* (national polity), which included two interrelated parts: *tennosei* (the emperor system, eternal and transcendent) and *kazoku seido* (the family system, worldly and local).

These inter-relations are widespread but not universal. Although every society has some sort of father function embedded in its kinship arrangement, domestic (familial) structures of identification with the father vary. Much like the political father/leader's embodiment of transcendent and national-territorial authority, domestic forms of the father take form in specific cultural-historical projects. However, if the domestic father does claim to represent supreme authority, cultivation of a relationship to transcendence appears equally important to his authority, as does instrumental action and raw coercive power. Identification with the father as transcendent infuses his authority with religiosity and serves the long-term legitimation of ruling strategies. In the Western world, the transcendent is often empirically associated with the divine or a Christian God, but this is in fact far too narrow a theoretical definition. The OED does not even mention God in defining the transcendent; instead it references two other senses: "pertaining to or belonging to the divine as opposed to the natural or moral world," and "abstract, metaphysical, vague, obscure." It is useful to retain both senses, as something divine or sacred and, in Kantian terms, something beyond the range or grasp of human experience or belief—hence, also abstract, vague, and obscure. Defined as such, identification with a transcendent can be with anything that surpasses those of its kind, anything invested with supreme authority such as, for example, the family, money, ethnicity, race, nation, class, the masses, revolution, historical process, culture, anticorruption, or environmental protection. The authority of the father, then, would depend at least in part on his ability to control the meaning of and identify himself with transcendent values.

The inter-mediate, or national-territorial, form of identification is historically novel, having crystallized first in the late nineteenth century. Anderson (1983) points out that after the birth of nations in the New World, they were re-exported to Europe where they replaced empires and various forms of dynastic or Christian monarchical organization. They have since proliferated as modular and formally translatable in sundry combinations throughout the globe. In Europe, at one level, the growth of the national father served as a substitute for the deposed king. But his appearance also coincided with a crisis in domestic and sacred authorities, hence providing a response to a need for new transcendent values during a period of radical questioning of "traditional" forms of authority. By the nineteenth century, traditionalists and revolutionaries within Europe agreed that the authority of the domestic father should be bolstered. It was assumed that, as Jules Simon argued in 1869, "authority must be made omnipotent in the family so that it becomes less necessary in the state" (cited in Perrot 1990: 167). The state was conceived as at best a proxy for the domestic father; it was to help maintain order within families. Hence, in the latter part of the nineteenth century, the authority of the husband over his wife and the father over his children was, in fact, extended.

Not until the twentieth century did the national form reach its apogee and achieve a kind of transcendent value, as embodying the site of the "political" over and above that of domestic and religious authorities. National leaders then sought not only to mediate between the domestic and transcendent, but also often to substitute national identification for one or both of the other levels. In regimes where the national form has been most totalizing, the carriers of "traditional" sacred and domestic authority, such as the minister or priest (for Catholics, the Holy Father) and the family father, have frequently been coerced into ventriloquating national prerogatives. There the husband's authority over his wife and children was frequently undermined and replaced by that of the state acting in the name of the national father/leader.

## National Trauma, Wholeness, and the Modern Subject

The mutual imbrication of national with transcendent and familial authority has had profound unforeseen effects on the development of modern subjectivity and of identification with totalities and fathers. In his 1962 examination of transformations in the bourgeois public sphere, Habermas (1991: 156–157) had already pointed to some of these effects: "the surreptitious hollowing out of the family's intimate sphere ... the dismantling of paternal authority and a tendency toward the leveling of the intra-familial authority structure." But to claim, as he does, that the "pedagogical functions" of the "bourgeois family" are being replaced "by extrafamilial authorities, by society directly," surely ignores the different performative occasions where there is no zero-sum game and state, society, and family function symbiotically or parasitically. These occasions include ceremonials (coronations, elections, military parades, political demonstrations, church services, school graduations) as well as family rituals (marriages, funerals, anniversaries) and everyday routines. They create the sense of modern temporality through a ritualization of the year (e.g., work, vacations, weekends, public holidays) and an institutionalization of the lifecourse (e.g., childhood, youth, years of military service, career, retirement). Frequently they have been the crucial vehicles for the exercise of modern sovereignty, both to teach and to display how citizen subjects come to identify with the symbolic forms of national authority. Modern political authority in the form of the nation, and modern domestic authority in the form of the family, were projects that presupposed each other.

While no specific institution has come forth to replace the nation-state and its familial subject, there are indeed many challenges to its primacy. One common approach has it that the nation has already reached its apogee as a world project in identification and its sovereignty and influence are waning. According to this logic, the nation-state model of political authority (hence, the national leader/father) is increasingly in competition with other institutions and forms of local and global identification, especially in the fields of sport and entertainment. Moreover, the domestic base of national authority is also challenged: the number of singles grows while nuclear families—with a clear father as head-of-household—decline; reproductive rights are increasingly denied men and attached to women alone; biomedical technology is radically refiguring the role of the genitor. The sex act is removed from reproduction, and reproduction is removed from the conjugal couple. Contemporary representations of the nation-state often focus on its problems: threats to its coherence, restricted powers of the executive or national governments generally, economic crises within welfare states, reethnicization of group belonging, often along nonterritorial lines, proliferation of alternative media with global reach outside any single state's control.

A more limited claim can be made with more certainty: that totalizing, patricentric variants of the nation form appeared as mirrors of a general crisis of symbolic identifications. The end of this type of political regime in the two waves of 1945 and 1989, the public face taken by the Death of the Father, serves as our point of departure. An anthropology of ends, however, must then ask the more unwieldy questions about transformations: how to conceptualize a rupture in authority and the effects of a presumed caesura on subjectivity. Here, I will suggest merely two relevant lines of inquiry, the first concerning effects of national trauma, lingering effects of the death and reproductive cults essential to patricentric rule; the second concerning effects of totalizing authority on the search for wholeness.

First, if these twentieth-century national forms were particularly traumatic, then one can assume that many of the lingering effects of trauma depend not merely on repressed memory but more specifically on "a temporal delay that carries the individual beyond the shock of the first moment" (Caruth 1995: 10). The repeated suffering of past events without the ability to recognize the experience that constituted them in the first place is conducive to repetition. People appear unable to grasp the effects of catastrophic events—ranging from brutal discrimination and exclusion to genocide, from coerced sterilization to naturalized reproduction—precisely because the experiences that constituted them resist recall and naming. Contemporary examples of traumatic effects are many: a series of revivals that include ethnonationalist unity movements organized around neofascist, Nazi, or imperial symbolism; the resurgence of racist xenophobia in the form of antiforeigner campaigns; nostalgia for the unity of the conjugal couple and nuclear family; revivalist crusades for pseudocollectives or strongmen leaders; reassertion of the authority of biological fathers and naturalization of reproduction; and movements for the domestication or "protection" of women and children.

The point is that specific totalizing, patricentric regime-effects will survive as traces of the past, embedded within the successor regimes, and they can be expected to have a long afterlife. Whether such traces will be determinative of the trajectory of change seems to depend, as Gal and Kligman (2000: 9) conclude, on how the "politics of reproduction" relates to newly constructed public spheres, where individuals recall experiences and retrospectively reconstruct them. The essays here suggest that a key to departures in regime transformation involves reworking the opposition set up between life-affirming and death-negating forces, which is often simply reproduced by substituting a reproductive cult for a former death cult.

Second, what does the Death of the Father suggest about the consequences for identification with regimes of self and politics that advance totalizing projects? As mentioned above, modern states made more extensive claims on the political loyalty of their subjects than did empires and kingships; they also demanded subjective identification with their national forms of culture. These claims were, above all, for coherence, wholeness, and a strong sense of "us" versus "them"—a sense of exclusive belonging. This modern subject, Ian Hacking (1995: 63–89) has written, implies a norm of the "whole person [as a] consensus of vital properties," an identity that coheres into a consensual whole. This whole derives from vital properties—biological (racial, genetic) or cultural (national, class, gender)—about which "we" normatively agree. Lacking these vital properties in their proper normative forms—what Charles Taylor, in his defense of the modern Self, calls "horizons" that include "strong qualitative discriminations"—results in damage to the Self. One might even extrapolate from Taylor's account of the sources of Self that "modernity" is the historical period in which "human personhood" or the "Self" (Taylor uses the terms interchangeably) enjoys the normal expectation that it will remain "undamaged." The goal of modernity, then, is ultimately an "undamaged human personhood," defined in terms of a specific moral orientation (Taylor 1989: 27).

Leaving aside the philosophical merits of Taylor's account, it describes a Self at odds with the empirical reality we seek to account for; the modern subject has hardly escaped this century's violent history whole and undamaged, especially in the traumatic and totalizing regimes we are examining. Indeed, the very expectation of wholeness as a "consensus of vital properties" may be one of the sources of this damage, for such irrational longing often feeds off of the abjection or cleansing of identifications or properties that disturb the presumed consensus (see Borneman 1997). In totalizing and patricentric regimes, the wholeness of modern subjects was linked to the political project of autochthonous, self-reproducing national wholes, and this despite the official rhetoric of transnational socialist unity. Resurgent nationalist longing in many former state socialist regimes is one subject-effect, and it makes sense only when understood paradoxically alongside its other effects: a skeptical relation to sovereigns, to consensus and the search for wholeness, and to political identification generally.

All of the authors in this volume move out of their own ethnographic and historical work, and therefore approach questions of sovereignty and identification in ways resulting from the specificity of their respective encounters. A comparative social anthropological approach seeks to explain the historical nature and socio-logic of differences in the way regimes end and are transformed, but it cannot uniformize the units of analysis. Such uniformization risks producing spurious ideal types based on deduced lowest common denominators or essences of regime types.[5] We hope that our focus on two historical ruptures, 1945 and 1989, will not foster the illusion of comparative uniformity and substitutability of type, for each case stands on its own processually, in its own historical and cultural context. Because some of the ends occurred within the last decade, others more than half a century ago, the authors also vary in their weighting of ethnographic and archival forms of evidence. For the remainder of this introduction, I place the various questions addressed in theoretical and anthropological discursive traditions, and, drawing from the various essays, I suggest ways in which a comparative social anthropology of the end might proceed. Although my approach has changed in interaction with the other authors and with their representations of different societies, it also grows out of my own analysis of a specific social formation—that in Germany—and my own reading of theory.

## The Name-of-the-Father and the Symbolic Order

The concept "Death of the Father" appeals to the fundamental and fruitful ambiguity of two psychoanalytic concepts—"death" with its associated terms of end, liberation, and loss, and "father" with its ties to human authority. "Of all the scenes of private life [in the nineteenth century]," writes Michelle Perrot (1990: 176), "the death of the father was the most significant, the most charged with meaning and emotion." This death was the moment of last farewells, transfers of power, and new beginnings. It invoked transcendent, national, and familial authority, and it was a moment when the dynamics of identification in the domestic group were performed. In classic Freudian theory, authority is first constructed in an elementary family. A child moves from a symbiotic relation of mother-child to a triadic relation of mother, father, child. Lacan, in his rereading of Freud, emphasizes the significance of language in the child's entrance into this triad. The child's identification with a father is simultaneously a departure and an opening, a movement out of a purely Imaginary realm and of a sole identification with the mother, an entrance through language into the Symbolic order and a relation to the father.

Accordingly, Lacan substitutes the "name-of-the-father" for Freud's simple "father," thereby properly (and entirely consistent with Freud) emphasizing that the father is not restricted to a biological person but is always himself a linguistic representation, a symbolic matrix for a series of other related symbols. The name-of-the-father represents not merely the "father" but also the locus of truth and meaning, the source of authority. Though a symbolic matrix for other symbols, the name-of-the-father is nonetheless always one instead of multiple, whole instead of dissoluble. The name-of-the-father may manifest itself, may find its locus of meaning or source of authority, in a biological father, but also in law, in God and nation (as Freud stressed), or in language, grammar, culture, and convention (as Lacan stressed), or even in the mother. The point here is that this type of authority, whether familial or national, is construed in the name of a symbolic locus, a linguistic source that finds expression in the actual person who embodies this authority.

Theoretically, the child's entrance into the Symbolic order, into language and symbolization, is at once negating and creative. Negating in its "break" with the mother and her exclusive hold on meaning, and as an exit from the closed world of the Imaginary register. Creative in its access to the Symbolic register and identification with the father. This opens for the child a possibility for otherness beyond the mother-child dyad; namely, the father is presented as a Third, a disturbing yet determinative frame within whose prescribed limits certain freedom is possible. That freedom, argues Crapanzano (1992: 89, 90), "affords the space of desire," a desire that compels the continual positing of others. In interaction with the desire of these others, he writes, the person "becomes a self ... It is only after this recognition of desire that we can begin to appreciate our occasional (if not permanent) nostalgias for Edenic conditions—or our ruthless denial of Edens."

What I take Crapanzano to suggest is that this nostalgia for Edenic conditions is always also a yearning for reentry into the Imaginary, for a return to a mother-child bond, a search for prior or future wholeness, a desire for completion within a determinative totality. Such yearning was a central trope in the appeal of totalizing, patricentric regimes, and it was in fundamental tension with the desire to exercise freedom. The way in which these regimes used the Imaginary and Symbolic registers was peculiar in two notable respects. For one, they attempted to reinscribe the longing for the mother-child bond onto a national-social plane (e.g., the German Volk, Yugoslav brotherhood, Romanian *patria*, Soviet Communist worker utopia). For another, each leader/father insisted on total authorial control of the mythology of rule through use of propaganda and language. Along the way, exorcisms and killings proved necessary to secure the desired unity and identification with the single leader. This century's advancements in the technologies of communication and public spectacle, along with novel uses of biopower, made possible a new scale of control of language and the space of freedom. Forms of language control and manipulation of the entire Symbolic register were not merely instruments for the construction of totalizing authority; they made this type of authority possible.

To summarize this paradoxical social psychology, then, totalizing and patricentric forms of national authority uniformly relied on appeals to

"Edenic conditions," in the form of future-oriented utopias such as communism or nostalgic Volk communities. These appeals recall an idealized mother-child bond; to a unified social community, ordered, secure, whole, and transcendent of everyday political divisions. Individual subjects could find their (lost) completeness in national wholes, superordinate wholes created by identification with repressive leader figures—fathers—who worked primarily in the Symbolic register, in language and law. Yet such utopian dreams are, in fact, based on yearnings to occupy the space of the pre-Symbolic, for a return to the mother and the Imaginary, away from the space of desire afforded by identification with the father. This process of identification differed across regimes, but the longer the life of the regime, the more difficult it became to reproduce identification with the father.

Many socialist regimes fostered an image of authority as parental, deploying a peculiar combination of bad Symbolic father and good Imaginary mother, or even a good/bad split within the leader himself. Despite variation across regime in the embodiment of this Symbolic father and Imaginary mother, the image of leadership was conceived as decidedly heterosexual, in complementary male and female qualities. In East Germany, for example, by the 1980s state and party leader Erich Honecker came to embody both a benevolent father and a stern disciplinarian. His wife, Margot Honecker, who served as minister of education, was closely associated with the bad father side of her husband. When the bad father image was connected to Stasi head Erich Mielke, the state itself (the German Democratic Republic/GDR) came to represent the good Imaginary mother. In a similar fashion, Nicolae Ceaușescu frequently claimed to embody the nation and defend Romanian soil, but he also came to represent the cruel and arbitrary tyrant. Often his tyrannical side was attributed to (and then excused by) the influence of his wife, Elena, who represented the wicked mother and onto whom many people projected the most evil aspects of the regime. When Elena took on these qualities, Nicolae became a good father.

Authority in the Soviet Union, by contrast, remained symbolically structured solely around the father-son relationship. Stalin initially embodied the good father, but after his death Lenin became the good father contrasted with Stalin the bad son. During Stalin's rule, there was, by definition, no successor, meaning that entire generations of future sons who might come to replace the leader had to be killed. Throughout Soviet rule, the good Imaginary mother was never embodied by a woman but remained Russia-the-country.

At another level, all of these leaders shared the role of guarantors of national revolutionary orders and of unity, and they claimed nearly unlimited power of the sovereign father over the son. The guarantor role provided them with justification for the desired abjection, exclusion, even murder, of the exteriorized other, as well as a locus for dreams of an undivided, whole self, united and further reproducing life with those of one's kind (Lefort 1986). This elimination of difference, or of the possibility that difference might emerge, in the name of, as Lefort calls it, "the People-as-One," was possible only through the suppression of memory and the rewriting, the falsification, of experience and history. Much as the new leaders and their assistants took upon themselves the task of organizing the new national life, they also appropriated for themselves the organization of all aspects of memorialization and mourning for the dead. Hence book burning, doctored photographs, Orwellian newspeak, along with a proliferation of memorial cults to those who served and died for the people.

Now we might better understand why all of these patricentric leaders also presented themselves as writers, philosophers, or published scientists, people with special access to the word, to language and knowledge. For in situating themselves as true scribes for the Word, sources of meaning and truth, they functioned as "spirit mediums" to the new promises of transcendence provided by an undivided People, a prehistoric Race, a Science outside of politics, or by the dream of wholeness in Modernity itself. It is not that each leader and movement shared "the same vision of perfection," writes Tormey (1995: 178), but only that they possessed "a vision" and the modern powers of inscribing it in law. The technology of writing, then, as the fixation of speech and the arresting of time, was a crucial instrument for the exercise of power. The utopian dream these leaders possessed rested "on the fiction of the perfect Legislator—the Founder," argues Goux (1990: 165): "Utopus is the father who creates the ideal organization, the optimal order to which social reality must conform."

In order for these (im)perfect legislators to sustain the illusions of their utopias, they had to constantly rework language and the Symbolic order. In this they functioned as fathers who demanded total and absolute authority for their word, and their authority rested primarily on the repressive powers of the pater. The end of these leaders and their regimes meant the death of the father, a sense of liberation with new types of freedom. As the authors in this volume make clear, the end of regimes everywhere resulted in the reintroduction of what had been formerly rejected, the modern type of freedom. As originally envisioned by Kant, this authority is not absolute, not patricentric and totalizing, but bicephalic, where the master, the rule, restricts and limits itself. To be sure, regime change merely introduces this freedom; it is never secure. And to the extent that freedom of this type is made possible, it is through a reidentification with another name-of-the-father, but with one who makes claims to limited authority and identification.

## The Genitor and Transcendence through National Reproduction

Perhaps this century's most radical changes in the authority of the father have been with respect to the genitor role, a function directly tied to the third level of authority, the transcendent. If one no longer lived for God, what became the dominant fiction that organized ultimate values? Although each of the national fathers embraced a different notion of reproduction, they shared in common a particular Zeitgeist: the late nineteenth-century concept of the autochthonous nation that reproduces itself through generational continuity. Accompanying the expansion of the nation model was the growth of interest in population sciences, civil marriage, eugenics, and procreative and "deviant" sex (Anderson 1983; Foucault 1978; Mosse 1985). As modern subjects became national, they increasingly defined themselves in terms of an authentic, reproductive, heterosexual wholeness.

What is historically new here is not the harnessing of reproduction for the service of a particular group or power, but the scale at which reproduction—now defined biologically and in terms of the conjugal couple—is asked to perform for, as Anderson aptly put it, this "imagined community" of strangers.[6] Each of the father/leaders had to maneuver within this dominant fiction of a new relation between reproduction of the "population" and transcendence for the nation (Kligman 1998). Each regime experimented with a new semantics of the father that redefined the individual's relation to gender, sex, reproduction, and community. In many cases, the pater, genitor, and identificatory function were relegated to the same man, with the woman defined only as a necessary complement to male wholeness. Di Bella (this volume) writes that the Italian futurist leader Marinetti's position on reproduction represented a "desire of male parthenogenesis." Indeed, in each regime theories circulated that displaced women's agency in reproduction to the level of biology, the species, the race, or the "new socialist man."

Here it is worth reiterating a fact often ignored by analysts: that the three leaders who did not die a natural death—Mussolini, Hitler, and Ceaușescu—carried their wives/mistresses with them into death. Each dictator in fact had a peculiar relation to the conjugal couple, marriage, and reproduction. Mussolini, for example, organized large collective weddings in the name of the people. On 30 November 1933, he staged a collective wedding with 2,600 brides and grooms, each of whom was rewarded a prize from *il Duce*. He himself enjoyed both a wife and a mistress and played the "mythical copulative intermediary between Italian men and women" (Di Bella, this volume). With his usual flair, the statesman Mussolini cultivated a virile image that could be directly carried into marital bed. The national leader became a symbol for the individual genitor in the family, and hence functioned as an analogue to stabilize the bourgeois family as transcendent form. But while Mussolini stood in for the symbolic genitor, he never fully embodied the law and the functions of the pater. In this vein, Eco (1994: 2–3) has characterized Italy as lacking a disciplinary father: "The father is the Law. Our country has never succeeded in identifying with the Law. [Italy never found a] paternal image [but remained] a confederation of uncles, with an indulgent mother, the Church."

In prewar Japan, the transcendent remained tied solely to the emperor's position, so that his reproduction alone counted for the nation.

The emperor alone belonged to an order above and beyond that of actual Japanese people. As in Italy, this structure of the leader as uncle can be found in several of the totalizing Asian regimes, including Ho Chi Minh's Vietnam, Mao's China, and Hirohito's Japan. Leaders there were addressed affectionately as uncles. Where these regimes differ is the extent to which the uncle also occupied the role of ultimate order and authority. As Han (this volume) points out, after the war, Hirohito distanced himself from the pater functions and retained authority by relying solely on the meanings of the uncle.

In many cases, leaders propagated myths of national reproduction while obscuring or trivializing their own origins and physical paternity. Often the leader would take on the image of a "transcendent genitor" and usurp functions from the biological father, which, in turn, frequently positioned him at odds with the newly ascendant bourgeois family form. In Nazi Germany, Hitler cultivated erotic attachments but sex was functionalized and desire displaced away from the pleasurable and sensual onto the Volk community. He forsake marriage until the very end to dedicate himself to the Volk, playing the transcendent genitor through whom some women were encouraged to impregnate themselves with any "Aryan" man and have babies for the Führer, whereas other, less racially desirable women were forced to abort or to be sterilized (Borneman, chapter 2, this volume).

In countries without a major discourse on sex, such as Yugoslavia and the Soviet Union, the practice of sex was never directly linked to reproduction and the symbolism of the individual genitor. There, sex was never confined to the procreative conjugal couple as effectively as it was in the Western European bourgeois project. Without recourse to the ideology of the procreative, nuclear family, regimes in these countries made other kinds of direct links between the state, its leader/father, and the baby. Tito, for example, constructed his authority around both a cult of the dead partisans (who fought against fascism and for "brotherhood and unity") and a universalistic peace cult. He was comrade, leader, and father of the nation's children; he represented freedom and justice, the future—as well as protection from the past. He kept his biological paternity private and separate from his highly publicized social paternity. He had children with women of different nationalities (including a "foreign" Russian woman), but he did not marry them all (see Bringa, this volume).

Ceauşescu's Romania and Stalin's Soviet Union carried the logic of the collective genitor to its most literal extreme by officially "adopting" orphans as state fathers, and then setting up large state-run child-care orphanages. This pattern was also true, though to a more limited extent, in East Germany. By the 1970s, the Ceauşescus, while presenting themselves as engaged in a benevolent paternalism, had resorted to coercive pronatalism to increase the population. Their ruinous economic policies actually made it difficult for some women to carry children to term and impossible for many others to keep their children, hence the increased number of state orphans. The "healthiest" of these were eagerly adopted by the state and rumored to be destined for the securitate, where they were raised to be devout to Ceauşescu and his family (Kideckel, this volume; Kligman 1998: 364–418). For many of these children from state orphanages, the state and its embodied leader became identificatory father.

In the Soviet Union, the optimism about this new genitor-nation and identification led Stalin to proclaim the achievement of a "new Soviet man," more advanced than all previous forms of human (Schoeberlein, this volume). Churches were turned into museums of atheism, and the progressive "history" mapped by the authors of the revolution was posited as the proper sphere of transcendence. The bourgeois family became, much like the individual, a relic of the past, a pre-stage to a communist future. The future, in turn, was guaranteed though sacrifice: honoring those who had fallen in service to the Motherland in World War II, killing those who were suspected of posing opposition to official doctrine.

In most cases, the death of each leader appears to have brought about an abrupt end to the particular meanings of patricentric authority, though not to totalizing appeals. What today is frequently represented as a reproduction crisis in many of these countries might more critically be seen as the end of the dominant myth of transcendence through national reproduction and of the male's loss of control over the genitor function. Patricentric, totalizing regimes did not invent this myth, but they carried nationalist pronatalism to an extreme, and in the process remade the relation between genitor and pater. Italy and Spain, the two most Catholic countries in Europe and both with fascist pasts, are now renowned for having the lowest birthrate in all of Europe, and the birthrate throughout East-Central Europe, especially in post-Soviet Russia and Romania, has also dramatically declined. After 1990, Romania engaged in an unofficial export of abandoned and handicapped babies from orphanages, many who were gypsy, reminding us of the continuing relevance of eugenic dreams of purity to modern forms of sovereignty. In Germany, while a baby boom followed the death of Hitler and World War II, the birthrate then sunk and has remained very low ever since. The end of the GDR in 1989, on the other hand, was accompanied by an initial dramatic decline in the birthrate, which has since risen some but remains among the lowest in Europe. These cases all attest to the decline in the power of the myth of transcendence through reproduction, or of the equation that reproduction equals life.

The cultivation of the genitor role in post-Tito Yugoslavia serves as a counterexample to the others. Until the last years of his life, Tito separated his embodiment as the "social father" of all the nation's children from his absence as father to his biological children. In fact, he even refused to produce children with Jovanka, his longtime companion. His encouragement of "mixed marriages" between the various regional, confessional, and ethnic groups (he himself was a product of such a marriage), indicated a certain disrespect for the symbolics of blood and lineages, and it offered a respite from what preceded and followed his rule (see Bringa, this volume). Following Tito's death there was a reaffirmation of reproductive ideology and a reassertion of medieval sovereignty, in particular by the leaders of Croatia and Serbia, who positioned themselves symbolically as sons of Tito while rejecting his legacy of "brotherhood and unity." In the Bosnian war, Serbian (and alternately, Croatian) nationalists within Yugoslavia, with the support of religious authorities, employed the older arguments of ethnically pure population reproduction to convince their subjects to support annihilationist state policies directed against ethnically defined "Muslims" or *Bosnjaks* (see Borneman 1998: 273–319). This strategy was subsequently applied to Albanian Muslims in Kosovo. The propaganda line of Croatian authorities during the Bosnian war was that the Bosnian Croats were the victims' victims, a weak minority that the Muslims wanted to eliminate. As the war progressed and most people involved in "mixed" marriages were ostracized, killed, or exiled, all three major politically organized groups turned to ethnic reproductive ideologies, explicitly to replace children who were killed (Borneman 2002b). In the Sarajevo area, for example, the birthrate during the war was the lowest ever recorded, but in 1997 it exceeded the previous record years, which were those following World War II.

What all this suggests is that national authority generally required ties to transcendent and familial authority. Yet following a caesura in the national regime, the particular de-linking of national to transcendent and domestic authority is by no means straightforward. Each death of the father was followed by a period of national instability and ambiguity about the powers of the sovereign, with immediate searches for other identificatory figures, frequently of an authoritarian type. In most cases, there has also been a resurgence of the ideology of the "traditional" bourgeois family and demands for the return of women to the home. In some cases, there has been a resurgence of traditional religious authority, or in faith healing or sorcery. Such sudden changes in political and domestic authority have, in turn, themselves proven unstable. Nonetheless, it seems likely that for now, at least, in these six cases, the particular conditions under which Edenic social orders—fascist, imperial, and communist utopias—have been imagined have largely disappeared.

## "Complex Structures" of Kinship and Political Authority

The dominant anthropological model employed to understand kinship divided it into "elementary" and "complex" structures, which were correlated with the temporality of tradition and modernity, and with the political order of statelessness and states. This model viewed elementary structures of kinship as organized by rules of exchange or descent, whereas complex structures, though containing "survivals" of primitive systems, tended toward a reduction in the significance and size of kinship units and toward their autonomization. Although these simple dichotomies contain elements of caricature, they have contributed to understanding the nature of elementary/kinship-based/stateless societies. But they have not been applied systematically and reflexively to state societies, nor have they been used to advance the understanding of complex structures. We might begin by elaborating on one major difference in the social psychology generated by kinship systems. In elementary structures, as Radcliffe-Brown and Lévi-Strauss, among others, noted, the father-function is shared by two figures: an "actual father" and a "father-substitute." In matrilateral systems, the father-substitute is also the identificatory father, usually the uncle (mother's brother), whose relation with his "nephew" is playful, loving, and joking. This contrasts with the son's relation to his "actual father," which is frequently tense and authoritarian, and therefore sometimes altogether disavowed. These distinctions in "elementary structures" alert us to three symbolic positions of the father: (1) the actual, or biological, father, who is opposed or complemented by (2) the father-substitute (frequently the uncle), and (3) the "identificatory father," who, in matrilateral systems, is the father-substitute.

I want to map these symbolic positions onto the distinction between pater and genitor. The pater, we might recall, is associated with authority and repression, whereas the genitor is the biological or reproductive father. If applied to the "elementary structures," the "actual father" is always genitor and usually pater, while the "father-substitute" is involved in neither discipline nor physical reproduction but is the man with whom the child identifies. He is the "identificatory father." The pater, who enforces rules and the law, takes a position that might also be occupied by other figures, such as the mother, or a totemic source such as a constitution. Borch-Jacobsen (1994: 276), elaborating on a discussion of this issue by Lévi-Strauss, concludes about simple structures, "Either sexual repression is exercised by another person ... or the assumption of the sexual ego-ideal is accomplished by an initiatory identification with a totem (that is, a pure 'symbol' or 'name of the father') different from the real father." In other words, the pater and the genitor, as symbolic forms and paternal positions, may be only tenuously related to the figure that stands as the "actual father" in the domestic unit. Hence, the pater need not be the identificatory father. As a matter of fact, the father functions are usually shared by several figures, each of which is formally independent of the mother.

These distinctions help to clarify the logic of authority and the meaning of the father in "complex structures" in two ways. First, rather than distribute the functions of the pater, genitor, and identificatory father into two or three symbolic positions, as they are in elementary structures, complex structures fuse (or ideally fuse) them into one person. This "actual father" is still considered incomplete—unless linked with a wife/mother in a conjugal couple that, together with children, becomes a nuclear family. Freud called this fusion of symbolic positions the "Oedipal complex." A peculiar problem in identification with authority immediately appears.

By combining the normalizing ego-ideal and the repressive super-ego into one "father," the subject in an Oedipal structure is required to identify with the father, who in turn prohibits this identification—a problem solved with a "substitute father" in elementary structures. The mother, in this triangulation, is the figure from whom the child must break in order to arrive at a normal identification. Women are, to be sure, important, but only in conjugality, as wives and mothers of sons to complete the adult male.

If the pater, genitor, and identificatory father are fused in a single figure as part of an Oedipal complex, the modern child will have the opportunity, it is maintained, to be successfully "normalized." But when this fusing does not work, which it never really does, the structure produces neuroses, as Freud argued, management crises in identification. Since the collapse of paternal authority is one of the characteristics of "modern" societies with states, these management crises are particularly prominent among peoples in state societies. There the process of identification is far more difficult to resolve than in stateless ones. The types of neuroses resulting from this collapse are reminiscent of Durkheim's term "anomie"—a generalized condition of alienation found in all twentieth-century state societies. Borch-Jacobsen (1994: 282) argues as well that modern societies "are defined by a general crisis of symbolic identifications—'deficiency' of the paternal function, 'foreclosure of the name-of-the-father,' perpetual questioning of the symbolic Law and pact, confusion of lineage and general competition of generations, battle of the sexes, and loss of family landmarks." Totalizing and patricentric regimes tried to arrest this particular crisis in symbolic identification by addressing the deficiency in the paternal function—speaking in the name-of-the-father, reaffirming the symbolic Law, reclaiming of lineage, denying generational or gender conflict, and monumentalizing national "landmarks."

The second sense in which these structures are "complex" and different from "elementary structures" pertains to the relation between domestic and political authority.[7] In both types, the authority of the domestic unit is in constant articulation with political and transcendent authority, but in complex structures this articulation is attenuated, if not denied. In liberal regimes, there is denial of the influence of government in producing specific forms of kinship; in totalizing regimes, the denial is of the influence of kinship organization in regulating government. Embedded in the ideology of modernity is the assumption that the political domain is autonomous and independent of the kinship domain. Liberal regimes assume kinship is the higher domain; totalizing regimes assume politics is the higher domain. For one, kinship entering into the political is condemned as "nepotism," whereas for the other, the political entering into kinship is condemned as a violation of the sanctity of the private. That the practices of the two domains are never entirely separable poses a problem only insofar as the principle of their separation is ideologically reiterated. Indeed, both liberal and totalizing regimes reiterated a commitment to a principle of separation of domains. But because totalizing regimes more consciously and explicitly violated that principle of separation, they exposed the instrumental character of their rule—hence delegitimating their authority.

In totalizing forms of authority, each leader presented himself as an identificatory "solution" to the "'deficiency' of the paternal function." At a more general level, in securing their rule, each leader appropriated the genitor role for racist and communal eugenic projects; each reformulated the meaning of reproduction—of the self and the community—thereby changing the relation of the genitor to the pater. For Lenin, Stalin, Hitler, Tito, and Ceauşescu, the leader tried to embody not only, as in matrilateral systems, an identificatory and substitute father, but also a pater. Accordingly, each national leader demanded a particular identification with himself as a superior substitute for the authority of the "actual father," and, at the same time, he sought to occupy the position of transcendence, a position beyond question, beyond the range of human experience or belief. The transcendent value embodied by the pater was located, in turn, in a genitor function: the social reproduction of the national community.

## On the End of Regimes and Democratization

To conclude, let us reconsider the question with which we began: What does the mode of death of the leader/father tell us about the art of regime end following national traumas? Two conditions stand out: First, a public, participatory death that can symbolize a radical break with the old regime and that is affirmed by the new political authorities seems preferable to a private death. Second, if the state withdraws from orchestrating mourning, a genuine public mourning process is more likely and a departure from national trauma appears more possible. Then the death is less likely to become the basis of a cult and less likely to be instrumentalized to reassert the old structures of authority. This said, neither all public modes of death nor all mourning processes are equally effective.

Consider the regime changes of 1945. Mussolini's private execution followed by the public exhibition and humiliation of his body (along with that of his innocent mistress) continues to haunt Italian politics today, but not merely because it was secretive. The execution had also been summary, without a trial or an opportunity for public witnessing concerning the crimes of the regime. Public humiliation of the bodies in Milan's center, and an unproblematic identification of the new regime with the Allies, substituted for a discursive process that might have facilitated personal reflection on the conditions that brought about Italian fascism. Nonetheless, the successor Italian state did withdraw from the organization of mourning and it has not returned to a form of legitimation based on the use of death cults.

The suicide of the newly wed Hitler (along with that of his wife, Eva Braun) also preempted forms of German public participation. And the

Allied-occupation policy of banning Nazi images furthered this preemption. Yet the occupation, along with the supranational Nuremberg Trials and subsequent German government trials of members of the political elite, created other conditions that symbolically cleansed the new regimes and strengthened those indigenous voices that sought a public discussion of the crimes of the old regime. These voices also happened to be largely democratic and participatory, and their critical discourse contributed to undermining the nineteenth-century concepts of German Volk and nation. Privatized mourning replaced state-orchestrated national death cults. These processes fostered the restructuring of German authority into more accountable forms, which themselves continue to undergo transformation (Borneman 1997; Borneman and Senders 2000: 294–317).

Hirohito's desacralization in 1945—by fiat, without trial and without public participation—enabled the entity the "Japanese people" to escape a critical discourse about its crimes, especially in China, Indonesia, and Korea. It provided, as did Mussolini's death, an alibi for the people. Yet there were international war crimes trials in Japan, and the new regime explicitly repudiated its former militarism and did not legitimate itself through links to death—even to the mass deaths of Hiroshima. Hirohito's "second," or biological, death in 1989 demonstrated that although the formal trappings of authority had remained remarkably intact, things never stay the same. Democratization after the war, under the tutelage of the Americans and the "internationalization" of Japan, has indeed created a public discourse about accountability and democratic authority (see Han, this volume).

The deaths of the fathers in "1989" continue to unfold in dynamic social processes. Successive attempts to kill the Soviet father, such as that by Khrushchev in 1956 and Gorbachev in the late 1980s, were always partial, since the state refused to proclaim a radical break in its form of legitimation. One integral aspect of this legitimation was the heroization of fallen soldiers from the revolutionary period through World War II. With the implosion of the Soviet Union in the early 1990s, its two major identificatory figures, Lenin and Stalin, have taken on different fates in the various republics. No revolution has replaced the great Communist revolution, and no pater has replaced the old iconic father. Since the former Communist Party no longer rules, other voices have challenged the instrumental use of mourning for the death of the Soviet Empire. Also, new sources of power, especially money, are generating new hierarchies. Since many of these new sources are global and come from without, they appear outside the control of any central political authority. Future executives are therefore likely to rule without the power that comes from affective ties, strong identification, and effective control of the Symbolic Order through its disciplinary institutions (see Schoeberlein, this volume).

In Romania, the dramatic trial and execution of the Ceauşescu couple formally resembled a public, participatory end. But the execution, though later televised in part, was a kind of voyeuristic public participation, and the trial, conducted by a self-appointed judiciary, actually preempted the formation of public judgment. After the impromptu court pronounced its verdict, it announced, "The forces of the people are now in control. In the name of the law of the people, you are condemned to death. All [your] possessions [are to be] confiscated and distributed among the people." Elena tellingly addressed her accusers, "Child, do not do this to me. Child, don't tie me up," while Nicolae insisted, "This is a coup d'etat." By fiat, the court took away from the Ceaușescu couple the power to act in the name of the people. Elena's appeal to a feminine authority of parental inclusion contrasts with Nicolae's appeal to the masculine authority of a father over his sons. Indeed, the mix of these two modes of authority had characterized their regime, as it did to a large extent the successor regime. The openness of the transformation is paralleled by an ambiguity about the source and directionality of Romanian political authority. This was revealed in 1990, for example, when the new leaders argued against employing the death penalty to punish wrongdoers, while much of the public seemed to favor its reinstatement to exact retribution on its former leaders. As Kideckel (this volume) argues, the meaning of the death and the trajectory of the democratization process in Romania remain ambiguous.

In Yugoslavia, the extensive mourning at the time of Tito's death, only partly state-orchestrated, was followed by a repudiation of his legacy, by a public discourse linking the immediate past to some future Yugoslav, meaning pan-Slavic, project. That said, Tito as symbolic father meant different things to people in the various republics. In Bosnia, his image was never successfully erased and he was widely mourned. But in the other republics, especially Serbia and Croatia, this mourning was immediately displaced, through the competition of Tito's "sons"—Milošević and Tudjman—for succession to his office, into yearning for the recovery of a pre-Tito social phantasm: ethnic wholeness. To achieve this required the resurrection of the People-as-One myth, along with an exteriorization of all internal differences. A struggle followed to replace the Yugoslav entity with the dominance of various patrilineal, centralizing authorities in-the-name-of ethnic-religious unity and of those sons lost in previous and present wars. The two most belligerent sons, Milošević and Tudjman, along with their counterparts in Bosnia (Karadžić) and Herzegovina (Boban), relied on death cults to prop up their authority. A renewed reckoning with the death of Tito and the meaning of the end of the Yugoslav regime was perhaps possible only with the signing of the Dayton peace accords of 1995, which stopped the war of aggression in Bosnia and set up Bosnia as a United Nations protectorate. But then, the most recent losses in the series of wars had created other needs to mourn. And in 1998, Milošević initiated another war, in Kosovo. Not until public demonstrations in Serbia in 2000 brought down Milošević's regime was there an actual end to symbolize. Much as in Germany, Italy, and Japan after World War II, an external authority (the UN and NATO) was "called in" to force an end to an attempted genocide and to mediate the dispute concerning the form of successor regime. Here the variations in the transformative process in each successor republic require separate analyses. In Sarajevo during the war, the fact that many youths resorted to "Fuck Tito!" as a popular curse signifies not only the ambivalence attached to an identification with him but also that he was not yet properly buried (see Bringa, this volume).

Finally, the ends of 1945 and 1989 should be recognized as ruptures that present historical opportunities for transformation: a displacement of identifications and a turn toward more democratic forms of authority. The major differences in country-specific forms of authority, and the instability of identifications, should make us wary of any universal predictions. Since identifications with authority are always multiple and conflictual, they are in constant need of management. What appears to be a permanent identification with, for instance, the transcendent father, is often quickly dislodged by another attachment to such figures as the national or the family father. In the particular cases with which we are concerned, the totalizing aspirations of the father included an attempt to control the conflict of identification by fusing multiple father-functions into the national leader. This aspiration was hardly realized. Nonetheless, as Fuss (1995: 49) writes, what is "'repudiated and even overcompensated can reestablish [itself] once again much later. The history of the subject is therefore one of perpetual psychical conflict and of continual change under pressure." It follows that the deaths of these national leaders/fathers, and the ultimate failure of totalizing political projects, should not be mistaken for a closure and an end of crisis. It is likely, as Chirot (1994: 427) concludes in his massive study of modern tyranny, that humans will create other, equally inventive forms of tyranny in the twenty-first century.

Even if all successor regimes today appear to be grappling with democratizing processes, we must remain skeptical about emergent forms of political authority. Democracies themselves do not perform the same way in every situation, meaning that they, too, may become less or more democratic over time. We must therefore examine them critically with respect to their trajectories and the effects of "the end" in specific historical-cultural situations.

# Notes

1. I am much in agreement with a revised definition offered by Friedrich (1969: 136): "Totalitarian dictatorship is a system of autocratic rule for realizing totalist intentions under modern technical and political conditions. Since modern political conditions signify a general acceptance of democracy, a totalitarian dictatorship can also be described as a 'perfect democracy' in the sense that the people, represented by the party, which in turn is represented by its leaders, exercise total and unrestrained power." Friedrich here shifted the definition away from his earlier concern (Friedrich and Brzezinski 1956) with the primacy of ideology, the domination of people's thought and minds, to an emphasis on legitimacy and consent.
2. I use the term "Father" when referring to the authority embodied in the leader who invokes a line of descent through equivalent political, religious, and domestic fathers.
3. As Benveniste (1973: 175–204) demonstrates for Indo-European concepts, father and mother (pater and mater) are neither parallel nor complementary terms. "[T]here was no authority or possession that belonged to the mother in her own right" (175–176). Moreover, Indo-European has no terms for "husband," "wife," or for "marriage." The "conjugal couple" is indeed a very modern invention.
4. I owe inspiration for this threefold sociological model of sovereignty to Baber Johansen.
5. Such reductions include attempts to characterize regimes by their "totalitarian ideology" or "cult of personality." These regimes did in fact create totalizing ideologies in support of one-man leadership cults, and they demanded a personal commitment to national identification. But they were, in Walzer's insightful characterization, a "living tomb of a utopian—or better, of an anti-utopian project" (1983: 118). In other words, they were examples of "failed totalitarianism." There was always considerable discrepancy between leaders' visions, what the political regimes actually did, and the specific psychologies, identifications, and behaviors of their modern subjects (cf. Bracher 1981; Kolakowski 1989; Tucker 1983). Patricentric leaders in these totalizing regimes turned to terrorizing their own subjects—the famous "purges"—only when (and because) it proved impossible to achieve the desired certainty of total ideological control. We draw attention to the attempt to narrow the discrepancy between cult vision expressed in ideology and people's behavior, and the simultaneous normalizing and neuroticizing effect on identifications.
6. See the volume edited by Yanagisako and Delaney (1994) for a wide range of ethnographic studies about the importance of gender and reproduction for naturalizing social inequalities.
7. Michael Herzfeld (1993) offers another, fruitful approach to the study of complex kinship structures, finding in them the "symbolic roots" of modern forms of bureaucratic and national authority. In this volume, we instead focus less on the roots or continuities in bureaucratic form than on issues of transformation from one bureaucratic form to another, from totalizing to democratic authority.

# References

Agamben, Giorgio. 1998. *Homo Sacer: Sovereign Power and Bare Life*. Stanford: Meridian.
Anderson, Benedict. 1983. *Imagined Communities*. London: Verso.
Arendt, Hannah. 1973 [1951]. *The Origins of Totalitarianism*. New York: Harcourt Brace.
Aries, Philippe. 1981. *The Hour of Our Death*. New York: Knopf.
Benveniste, Emile. 1973. *Indo-European Language and Society*. Coral Gables, FL: University of Miami Press.

Borch-Jacobsen, Mikkel. 1994. "The Oedipus Problem in Freud and Lacan." *Critical Inquiry* 20 (Winter): 267–282.

Borneman, John. 1997. *Settling Accounts: Violence, Justice, and Accountability in Postsocialist Europe*. Princeton: Princeton University Press.

———. 1998. "Toward a Theory of Ethnic Cleansing: Heterosexuality, Territorial Sovereignty, and Europe." In idem, *Subversions of International Order: Studies in the Political Anthropology of Culture*, pp. 217–319. Albany: State University of New York Press.

———. 2002a. "Introduction: German Sacrifice Today." In *Sacrifice and National Belonging in Twentieth-Century Germany*, ed. Greg Eghigian and Matthew Paul Berg, pp. 3–25. College Station: Texas A & M University.

———. 2002b. "Reconciliation after Ethnic Cleansing: Listening, Retribution, and Affiliation." *Public Culture* 14 (2): 281–304.

Borneman, John, and Stefan Senders. 2000. "Politics without a Head: Is the Love Parade a New Form of Political Identification?" *Cultural Anthropology* 15 (2): 294–317.

Bracher, Karl-Dietrich. 1981. "The Disputed Concept of Totalitarianism: Experience and Actuality." In *Totalitarianism Revisited*, ed. Ernest A. Menze. London: National University Publications: Kennikat.

Caruth, Cathy. 1995. "Introduction." In *Trauma: Explorations in Memory*, ed. Cathy Caruth, pp. 1–10. Baltimore: Johns Hopkins University Press.

Chirot, Daniel. 1994. *Modern Tyrants: The Power and Prevalence of Evil in Our Age*. Princeton: Princeton University Press.

Crapanzano, Vincent. 1992. "The Self, the Third, and Desire." In idem, *Hermes' Dilemma and Hamlet's Desire*, 71–90. Cambridge: Harvard University Press.

Eco, Umberto. 1994. "Interview by Eugenio Scalfari." *La Republica* (Rome), 3 March, pp. 2–3.

Foucault, Michel 1978. *The History of Sexuality*. Vol. 1., *An Introduction*. New York: Random House.

Friedrich, Carl J. 1969. "The Evolving Theory and Practice of Totalitarianism." In *Totalitarianism in Perspective: Three Views*, ed. Carl J. Friedrich, Michael Curtis, and Benjamin Barber. London: Pall Mall Press.

Friedrich, Carl J., and Zbigniew Brzezinski. 1956. *Totalitarian Dictatorship and Autocracy*. Cambridge: Harvard University Press.

Fuss, Diana. 1995. *Identification Papers*. New York: Routledge.

Gal, Susan, and Gail Kligman. 2000. "Introduction." In *Reproducing Gender: Politics, Publics, and Everyday Life after Socialism*, ed. Susan Gal and Gail Kligman, pp. 3–21. Princeton: Princeton University Press.

Gellner, Ernest. 1983. *Nations and Nationalism: New Perspectives on the Past*. Ithaca: Cornell University Press.

Goux, Jean-Joseph. 1990 [1973]. *Symbolic Economies: After Marx and Freud*. Ithaca: Cornell University Press.

Habermas, Juergen. 1991 [1962]. *The Structural Transformation of the Public Sphere: An Inquiry into a Category of Bourgeois Society*. Cambridge: MIT Press.

Hacking, Ian. 1995. *Rewriting the Soul*. Princeton: Princeton University Press.

Herzfeld, Michael. 1993. *The Social Reproduction of Indifference: Exploring the Symbolic Roots of Western Bureaucracy*. Chicago: University of Chicago Press.

———. 1997. *Cultural Intimacy: Social Poetics in the Nation-State*. New York: Routledge.

Hobsbawm, E. J. 1990. *Nations and Nationalism Since 1780: Programme, Myths, Reality*. New York: Cambridge University Press.

Kantorowicz, Ernst. 1957. *The King's Two Bodies: A Study in Mediaeval Political Theology*. Princeton: Princeton University Press.

Kligman, Gail. 1998. *The Politics of Duplicity: Controlling Reproduction in Ceauşescu's Romania*. Berkeley: University of California Press.

Kolakowski, Leszek. 1989. "On Total Control and Its Contradictions: The Power of Information." *Encounter* 73 (2).

Koselleck, Reinhart. 1994. "Einleitung." In *Der Politische Totenkult: Kriegerdenkmaeler in der Moderne,* ed. Reinhart Koselleck and Michael Jeismann, pp. 9–20. Munich: Wilhelm Fink Verlag.

Lefort, Claude. 1986. *The Political Forms of Modern Society: Bureaucracy, Democracy, and Totalitarianism.* Cambridge: MIT Press.

Luhmann, Niklas. 1990. *Political Theory in the Welfare State.* New York: Walter de Gruyter.

Malinowksi, Bronislaw. 1955 [1927]. *The Father in Primitive Psychology.* New York: W.W. Norton.

Minkenberg, Michael. 1997. "Civil Religion and German Unification." *German Studies Review* 20 (1) (February): 63–82.

Mosse, George. 1985. *Nationalism and Sexuality.* New York: Basic.

Perrot, Michelle. 1990. "Roles and Characters." In *A History of Private Life, Vol. 4, From the Fires of Revolution to the Great War,* ed. Michelle Perrot, trans. Arthur Goldhammer, pp. 167–338. Cambridge: Harvard University Press.

Reich, Wilhelm. 1970 [1946]. *The Mass Psychology of Fascism.* New York: Farrar, Straus & Giroux.

Taylor, Charles. 1989. *Sources of the Self: The Making of Modern Identity.* Cambridge: Cambridge University Press.

Tormey, Simon. 1995. *Making Sense of Tyranny: Interpretations of Totalitarianism.* New York: Manchester University Press.

Tucker, Robert C. 1983. "Does Big Brother Really Exist?" In *1984 Revisited: Totalitarianism in Our Century,* ed. Irving Howe. New York: Harper & Row.

Verdery, Katherine. 1996. *What Was Socialism and What Comes Next?* Princeton: Princeton University Press.

Walzer, Michael. 1983. "On 'Failed Totalitarianism.'" In *1984 Revisited: Totalitarianism in Our Century,* ed. Irving Howe. New York: Harper & Row.

Yanagisako, Sylvia, and Carol Delaney, eds. 1994. *Naturalizing Power: Essays in Feminist Cultural Analysis.* New York: Routledge.

# CHAPTER 1

# From Future to Past:
# A Duce's Trajectory

*Maria Pia Di Bella*

At the dawn of the twentieth century, groups of dashing young European men propelled themselves to the front of the political scene to play a role that would have been beyond their reach if genealogical rules had to be followed. Thus an era of effervescence started, breaking normative ties that seemed to be everlasting. Nowhere was this breach brought about in a more fruitful way and in more spheres of the intellectual, political, and artistic life than in Austria. Names such as Sigmund Freud, Joseph Roth, Stefan Zweig, Robert Musil, Ludwig Wittgenstein, Oskar Kokoschka, Gustav Mahler, Arnold Schönberg, and so forth, only point to the richness of the period in that country. But it was also in Austria, in 1914, that its emperor, Franz Joseph, whose long reign went from 1848 to 1916, declared war on Serbia, after the assassination of the emperor's nephew (28 June), the archduke Frantz Ferdinand, in Sarajevo (Bosnia). For the old emperor understood that the two bodies of the Habsburg's monarch (Kantorowicz 1957) were now permanently torn apart and that the Habsburg's rule would probably end with him. The Great War he decided upon has also to be seen as a loud utterance of grief for his dying dynasty, a grief that took the lives of millions of young men. In this period of convulsions—before democracy was finally accepted as the best way to govern—men eager to establish new hereditary lines but with no pedigree came along, boasting that they would be their country's saviors. After Lenin, but before Hitler, Benito Mussolini was one of them.

One of the most striking differences between the patriarchal monarchs who ruled Europe from the early modern period on and the dictators of the twentieth century, is the role ascribed to the ruler's image. Sovereigns—if we follow Jean Bodin's model (1986: iv:157–159)—were advised not to "communicate" directly with their subjects but only with their "intimates" who served them to relay their messages to the public. Thus, the sovereigns had to speak "little" to the crowd and to show themselves "rarely" to it. They had to follow the example of God, who revealed his word only via his messengers and his power only through the effects of his creation. The illegitimate successors of our century, on the contrary, had to build their legitimacy on their own image. The creation of their image—which combined visual and vocal skills—was the epicenter of their politics. Hence, they legitimized their accession to power through the use of images and symbols of their own bodies (Freedberg 1989; Gruzinski 1990). The representation of the created images was conferred to partisan artists. Later, it was spontaneously used on a larger scale by artists and citizens alike, as an icon embodying their personal and political aspirations. The dictators' image policy did indeed enjoy success. But they forgot Jean Bodin's warning: too much "communication" exposes the kings to the risk of ridicule, disrespect, and disobedience.

Here, we will highlight the way Mussolini wanted to present himself to the Italians in order to fulfill the role of a leader; we will present the multiple models and often contradictory strategies that he used for this purpose (Milza and Berstein 1980; Palla 1994). While doing so, we will keep in mind that Mussolini knew all along that he was usurping a function that he could assume only because he had created a combative party strong enough to uphold him and to mobilize people around him (Paris 1968). At the same time, his access to power was made possible thanks to King Vittorio Emanuele III, who, by accepting him as prime minister, granted him legitimacy (Valeri 1962). This old paternal figure maintained his privilege of representing the Italian state and nation, not allowing Mussolini to exercise this function exclusively by himself.

Mussolini therefore created new, imaginative ways to seduce his countrymen (Lepre 1995). When his power to do so ceased, in the face of the grim reality of World War II, he was executed by the Italian resistance. Nevertheless, the interest in Mussolini's personage was passed on from one generation to the next, part of a permanent effort to solve the riddle of the Duce's illegitimate presence in Italy's past (De Felice 1995).

## The Futurist Model

The genealogical rules that were followed in the Occidental world incorporated the idea of a "trinity" of fathers. As we know, this idea was successful enough to remain valid until the Great War. Its success in German society—exemplified in Joseph Roth's magnificent novel *The Radetzky March*—persisted during the Nazi period, though the nexus between the great-grandfather and the grandfather, which represents the religious and the political spheres, was torn apart. The idea of a "trinity" of fathers, so important in the foundation mythology of the Roman Empire,[1] seems to fade completely also from the Italian horizon before the Great War, as angry young men, such as Umberto Boccioni, Carlo Carrà, and

Luigi Russolo, followed by Giacomo Balla, Gino Severini, Fortunato Depero (Belli 1996), and Enrico Prampolini, led by Filippo Tommaso Marinetti (1876–1944), proclaimed their movement, Futurism, with the ambition of totally disregarding the past.

More should be said about this artistic movement since many ideas, developed at an early stage by Marinetti and his friends, were integrated later on by Mussolini in the construction of his own image. These ideas appeared first in the Futurism manifesto, written by Marinetti and published on the front page of the French newspaper *Le Figaro* (20 February 1909; see also Marinetti 1983). The manifesto starts by saying that Mythology and the Mystic Ideal are behind us, that scent alone is enough for wild beasts, and that we should break out of the horrible shell of wisdom altogether. Eleven intentions follow a brief introduction:

1. We intend to sing the love of danger;
2. Courage, boldness and rebellion will be essential elements of our poetry;
3. We intend to exalt aggressive action, feverish insomnia, the racer's stride, the somersault, the punch and the slap;
4. We affirm that the world's splendour has been enriched by a new beauty: the beauty of speed, for a racing car is more beautiful than the Victory of Samothrace;
5. We will hymn the man at the wheel;
6. The poet must spend himself with ardour, splendour and generosity, to swell the enthusiastic fervour of the primordial elements;
7. Except in struggle, there is no more beauty;
8. We stand on the last promontory at the end of centuries! Why should we look back? Time and space died yesterday. We already live in the absolute, because we have created eternal, omnipresent speed;
9. We will glorify war—the world's only hygiene—militarism, patriotism, the anarchists' destructive gesture, beautiful ideas worth dying for, and the contempt for women;
10. We will destroy the museums, libraries, will fight moralism, feminism, and every opportunistic or utilitarian cowardice;
11. We will sing of great crowds excited by work, by pleasure, and by revolt; we will sing of the vibrant nightly fervour of arsenals and shipyards blazing with violent electric moons; greedy railways that devour smoke-plumed serpents; factories; bridges; steamers; locomotives; planes. (Hulten 1986: 514–516)

After this list of self-asserted commandments, the Futurists explain the objective of their movement: freeing Italy from its foul gangrene of professors, archeologists, guides, and antiquarians, and from the museums that cover the country like so many graveyards. To do so, their country's most potent forces should not be wasted in the futile worship of the past. Libraries should therefore be set on fire. Museums should be flooded with water where glorious old canvases would bob adrift. "The oldest of us, they said, is thirty years old; we have at least a decade to finish our work. When we are forty, they added, other younger and stronger men should throw us in the wastebasket like useless manuscripts" (Hulten 1986: 515).

The Futurists concluded their manifesto by reiterating that "our fine, deceitful intelligence tells us that we are the sum and continuation of our ancestors." To which they replied: "Perhaps! Let it be so! Who cares? We don't want to hear it! Let nobody say those infamous words to us again! Lift up your heads! Erect on the summit of the world, again we hurl our challenge to the stars!" (Hulten 1986: 516).

From 1909, the date of the manifesto of the political Futurist Party, to 1918, Marinetti and his friends were busy on all fronts, artistic and political, publishing and republishing, in different languages, their numerous manifestos. Marinetti went to Libya as a journalist, to describe the hostilities between Italians and the Ottoman Empire, participated with his sympathizers in many demonstrations in favor of Italy's entrance into the war, on the French and British side, and, in February 1915, was arrested in Rome, along with Mussolini. Finally, he went to war in July of the same year.

In December 1918, about twenty organizations, called Political Futurist Fascists (Fasci politici futuristi) were founded. On 23 March 1919, Mussolini laid the foundation of the Italian Fighting Fascists (Fasci Italiani di combattimento), in which Marinetti participated (Milza 1999: 237–238). Though Marinetti underlined (in a collection of articles published as a book in 1924, under the title *Futurismo e Fascismo*), the predominant role of the Futurists in the fascist movement, he and his sympathizers decided nonetheless to quit the "Fasces of combat" (29 May 1920), for they disapproved of Mussolini's appealing to the "fastidious remembrance of the old romanity" instead of the "greatness of Italy, [a] hundred times bigger" (Marinetti 1924: 243), his acceptance of the monarchy, and his desire to deal with the clergy. They wanted an Italian empire that would be "antisocialist, anticlerical, antitraditional, with all liberties and all progresses integrated in an absolute patriotism" (ibid.: 244). From that period on, Marinetti and his followers had no real political importance and he drifted apart from Mussolini. Yet they retained a certain mutual admiration for each other, and in March 1929 Marinetti was even nominated to be a member of the Italian Academy. Moreover, Mussolini never sanctioned Marinetti for his "negative" initiatives. For example, being intensely anti-German, in 1938 Marinetti openly opposed the racial laws and the formation of the Berlin-Rome Axis (De Felice 1988). In 1943, when Mussolini was deposed, Marinetti frequently visited him, either at the Villa Feltrinelli at Gargnano on Lake Garda, or elsewhere, and he supported unreservedly the "Social Republic of Salò" until his death, on 2 December 1944, in Bellagio (Lemaire 1995: 11–33).

## Mussolini's Use of Futurism

We find in Futurism four main ideas that Fascism appropriated, and these four ideas are clearly interdependent: the first and main idea is the complete rejection of tradition, the positing of a radical tabula rasa of the past, done in an iconoclastic way, by denying all heritage of the past. Since the past is eradicated, the present, and especially the future, find their place in their Weltanschauung: the Futurists sing the praises of all exterior signs of modernity and modernism, thus creating a cult of youth and machines. The "beauty of speed," along with the love of danger, temerity, audacity, and rebellion, are the new attitudes young men should have. These attitudes find their natural outcome in a hymn to war: war to the excess is their credo, a war that would always allow them to pursue the recommended conduct (Lemaire 1995: 30–32).

Did Mussolini stage these Futurist ideas in his lifestyle, ideas that he seemed to share totally, at least until the end of the 1920s? According to Margherita Sarfatti,[2] who remains for contemporary historians one of the most reliable sources on Mussolini's life, though until 1934 she was one of his official biographers and a fervent admirer, Mussolini frequently said, when he was questioned on his past: "You know, I never remember anything, the past does not interest me—does not exist for me—only the future exists" (Sarfatti, 1926: 15). Mussolini also claimed, as reported by Sarfatti: "The past is a point of transition of an unlimited line called progress. To pause on it means to regress; on the contrary, we have to proceed, to improve, to elevate ourselves, always, always more" (ibid.: 11). Sarfatti herself comments: "Mussolini lives so rapidly, that in the present he already anticipates the future with full evidence, what is more, he thinks he is already there. The events that are to come do exist, but when they happen, they do not interest him any more" (ibid.: 192). Margherita's echoing admirative cheers must have certainly reproduced, in her many readers, the exact image Mussolini wanted to propagate.

It is important to emphasize that for the Futurists, the cult of youth and machines replaced the abolished cult of the past (Bidussa 1994). How did Mussolini handle this imperative? After all, he was born in 1883. At the time of the Black Shirts' (camicie nere) March on Rome, on 28 October 1922, Mussolini was already thirty-nine years old. Since he was supposed to be on the brink of being "thrown in the wastebasket like a useless manuscript," according to the Futurist manifesto, he decided to give the Italians a young, athletic, courageous image of himself. Mussolini "is never tired," he used to reply if anyone ever dared to suggest he might be.[3] Mussolini hated and dreaded the idea of old age: in fact, he never wished journalists to be precise about his real age, nor did he ever give birthday parties. On the contrary, he used to exhibit himself for photographs in different plastic attitudes to underline his ever-fresh vitality. From 1929 on, he used to gather journalists at Villa Torlonia to show them his athletic, youthful shape (Cervi 1992: 147).

Mussolini's past as a *bersagliere* during World War I was always emphasized to Italians.[4] Until 1938, when visiting his old regiment, he used to run in the typical bersagliere way. From his army past, he also kept a liking for uniforms, which he wore on different occasions, and a sharp desire for military command and strategy. Though mechanical weapons and mechanical sports always attracted him, he was also fond of horse riding and fencing; in fact, he fought many duels before coming to power. His passion for guns and canons was well known, as was his penchant for rapid sports cars—he drove fast in a red Alfa Romeo—for planes that he used to pilot himself, and for motorcycles; he was, he believed, Italy's first "centaur." He also loved to be seen swimming, strolling on the beach, skiing, playing tennis, and, most of all, playing soccer, thus encouraging what was already a very popular sport in Italy (Cervi 1992: 144).

Mussolini also had very specific ideas about the image pictures should convey of himself; for this reason he used to examine all of them attentively, granting or refusing permission to print them (Malvano 1996). As stated previously, he privileged the young, athletic, courageous images of himself. But he also wanted his capacity as a ruler to be portrayed distinctly, either in his facial expressions—recall his compelling eyes and his determined jaw—or in his bodily bearing. He stressed his domineering capacities over Italians by symbolically always raising himself above them, on a podium, on a balcony, or, if these were not available, on a horse (Cervi 1992: 66).

## Mussolini as Genitor

While many of the features that Mussolini integrated into his public image were clearly compatible with his Futurist background, there is a striking difference between Futurism and Fascism and between the two men who represented them, Marinetti and Mussolini. This main difference is important since it touches on the topic of paternity. In his 1909 manifesto, Marinetti says clearly that he wants to "glorify the contempt of women" and "demolish feminism." He writes a special manifesto that he publishes again in 1924 (204–206): "Against Feminine Luxury." But his attitude toward women is clearly revealed in his novel, *Mafarka le futuriste, roman africain* (1910), in which he pictures Mafarka as a sanguinary warrior capable of begetting an immortal son, Gazurmah, all by himself, regardless of all biological laws. Women, as residues of the past, are—in this Futurist scenario—totally eliminated by this (impossible) desire of male parthenogenesis.

Not so with Mussolini. Though we do not have any novel or theatre play of his, we know, thanks to Margherita Sarfatti, that he imagined many plots in 1919, whose topics we can now compare to Marinetti's *Mafarka*. *La lampada senza luce* (The lamp without light) is the story of a father who does not wish to have a child from his wife since he already has one from a secret union and knows he is in weak health. But the maternal instinct of the woman is stronger, and finally she begets a blind female baby, who gives rise, among them, to bitter accusations and remorses while they suffer in the dark (Sarfatti 1926: 232). *Si comincia, signori!* (Let us start, gentlemen!) is a drama of jealousy and perhaps of incestous love, says Sarfatti. It is the story of an old street player who is attracted sexually to the young girl who accompanies him on his tours. The jealousy and the incestous love he feels for her (for this young girl may be his daughter) prevent him from agreeing to give her to a young man who sincerely loves her and wishes to marry her. The street player finally ends up by strangling her. *Vocazione* (Vocation) takes place during Christmas night, in the cell of a young nun who remembers, in front of the Divine child, the child of "shame" that she had and that she abandoned (ibid.).

These never-written plays refer to the same topics, which, according to rumors, played a major part in Mussolini's private life. As a young man, before his coming to power, Mussolini begot his first-born daughter, Edda (1910), five years before marrying the mother, Rachele Guidi. Ten years after his civil marriage, he married Rachele in a religious ceremony (1925). One month before his civil marriage, he became a father for the second time, but from another woman, Ida Dalser: he first gave her a monthly allowance of two hundred lire; then, in 1925, a sum of one hundred thousand lire. Rumors that he was the father of the daughter of Angela Curti Cucciati, with whom he had a relation from 1921 on, were persistent. Most of all, rumors that he had a relation with his father's concubine, Anna Guidi, the mother of his own wife, Rachele, added an incestuous flavor to his marriage with Rachele (Cervi 1992: 199).

But apart from Mussolini's private life,[5] these scenarios can also be analyzed for their own content. The first thing to be underlined is the fact that, as in *Mafarka*, we completely lack the idea of a "trinity" of fathers. Mafarka produces a son, all by himself, without caring about his grandfather or great-grandfather, and without any help from an eventual mother.[6] The male personages of Mussolini's plays still need a mother to beget a child, but this presence is not a strong one, for the woman is never comforted by her role in the couple. In the first story, the husband refuses the wife the possibility of becoming a mother; in the second, we see the father but not the mother; and in the third, it is the reverse—we see the mother but not the father.

It is time, in order to better understand these plays, to introduce a classic Roman dichotomy between what Romans called pater and genitor: the first one, pater, being the person who transmits to the child all social advantages (education, name, status), while the second, genitor, being only the procreator.[7] With this dichotomy in mind, we can clearly see that the role of genitor is favored in Mussolini's eyes. In the first play, the husband refuses the eventual role of a father since he is already a genitor; in the second play, we see a genitor who lives and works with his daughter, though she ignores the fact that she is his daughter; while in the third play we see only the "shameful" mother, for the genitor is absent.

Apart from Mussolini's preference for the role of genitor, we can also notice a second important difference between his plays, Marinetti's novel, and the model of a "trinity" of fathers. This is the fact that all of these genitors seem to beget daughters instead of sons, a daughter whom the genitor, not being the pater, can eventually desire sexually. And if a man has to enter into a role of pater, due to his wife's persistence, he will beget a handicapped daughter so as not to be allowed to desire her sexually; her handicap protects her virtue by giving him a culpability complex. For all these reasons, the role of pater seems to be an undesirable one.

## The Duce as the Mythical Copulator

As suggested, the idea of a genealogical rule ("trinity" of fathers) and of an authoritarian patriarchal father faded out at the beginning of this century, before the advent of Lenin, Mussolini, and Hitler. Just before World War I, a new, younger generation came to the front stage, subverting existing traditions in all categories of social and cultural life. It was with this new, younger generation, that Mussolini entered into history (Setta 1993). It was with the help of a paternal figure such as King Vittorio Emanuele III that he was allowed to have access to power. Before this background, we can clearly perceive that Mussolini developed the role of genitor in order to conquer a dominant position in Italian society. For, on the one hand, the role of the fatherly political authority was weakened by World War I, and what remained of it was fulfilled by the king.

We are not suggesting that Mussolini purposely decided that the role of genitor befitted him and this was the one he had to play in order to seduce all Italians. But, objectively, it was the only role he could assume in front of the masses if he wanted to reign on the same level of political and social importance as the king. First, without irritating the king, and second, without ever losing, in the eyes of women and children alike, the aura of eternal youth that he wanted to keep at all costs and that paternal figures lacked, especially in his time. Mussolini's past as a seducer (Rafanelli 1975), his illegitimate children, easily upheld this project. His virile postures, not yet seen as machismo nor targeted as politically incorrect, were openly exhibited in a country in which men and women considered them to be attractive (Gilmore 1990). Italian women therefore offered their charms to the Duce, who simply had to choose among the numerous love letters he received (Boatti 1989), which he did. Therefore, during those years, he daily invited one of them—a different one each day[8]—in a special lounge of Palazzo Venezia in Rome (*la sala del mappamondo*). If, on the one hand, the hectic sexual life of the Duce was determinant in stressing his stallion qualities, on the other, it encouraged the idea that he was the procreator of Italy.

In fact, tales of his ever-flowing fertility and the media's constant focus on his omnipresent virility made Mussolini also the mythical copulative intermediary between Italian men and women when they were having sexual intercourse. Young children, at that time organized by the Fascists in a national youth organization called Balilla,[9] used to celebrate this virtue:

"The Duce's eyes shine/fixed on his Balilla/we are the love spark that one day/sprung from his great heart, yes yes" (Cervi 1992: 165).

Two more examples support my point. In November 1933, 2,600 couples came to Rome to get married and to receive a special prize from the Duce's hands. That same night, Mussolini received a telegram from each couple promising him 2,600 Balilla in nine months' time (Cervi 1992: 165). In December 1935, Italians were asked to give up their golden wedding rings to help the state against the sanctions taken by the League of Nations after Italy's invasion of Ethiopia. The Duce himself participated in the collection of these rings, which was exclusively represented in pictures or in movies through female figures offering their rings. The first one to do so was Queen Elena (Colarizi 1991: 195).

The construction of a public image based on the elements described above was extremely successful (Bollati 1984). The majority of Italians came to consider Mussolini as a mythical leader, Duce, not only in the sphere of politics but also in the culture of virility (Mosse 1996) and procreation. Children read about his heroic acts in books where he was usually pictured on a silver horse. Poets, such as Curzio Malaparte (1928), sung the deeds he performed while riding his white horse. The Duce himself gradually started to dress more and more in white and to ride only white horses, to accentuate his radiance and his representation as a sacred personage.

## To Build a Genealogy

From 1928 to 1932, a series of biographies, pictures, films (Luzzatto 2001), and journalistic reportages contributed to transform Mussolini's birthplace and that of his parents, Predappio, into a site of a new cult (Baioni 1996). Luisa Passerini underlines the fact that, at the beginning, lay themes were predominant, whereas from 1932 on, Mussolini's "parents are invested by a wave of deification" (1991: 90). It is with the biography of Antonio Beltramelli, *L'Uomo nuovo, Benito Mussolini* (1923), that the figure of Rosa Maltoni, Mussolini's mother, a schoolteacher who died in 1905, is emphasized for the first time. Her life is described by the author as a "vocation" and her tomb as "an altar" (Passerini 1991: 48). The figure of Rosa is associated with the world of religiosity and with love of the fatherland. Mussolini himself is supposed to have said, according to Beltramelli: "To renounce the Fatherland means to renounce one's mother" (Passerini 1991: 49). Later on, the figure of Mussolini's daughter, Edda, will be "like a pendant to the figure of the Duce's mother" (ibid.: 94).

It is, in fact, the figure of Mussolini's father, Alessandro, a blacksmith, that does not come through properly, being less appealing and certainly more prosaic than the one of his mother (Passerini 1991: 48). Many efforts and many indications are given to authors and journalists to stress the importance of this figure, but it is only from 1934 on, with the biographies by De Begnac, *Trent'anni di Mussolini 1883–1915* (1934) and *Vita di Mussolini* (1936), that there is a tentative success in giving the father a major presence (Passerini 1991: 161). And in Edgardo Sulis's book, *Imitazione di Mussolini* (1932), the parents appear tied together in a religious aura. Sulis in fact presents them this way: "Alessandro Mussolini and Rosa Maltoni are nothing but Joseph in front of Christ: instruments of God and of history to take care of one of the greatest national Messiahs. And certainly the greatest" (Passerini 1991: 90).

The blurring of the father's figure is probably due to the fact that he was a fervent socialist, an artisan (instead of a schoolteacher, like his wife, an "instructor of souls"), a man who dared to live with another woman after his wife's death. And, if we follow our model, a pater instead of a genitor.

## The Duce as a Statue

During the period of "deification" (from 1931 on), Mussolini seemed to gradually lose the characteristics that helped to bring him to power. He had become, as Giménez Caballero said, "marble like," "the statue of himself." Or as Bottai said about a private meeting with the Duce that "hurt him": "Not the man but the statue was in front of me." Mussolini had transformed himself into a statue (Passerini 1991: 164–165). These personal impressions were reinforced by the massive use of the Duce's face, in drawings or paintings, always portrayed as if his face were marble-like; the Duce's statues, usually on a horse, for all to see; the first letter of his surname, "M," displayed in Fascists' public political rituals, along with the Latin equivalent of Duce, "Dux."

The statue reminds us of the famous plays built around the myth of Don Juan, so very popular in Europe, from 1630 on, the date of the first traceable written version, by a Spaniard, Tirso De Molina, *El burlador de Sevilla, y combidado de piedra*. After that date, many different versions, in Italian, French, and English, contributed to the development of the myth (Molière 1665; Goldoni 1736, etc.), while the Mozart and Da Ponte version of it as an opera (1787) made it universal. The play relates the conflict between Don Juan, a seducer, and the Commander, father of Dona Ana (a young woman seduced by Don Juan), who defends his and his daughter's honor in a duel with Don Juan in which he is put to death. Don Juan has three encounters with the statue of stone that represents the dead Commander: the first one is in the cemetery, in which Don Juan invites the statue to dinner at his home and the statue accepts; the second is at Don Juan's home, in which the statue comes as a guest (*convitato di pietra*) and reciprocates Don Juan's invitation by inviting him to dinner at his place; the third is the one in which Don Juan goes to the Commander's home and gives him his hand, at his request, but Don Juan is immediately burned without being granted a confession to repent from his sins (while later, with the great romantic conversion, it is Don Juan himself who refuses obstinately to repent) (Rousset 1978: 21–35).

The man of stone (*l'uomo di sasso*) is, in this South European myth, the punishing father, the man of traditions who obeys the traditions since they are the law. Metaphorically, he is the law, for the law was originally written on stone. This play can also be seen as the eternal conflict between genitor and pater, in which the first represents seduction, liable to destroy an honored society, while the second guarantees order. Thus Mussolini, by either shifting his role from a "seducer" to "a statue of stone," or by playing alternatively one or the other role, probably thought he could control the imagination and the reality of all Italians.

## Years of Diarchy

If Mussolini, on the one hand, shifted from one role to another, thus occupying different positions in the cult of his person, on the other—and surprisingly so—he always seemed to share with someone else the high moments of his existence. Though he was seen as a dictator and though his aides, especially Bottai, feared that Fascism would not survive the death of its leader (Luzzatto 1998: 129), the public life of Mussolini, to his execution, is generally tied to a second person. The most obvious person was the king, Vittorio Emanuele III, with whom Mussolini ruled diarchically. Ruling seemed so evidently to rest in Mussolini's hands that the king's authority, not to mention his (future) historical prestige, suffered badly from it. But in moments of crisis, the king's arbitration was sought, thus underscoring the fact that Mussolini's legitimacy was in the king's hands. For if the king allowed Mussolini in as prime minister on 29 October 1922, it was still the king, on 25 July 1943, who signed his deposition order after the Gran Consiglio (Grand Council) voted for it.

In the eyes of Catholic Italians, Pope Pius XI was certainly an important moral figure and Mussolini was painfully aware of this. Though his political legitimacy did not depend on the pope, the Duce knew that a conciliation between church and state was a necessary step to attract Catholics into the Fascist Party. For the church, it was the only way to become a state religion and, as such, manage all citizens' births, marriages, and deaths. Therefore, on 11 February 1929, Mussolini and Pius XI signed the Lateran Pact. Though this "political coup for the fascist regime ended the seventy-year old schism between church and state," it also "paved the way for the Fascist Party to accelerate its infiltration of Catholic civic and voluntary organizations" (Berezin 1997: 50). Mussolini in fact tried, from 1929 to 1931, to impose the Fascists' youth organization, Opera Nazionale Balilla, as the only eligible one in Italy, thus giving rise to bitter opposition between him and the Vatican (Colarizi 1991: 116–132), until a compromise was found with Pius XI. Though the Azione Cattolica finally seemed to give way to the Opera Nazionale Balilla, Mussolini's victory was short lived, for the church succeeded a few years later in recovering part of its lost influence over youth organizations (ibid.: 131).

If the presence of both the king and pope legitimized Mussolini, one politically and the other religiously, the two other persons with whom he associated from the middle of the 1930s until his death, Hitler and Clara Petacci, had the opposite effect, for they gradually alienated him from many Italians. When Hitler came to power in 1933, the relationship between the two men seemed an even one, for Hitler admired the achievements of his elder. But Hitler's aggressive attitude inside and outside Germany obliged Mussolini to be more aggressive in foreign policy in order not to lose his prominent international position. Mussolini seemed not to realize that these choices succeeded only in cutting him off from the realities of his country (Zangrandi 1963). From 1935 on, Mussolini made a series of decisions that accentuated this gap: invading Ethiopia; proclaiming the Italian Empire and giving King Vittorio Emanuele III the title of emperor of Ethiopia (9 May 1936); participating in the Spanish Civil War (1936–1937); signing the Rome-Berlin Axis (24 October 1937); decreeing the racial laws against Jews (17 November 1938); and declaring the war on the German side (10 June 1940).

During Hitler's famous visit to Rome (9 May 1938), the Führer was shocked to see that the king still held a superior position during all public events, while Romans were shocked to see that the Duce was visibly imitating his German counterpart; they dreaded the consequences. Two months later, the publication of the *Manifesto della razza* (Race manifesto) only helped to disclose the grim reality of a regime that ultimately shed all literary metaphors and embraced a criminal scheme (Di Cori 1996). One of the people who tried to counter the influence of the manifesto and the application of the racial laws, by repeating obsessively until his death on 10 February 1939 that "there is only one human race," was Pope Pius XI (Loy 1997: 45–81). Not until 1959 did Pope John XXIII produce Pope Pius XI's speech, specially prepared to introduce the encyclical to all bishops, entitled *Humani Generis Unitas* (The unity of humankind). The speech had neither been delivered nor disclosed before that date (ibid.). But with the enthronement of Pius XII, a fervent admirer of German culture, the ties between the Vatican and the Duce became more cordial again.

Clara Petacci was first introduced to Mussolini in 1932, when she was barely twenty years old, on the road to Ostia, where he was driving his red Alfa Romeo. After that first glimpse, she showered him with poems and romantic letters.[10] An unhappy marriage that lasted four years separated her from finally being Mussolini's mistress, his *favorita*, meeting him regularly in the Cybo apartment of Palazzo Venezia (Cervi 1992: 218, 227) or at the Villa Camilluccia (Luzzatto 1998: 193). Her constant presence beside him disturbed Italians who had to accept the idea that his virility—which was assumed to belong to all—was now reserved for her.[11] Their shock was so great that they started to see him as an adulterous and unfaithful husband, and they called him by these names. From

1939 on, as Mussolini's external and internal political choices created great anxiety and dissatisfaction among the people, Clara Petacci became, in their eyes, responsible for what was considered to be Mussolini's change. "The male conqueror has been turned into a moron," people kept saying (Colarizi 1991: 400). Rumors of his syphilis were ever more persistent,[12] as were those of a "mortal disease," or of brain cancer, all carrying him to an imminent death, which would have meant, according to the majority of Italians, the end of the war (ibid.: 401; Imbriani 1992: 170–193). But war had only just begun, and Italians had to go through the dramatic experience of a civil war before regaining peace, while Claretta Petacci had to pay with her life for having believed, in an overly romantic way, the Fascist myth of the Duce.

## The Duce's Fall

On 10 June 1940, when Mussolini declared war in a united front with the Germans, the German army had already won an impressive series of battles. Mussolini decided to participate in the war to share in the German conquests, but with the evident aim of leading a parallel war to preserve his national and international leadership (Colarizi 1991: 342). This constant drive for leadership disposed him to open new fronts, without Hitler's consent, which his demoralized and badly equipped army was unable to sustain. Therefore, the Germans were obliged to come to the rescue, making Mussolini ever more subservient to Hitler.[13] For "if the outcome is success, the laurels will go once more to the Führer. Now Mussolini feels like a vassal—and not even an appreciated one—of Great Germany" (ibid.: 345).

But the outcome was not a success. All fronts were gradually lost, and after October 1942, Italy itself became the constant target of aerial bombardments, first by the British, and later by the Allied forces. The Duce's silence during those long and difficult months—his last speech was heard on 10 June 1941, to celebrate the first anniversary of his declaration of war—worried Italians, and it unleashed all sorts of rumors concerning his person. Finally, on 2 December 1942, Mussolini spoke to the Italians via the radio, from the Chamber of Fasces and Corporations (Imbriani 1992: 173). The moment was highly dramatic, and the imagination of the urban population was overflowing with different and contradictory expectations. But Mussolini was unable to give his audience what they were looking for. His hatred for the enemies, especially the British, whom he depicted in a strongly racist light, revealed, at the same time, his contempt for Italians.[14] Still in shock, Italians' comments were "it was not Him," "not His voice," surely "another," "a double" certainly, for "He is sick," possibly "already dead" (ibid.). To the people suffering from air raids, the Duce's only advice was to evacuate town. Visibly, neither the refugee issue, nor that of anti-aircraft defense was tackled by the Fascist government (ibid.: 176). Italians understood, for the first time, that war had been engaged with no serious defense preparations. The Duce had never really bothered to prepare for a "long" war to be endured mainly by the civilian population. He assumed Italy was sure to win rapidly, since the German allies seemed invincible. But now the civilian population was living under constant air attacks, helpless. And the Duce's only answer to their fears was that they should have long-sought refuge "in our beautiful countryside" (ibid.: 178).

We can safely say that the love Italians had for their Duce turned to hatred from that day on, for a major inversion took place that changed all his attributes from positive to negative. Italians turned to the king hoping for an intervention that would save their lives. The genitor having failed, they remembered the pater. But they had to wait almost eight months before the king finally signed Mussolini's deposition order, on 25 July 1943, and he managed to do so only after the Allied forces, led by Patton and Montgomery, landed in Sicily (10 July 1943), and only after the vote for Mussolini's deposition was brought about by Dino Grandi, Giuseppe Bottai, and Galeazzo Ciano during a meeting of the Gran Consiglio. "When on Sunday evening the radio announced Mussolini's resignation, all the [Roman] population immediately opened the balconies to clap hands and shout aloud 'Long live the king, long live Badoglio.' All were crying with joy and kissing each other" (Imbriani 1992: 198). In the major Italian cities, the popular outburst went on for many days; the Duce's pictures were burned, and his statues and busts were thrown on the ground and smashed (ibid.: 199).

## The Duce's Last Two Years

While Mussolini was carried to the islands of Ponza—and subsequently to the Maddalena (Porta 1996)—as a prisoner, the new government, led by Marshal Badoglio, was already negotiating secretly with the Allies. By 8 September, they had signed an armistice, which in fact divided Italy in two: the southern part of the Gustav line (from Naples to Pescara) was to remain under Italian control, while the northern part was left in the hands of the Germans. A few days later, Mussolini was liberated by the German commando of Skorzeny from his Gran Sasso prison, by plane, and taken to Vienna, Munich, and finally Rastenburg, to meet Hitler. Before the end of the month, Mussolini founded the Social Italian Republic in Salò (Garda Lake).

The last two years of Mussolini's life reveal a man who was a prisoner of his past, unable to make new and radical decisions that perhaps would have saved, if not his life, at least his image. The public figure was, for one, prisoner of the Germans,[15] who needed him badly in order not to appear as illegitimate conquerors and, thus, manipulated him like a puppet to achieve their means. For another, Mussolini was prisoner of the "fundamentalist" supporters of the new Fascist government, grown-up *balillas* who constituted an important faction of the Social Italian Republic; they were eager to show that the party leaders during the last twenty years were, compared to them, dishonest and had no real ideology. As a private figure, he was also torn between the family man (husband, father, and grandfather) and the lover of the young and beautiful Claretta Petacci, who was living a few miles away, in a villa in Gardone ("The deads' villa"), well protected by the Germans.

These tensions proved negative for Mussolini himself, the people around him, and to all Italians, for they contributed to erasing the frontiers between private and public and to installing vengeance as the principal means of government. To this hubris two figures were sacrificed: Galeazzo Ciano, Mussolini's son-in-law, and Claretta Petacci, his mistress. The first one, a well-known anti-German who suggested Mussolini's deposition in order to repel the Germans from Italy (Guerri 1995: 252), was condemned to death in a mock trial and executed in Verona (8–11 January 1944), along with four other "traitors"[16] of the famous Gran Consiglio meeting of 24 July 1943. If, on the one hand, the execution of the "traitors" was meant to point to their responsibility for the fall of the Fascist Party, thus absolving Mussolini (ibid.: 269), on the other, when it came to Ciano, it was to punish him personally for having been anti-German and also for having been, in the eyes of Italians, one of the Duce's potential successors (Colarizi 1991: 315). The aristocratic lineage of Ciano played against him in this fanatic period of a "return to the origins" called forth by the former balillas, supporters of the Social Italian Republic. Ciano's marriage with Edda, the eldest of Mussolini's children, and possibly his ease in handling the world's greatest men of state when he was minister of foreign affairs, must have created a front against him that was difficult to oppose, even for the Duce—if we wish to believe, as some do, that the latter was willing to pardon him after the trial but could not manage to do so. Edda did not believe so. She tried everything to save her husband's life, even to threaten her father with the publication of her husband's diary. But her husband was executed, and Edda, psychologically shaken, left Villa Feltrinelli where her parents lived to flee to Switzerland, far from her father, the Fascists, and the Germans. This dramatic event was never completely overcome by the family, and Edda's publication of Ciano's diary, after the war, had disruptive effects on the family for a long time.

The Duce's image was now in the hands of the "fundamentalist" grown-up balillas, supporters of the Social Italian Republic (Guerri 1995: 260–262). Those children who used to sing "we are the love spark that one day/sprung from his great heart" were distrustful of Mussolini's legitimate and illegitimate ties. Both, according to them, had to be controlled in order to fulfill the expectancy they had put in Him. Thus, once Ciano and the "traitors" case was solved, there remained the problem of Claretta's presence beside Mussolini. Vittorio, Mussolini's first son, writes, "The really fanatical Fascist Republicans were convinced she wielded [an] influence [over my father]—the Badoglio Government's propaganda machine having exploited the scandal—and to them Clara Petacci was a disgrace and a source of danger" (1973: 51).

For "they swallowed the story of their leader being twirled around the little finger of a woman," but, as Vittorio confesses a few lines later, "even I, in a way, had caught the same disease." He decides to go and see his father "to make a clean breast of all [his] worries and bitterness" (V. Mussolini 1973: 51). He does. Though "with every word [he] felt more embarrassed," he tried to be "calm and logical" since it was "one of the very few times that [his] father and [he] talked man to man, as equals," and he "begged him" "to sacrifice this woman's love and compel her to leave Gardone."[17] The father "went to some length to reassure [him] on the … family aspects of the situation, reaffirming that nothing had changed and nothing would change toward [his] mother and the rest of [them]." But "he talked to me about Clara in a very human way and very calmly … with the respect that any real man owes to a woman … who really loves him.… He had a deep affection for Clara Petacci, perhaps because she was the first woman … who loved him without thought of advantage."

In the end, the father added "that he had nothing against sending Clara away from Gardone" (V. Mussolini 1973: 52–53). Two days later, Vittorio received a seven-page letter from Claretta, which "rebuked [him] for being small-minded in judging a human situation," writing, "I ask nothing from your father and I would have you know that I would give him anything, including my life" (ibid.: 53).

The pressure of the "fanatical Fascist Republicans" must have been unbearable, for after a certain span of time it was the wife/mother herself, Rachele, who decided to go to Claretta's villa "to confront her rival and order her to go away" (V. Mussolini 1973: 54). But it was not easy to order Claretta to go away. During the confrontation between the two women, which lasted more than three hours, "a dramatic, almost desperate" (ibid.: 55) one, every time Rachele obsessively repeated to her rival that she should "do a sacrifice" if "she really loved him" and therefore "renounce to see him," Claretta would inevitably faint in her armchair while Buffarini-Guidi would serve her some cognac to recover her spirits. It is through Rachele's version of the encounter, published fourteen years later, that we follow the dispute (R. Mussolini 1958: 244–251). According to Rachele, she depicted to her rival all the dangers that were awaiting her if she persisted staying in Gardone, since "she was hated by everybody, by the Fascists and by the partisans: her life was in danger" due to some of the Duce's faithful who had "sworn to kill her to save him from a scandal"; all "her phone calls to him were recorded and five different copies of the text sent to the German commanders" (ibid.: 248); the Allies were following her "to track him down"; she had to "mistrust everybody" for she was "surrounded by traitors." Claretta went on fainting or crying feebly. Obviously, Rachele could not confront her directly, for the young woman eluded her blows through her repeated "absences."

Finally, Rachele got up "with a flaming head and a heart that was pounding hard" and told Claretta, "You will end up badly, Madam," and repeating a refrain she had just read in an anonymous letter sent to her, probably by a partisan,[18] she added, "They will take you to Piazzale Loreto" (ibid.: 249). This prediction did not seem to scare Claretta, for she remained in Gardone.

The war was coming to an end, but the Duce was still hoping that the Germans' "new weapons" would change the outcome of the war. This is what he promised in his last speech to the Milanese population, in mid December 1944, during his three-day visit to the town where he was still surrounded by some admirers (Cervi 1992: 49). But in Northern Italy, the civil war was at its height, for although General Alexander requested the adherents of the armed Italian resistance to demobilize, his appeal remained unheard, since the partisans decided to put all the weight of the popular masses in the fight (Carocci 1975: 392). By mid April 1945, the Allied forces managed to break open the German lines and invaded Northern Italy (ibid.: 393). On 25 April, the partisans proclaimed a general insurrection and liberated the major northern towns (ibid.). This moment was highly dramatic due to the competition between the partisans and the Allied forces, which were trying to control the situation, raising all stakes. And what was at stake was Mussolini's life. For the Comitato di Liberazione Nazionale dell'Alta Italia (CLNAI), it was out of the question to let him fall in the hands of the Allies. A trial was out of question as well. Mussolini seemed aware of the dangers awaiting him. On 18 April, he left Gargnano for Milan. He thought of possible scenarios for escape, but he had to follow the German troops, for they were not willing to let him go. The first attempt, in the Valtellina region, failed. The Como region was then chosen because of its easy access to Switzerland. His wife and three of his children tried to reach Switzerland on their own but were not allowed in. On 27 April, though he was disguised as a German soldier and his famous bald skull was covered with a helmet, Mussolini was recognized and captured in Dongo, along with Claretta and some party leaders.

## The Debate on Mussolini's Last Two Days

Mussolini's last two days—on Lake Como—became a matter of fierce debate among left-wing and right-wing politicians and historians, who each tried to present an authoritative image of his personality and his execution in order to build a "foundation myth" of this important moment in Italy's history, either to secure democracy or to re-create a Fascist order. To the classical versions written in the 1960s, one by Pier Luigi Bellini delle Stelle and Urbano Lazzaro, *Dongo, la fine di Mussolini* (1962), another by Franco Bandini, *Le ultime 95 ore di Mussolini* (1963), today new books reply by giving a different interpretation of these historical moments, such as the one written by Giorgio Pisanò, *Gli ultimi cinque secondi di Mussolini* (1996).

According to the classical version, also upheld by the executioner of Mussolini, Walter Audisio (known as "Colonel Valerio"), in three long articles published by *L'Unità*, the Italian communist newspaper (30 April 1945; 18 November 1945; 28 March 1947), and in a book, *In nome del popolo italiano* (1975), Mussolini and Claretta Petacci were executed together at Giulino di Mezzegra (Como), on 28 April 1945, at about 4 P.M., before the garden gate of the Villa Belmonte, after having been retrieved at the house of the De Maria where they spent the night as prisoners of the partisans of the 52nd Garibaldi Brigate that captured them at Dongo the day before.

A different version states that according to a witness, Dorina Mazzola, Mussolini was executed on 28 April, but at 10 A.M., in the garden of the De Maria house, at Bonzanigo di Mezzegra, while Claretta Petacci was killed at noon on the street corner Rimembranze/Riale just outside the garden of the De Maria house. Though the witness was unable to see the executioners, Pisanò (1996) suggests that the real killer must have been Luigi Longo, the president of the Comitato Insurrezionale Antifascista, who became secretary of the Italian Communist Party at the death of Togliatti, in 1964.

These different versions of the same event reproduce the usual contradictory accounts of the images that friends or foes wanted to communicate about the Duce. First, the executioner. If for one party "Colonel Valerio" was very appropriate as a representative of the Italian nation taking vengeance on the tyrannical dictator, for others the political stature of Walter Audisio seemed insufficient, and inevitably a greater figure was envisaged. Luigi Longo seemed to fit that role, being not only one of the founders of the Italian Communist Party in 1921 but also president of the powerful Comitato Insurrezionale Antifascista, along with Emilio Sereni, Leo Valiani, and Sandro Pertini.

Second, the place and hour of the execution. One version offers a romantic flavor to the whole episode, with Claretta Petacci throwing herself on Mussolini to protect him from the bullets, thus being killed together with him. This version deleted all discussion of political or moral responsibility for her execution.[19] The opposing version, on the contrary, opens up a discussion of the moral or political responsibility pertaining to her actual death.

Third, the way Mussolini was shot. "Shoot me in the chest," urged Mussolini to his executioner (Pisanò 1996: 170), but was he shot in the chest? If we compare all the different versions of the execution, we may conclude that a majority of the descriptions confirm this hypothesis, as does the medical autopsy done by Dr. Cattabeni (30 April 1945), which explicitly states that the chest of the executed was exposed to the guns. On the contrary, we know that in Dongo, on the same day as Mussolini's execution, important Fascists' party leaders were shot, by a firing squad, in the back. But on one specific point Pisanò has to contradict Dr. Cattabeni's autopsy: the latter says that the two bullets on the Duce's forearms were probably caused during his execution by "an instinctive gesture of protection done with the right arm" (ibid.: 192), while the former insists that Mussolini most likely was hit in the forearm in the "extreme attempt to disarm the person who was shooting him" (ibid.: 81).

## Piazzale Loreto

If Mussolini's last two days became a matter of debate among left-wing and right-wing Italians, the "infamous" exhibit polarized the attention of all. "[For] the bodies of Mussolini and Clara Petacci were brought down the narrow road to the waiting truck [filled with a pile of Fascist party leaders' bodies shot in Dongo] that drove off to Milan. The next morning [29 April] all the bodies were found laid out in the same Piazzale Loreto where on August 8, 1944, the Germans [and the Fascists] had shot fifteen hostages. The bodies of Mussolini, Clara Petacci, and of others,[20] were strung up by the feet from the iron roofwork of a filling station" (Marshall 1970: 240).

We know that this way of hanging, a medieval North Italian tradition, was habitually reserved for bankrupts or crooks, persons who had abused community trust by first amassing a large amount of capital through borrowing from and lending to their townsmen, then declaring themselves bankrupt, and consequently fleeing the communal town to avoid any punishment. This particular way of hanging was meant to stress the "infamy" that befell men incapable of keeping the word given to their fellow citizens (Ortalli 1994). But in Piazzale Loreto, on that famous day, 29 April 1945, was it meant that way? And was it understood that way? There appears no clear answer to these two questions. Though the executioners always insisted that they had to pull up the bodies to protect them from the mob's wrath—which seems to be the plain truth when one looks at the movie shot during the event—on the other, the Italians at large who saw the movie or the pictures portraying the event were deeply shocked by it. Not all people, however, according to Luzzatto (1998: 71), who shows how quickly and how well "a real market of the Piazzale Loreto images" spread throughout Italy, two of them becoming "postal cards reproduced with the authorization of the Corpo Volontari della Libertà propaganda office." "Italians were eager to appropriate for themselves," he concludes, "the Duce's dead body." But the threshold of historiography was difficult to trespass, for to this day it is rare to see in a history book on the period a large picture of the hanging. If one is reproduced, it tends to be microscopic; the reduction in size makes it unavailing.[21]

But the display of the corpses in Piazzale Loreto was certainly meant to show the Italian population that the Duce and his regime were really dead, in order to avoid any speculation on a possible return of either one. Also, it had to be the foundation myth of the Italian Republic to come.

Thus, the image Mussolini tried to build for himself during his twenty years in power was dramatically inversed in order to show, once and for all, that the Duce was pushed off from his horse to bite the dust. A dictator of his importance, who had during all his political career so skillfully used images to build his reputation, could not but be executed through an image that imprints itself, indelibly, in all memories.

This display, the hanging, also came as the last important event of a long war that divided Italy into two. The question that it raises, Was it justice or was it vengeance? was inevitably deleted in the aftermath that this terrible war had created in all spirits. The announced execution—in the refrain "We will take them all to Piazzale Loreto," sent by a partisan in an anonymous letter to Rachele Mussolini—was duly carried out. The fifteen hostages that had been shot on 8 August 1944, by Fascists and Germans alike, in the same Piazzale Loreto, were avenged. War had come to an end, but the premises of a permanent feud were also laid down.

## Mussolini's Hidden Corpse

While an anti-fascist coalition governed Italy with the firm intent to overcome its past, Mussolini's body was stolen, barely a year after its burial, from its secret grave in Milan's Cimitero di Musocco—on Easter night, to signify His resurrection, to underline "the persistent vitality of Mussolini's ideology" (Luzzatto 1998: 99). The moment was timely, for two months later, Italians had to express themselves, through a referendum, on their choice between a monarchy and a republic. They indeed chose the latter on 2 June 1946. The new king, Umberto II, was sent into exile along with his family. On 12 August, Mussolini's stolen corpse was recovered in Pavia. After a second autopsy, done in order to confirm the identity of the corpse, it was buried once more, but this time in a place unknown to all, Mussolini's family included. For the next eleven years (ibid.: 120), the mortal remains were "discovered" in different parts of Italy: Monte Paolo, Tivoli, San Cassiano, Predappio (R. Mussolini 1958: 300–302).

During this period, Mussolini's hidden corpse became the focus of major topics of discussion among Italians, passionately debated by antagonist political parties in the press. These topics were moral issues to many, or confrontations useful to unriddle their pasts. Fascists complained often in their diaries that the Duce died in an "ugly way." Bottai, a party leader, criticized Mussolini's running away disguised as a German soldier, his carrying along Clara Petacci to Dongo: "the last act of Mussolini's life was performed without greatness or magnanimity" (Luzzatto 1998: 191). Vincenzo Costa, a federal official in Milan during the German occupation, after noting his own deception over the Duce's behavior, adds, "It should not have ended this way … it should not have ended this way!" (ibid.).

The anti-fascists used the same last events to pinpoint Mussolini's three crimes: treason, fraud, and adultery. Because these events were of major importance to the Italian nation, they were rapidly inflated and distorted. Italians were so shocked at the idea that the Duce tried to avoid his capture by wearing a Luftwaffe coat that rumors spread that he tried to flee wearing a woman's garment or a monk's attire (Luzzatto 1998: 192). The money found with Mussolini and his party leaders at the moment of their arrest gave way to legends of "hidden treasures" to be carried out of Italy, or of jewels stored in Claretta's brassiere (ibid.). Finally Claretta's presence in Dongo beside Mussolini instead of Rachele's on the one hand contributed to underlining the Duce's duplicity; on the other, it established for the couple a reputation of "brothel lovers" (ibid.), which burdens Clara Petacci's memory to this very day.

Then the imagination gave way to what was (historically) absent: "testaments" and "trials" that flourished as a genre. Sergio Luzzatto (1998: 121–128) gives us a list of the most representative of these "testaments," from Indro Montanelli's *Il Buonomo Mussolini* (1947), to Gian Gaetano Gabella, the last one to interview the Duce in Germasino (*Il testamento politico di Mussolini*, 1948), from Giovannini's article in *Oggi* (1948), to Curzio Malaparte's *La Pelle* (1949). The "Testament of Germasino" (near Dongo) is supposed to have been dictated by the Duce himself on 27 April 1945, and it is handed out as a brochure to all visitors in Predappio's cemetery. Mussolini's image is once more polished by these authors. Some highlight the fact that he sacrificed his life to save Italians, or that he confessed to a priest in mid April 1945 to stress his "return to God," or they decree, like Malaparte does, that "the human value of the losers is superior to the one of the winners." (1949). Others, such as Carlo Emilio Gadda, have built a literary career with *Il primo libro delle favole* (1952), *Eros e Priapo* (1955), and *Quer pasticciaccio brutto de via Merulana* (1957), on the "visceral hatred for the Duce's soul and body" (Luzzatto 1998: 133).

The posthumous "trials" of the Duce were evidently a way of absolving Mussolini and of suggesting that, had he been judged, he would probably have been acquitted (Luzzatto 1998: 141). The genre first found its way on the radio, where the arguments in favor of the Duce were mainly the same as the ones promoted by Montanelli in *Il Buonomo Mussolini* (ibid.: 140–142). In Malaparte's *La Pelle* (1949: 400–408), an entire chapter is dedicated to this trial, and Mussolini is metaphorically represented as a fetus, judged by a jury of fetuses. The author, as Mussolini's lawyer, suggests that "nothing is more beautiful and noble, in the world, than a man, a nation, defeated, humiliated, reduced into a fist of rotten meat" (ibid.: 406; also Luzzatto 1998: 142–144). Both Gadda and Malaparte were deeply disenchanted by the twenty years of Fascism their country went through, but both succeed in reproducing, through their explicit metaphors, the image of the genitor that Mussolini had conveyed so well. From Priapos (god of procreation) to fetus: the riddle of the Duce's illegitimate presence in Italy's past is brought forward repeatedly, giving rise to the same old answer.

## The Return of the Corpse

It was on 30 August 1957 that Mussolini's corpse and brain were delivered to his widow, Rachele, in Predappio. The funerals took place the next day. This conclusion seemed inevitable to many Italians, and was brought about, according to Luzzatto (1998: 194), by the fact that during the 1950s the "hegemonic culture was completely impermeable to the epos of the Resistance, while in the magazines a new brand of flour was ground, compassion, around the corpse of the Duce." A veil of acquittal gradually covered Mussolini's three crimes: treason, fraud, and adultery. The veiling was accomplished by denying all charges: no proof was produced that at his arrest he really wore a Luftwaffe coat; if he drove to Dongo on a German lorry, it was because Clara Petacci insisted; never in his life did he have any money on him, and if he had had any, it would inevitably have fallen out from his pockets in Piazzale Loreto; the passion between him and Claretta was only unilateral, for he had many other mistresses (ibid.: 194–199).

But the pardon Italians requested, initially in December 1954, by signing petitions for Mussolini's corpse to be returned to his family (Luzzatto 1998: 190), was essentially due to the efforts of his widow, Rachele. In the twelve years after his death, Rachele was followed by photographs and journalists alike, in order to portray her daily life to an ever larger audience of popular magazines (ibid.: 196). Seldom seen without her apron, always smiling, and always busy, either washing dishes or cutting salads in her kitchen garden, with gray bound hair, surrounded by her children, especially her last-born, Anna Maria, handicapped by poliomyelitis, Rachele managed to overcome her husband's last image, the one of treason-fraud-adultery, by suggesting constantly that this image was simply not true. Rachele also talked to journalists, especially Anita Pensotti, publishing books out of their long interviews, the first one, in 1948, being *La mia vita con Benito* (My life with Benito), in which she portrayed her role as one of a precious aid, dealing with all aspects of his life, the political ones included, for she knew better what Italians thought or felt since she was a perpetual intermediary between Him and them. Claretta's problem was solved through a "last" letter sent to Rachele by her husband in which he writes that she is "the only woman he ever loved" (Luzzatto 1998: 197). A few years before her death, Rachele admitted that this letter, which had been published in the meantime in all major magazines, was a fake (ibid.: 198).

After the return of Mussolini's corpse, Rachele published *Benito il mio uomo* (My man Benito), to relate the actual event and also to stress the fact—evident from the title—that she had finally become his official and only vestal. She describes how she solicited all government agencies responsible in order to get his mortal remains: letters were sent to Nenni, De Gasperi, Scelba, Andreotti, Zoli. Finally, the time was ripe, and Zoli accorded her request. Rachele had to leave her place of confinement, Foro d'Ischia, in great secret, on 29 August 1957, with three bodyguards, to go to Predappio to wait for his mortal remains. The next day at noon, the corpse of Mussolini was officially handed to her, and Rachele, after opening the container to check that the corpse was really the one of her late husband, finally covered it with the linen sheet she had embroidered, alone or in front of photographs. Professors Cattabeni and Cazzaniga, who had performed the three autopsies that the corpse underwent, were also present and gave Rachele Mussolini's brain, which they had carried from Milan in a glass vase, covered by a newspaper. Vincenzo Agnesina, responsible for the whole operation, typed a statement that was signed by the seven persons who participated in the event.

The next day, funerals were held in front of photographs and journalists, as well as nostalgic fascists,[22] whose presence, says Anita Pensotti, annoyed the widow with all their "Alalà" or "A noi!" (1983: 164–179). Finally, on 25 March 1966, Rachele received the visit of two "foreigners" who gave her a tiny box in which the last piece of Mussolini's brain, which was removed in 1945 to be analyzed in the United States, was kept in a piece of cellophane (ibid.: 200–201).

## Conclusion

During the last two years of the war, the grown-up balillas were engaged in a fratricide, either on the side of the Social Italian Republic, initially founded by Mussolini or on the opposite side, the one of the Resistance. The end of this fratricide was sealed in a dramatic way—the "infamous" hanging in Piazzale Loreto—which contributed to keeping the sides apart. The Fascists swallowed deep feelings of bitter vengeance, which were poised for statement at the first opportunity. As for the partisans, especially those near to the Communist Party, they lost their place in the government after the first general elections of April 1948. Only sixteen years later, in 1963, did a coalition of center-left come to power (Colarizi 1996).

By the 1960s the "grandchildren" of Mussolini were arriving on the political stage, far from parental guidance, but deeply embedded in the ideology of their milieu. The time had come for retaliation. From 1969 to 1983, "red" or "black" acts of terrorism appeared on the front pages of newspapers daily, replicating images of carnage still vivid in Italians' memory. From Milano's Piazza Fontana in December 1969 (twenty-seven dead, eighty-eight wounded), the kidnapping and assassination of Aldo Moro in Rome, from March to May 1978 (six dead), and the bombing of Bologna's station in August 1980 (eighty-five dead, two-hundred wounded), Italians had to pay a heavy toll in order to allow this generation to overcome their parents' feud. The terrorists themselves paid dearly. Among them, the most prominent one was Giangiacomo Feltrinelli, a well-known left-wing publisher, son of the rich Fascist Feltrinelli family, who had given the family's Gargnano villa to Mussolini from 1943 to 1945. Being eager to wash away his parents' "guilt," Giangiacomo Feltrinelli became the leader of the terrorist group Nuclei armati proletari. He inadvertently killed himself in March 1972, while placing a bomb along a railway track.

During the first years of terrorism, the "red" current claimed the heritage of the Resistance in order to fight an authoritarian "violent" state that did not respect the rules of democracy (Della Porta 1997: 378), while the "black" current followed the Fascist heritage of denying the Left the right to exist. Whereas the first concentrated on destroying "objects," the second was already attacking the crowd indiscriminately (Piazza Fontana, 1969). But from 1976 on, the Brigate Rosse, the most important terrorist group of the "red" current, committed homicides, the first being the killing of Judge Francesco Coco (ibid.: 389). Gradually, as Della Porta stresses, "red" and "black" terrorists shared the strategy of "attacks against the state" while "violence became an end in itself" (ibid.: 399), "justified by its aesthethic" (ibid.: 418). The escalation of violence in the "red" and the "black" currents was justified by such statements as "it is not towards power that we tend, and not even towards the creation of a new order.... We are interested in the fight, in the action itself, in the daily struggle for the affirmation of our nature" (ibid.: 413). This cannot but remind us of the Futurism manifesto of 1909, in whose images also the "grandchildren" dissolved their expectations.

The grip of the past loosened as the dissolution of the differences that liquefied the terrorist movements touched all political camps. Signs hinted that a page had been turned. The major political parties changed their names and their emblems, in a wish to cut the ties with their past and seek a new beginning. This movement to break with the past also generated many trials—against terrorists, Mafia members, and some of the people implicated in the "Mani pulite" anticorruption investigation. In this vast operation of washing away the "hidden" sins or compelling the culprits to denounce them (Di Bella 1987–1988)—by repenting and confessing the "truth"[23]—Italy was helped by magistrates, such as Giovanni Falcone and Paolo Borsellino, both assassinated by a Mafia fearful of being eradicated, or Antonio Di Pietro, who, by starting the "Mani pulite" investigation, had become Italy's good conscience before being forced to resign.

Thus, although the young generation of the 1990s has developed the capacity to judge their grandfathers' and fathers' past in the light of contemporary values, today old phantoms resound in an attempt to resurrect Italy's hideous past, and these efforts, ridiculous as they may rightly appear to the objective observer, remain dangerous, precisely because their new forms are acceptable to some sectors in Italy and elsewhere in Europe.

# Notes

I would like to thank John Borneman for inviting me into the group that worked on the Death of the Father. My exchange with him and the members of the group was a very enriching personal and scholarly experience. In particular, I want to mention Linda Fisher, whose attentive camera helped us never to get lost. Ms. Gianna Celli and M. Pasquale Pesci of the Rockefeller Foundation's Bellagio Center were the best hosts one could possibly hope for. I also want to thank the Watson Institute (Providence) for inviting me as a visiting scholar (September–October 1998). The daily use of Brown University's library was crucial in preparing this essay for publication, and I thank Professor Anthony Oldcorn for inviting me to give a lecture on the topic (Department of Italian Studies, Brown University). I am grateful also to Professor Anthony Molho (EUI, Florence) and Professor Luisa Accati (Trieste University) for recommending Luzzatto's book, *Il Corpo del Duce*, to Professor Michela De Giorgio (Sassari University) for recommending the *Annali 12: La criminalità* of the *Storia d'Italia*, and to Professor Leor Halevi (Texas A&M University) for recommending Lynn Hunt's *The Family Romance of the French Revolution*.

1. In ancient Rome, three fathers are necessary to gain or to lose one's legitimacy. If we recall the way Aeneas was always represented, we may remember that he carries his father, Anchises, on his shoulders, and his son Ascanius by the hand. Anchises himself carries the ancestral sacra and the son the *lituus*, an inaugural stick, emblem of foundations to come (Thomas 1986: 204, 229). Therefore, a Roman had a pater, an *avus*, and a *proavus* to legitimate his claims, while Rome had Aeneas, his father, and his son. Later, Augustus associated his family's gods with those of the state when he became *pontifex maximus* (from 12 B.C.), clearly identifying himself as the *pater patriae* (Lacey 1986: 139).

2. Margherita Sarfatti (1883–1961) herself, one of Mussolini's best known mistresses, who is still considered as having been his principal consultant on art (Berezin 1997: 82), preferred the literary circle called Novecento to the Futurists. The name "Novecento" was taken from the name of the journal created in Rome in 1926 under the direction of Massimo Bontempelli and Curzio Malaparte.

3. During the high days of Fascism, Mussolini's office window in Palazzo Venezia (Rome) was kept lit all night long to give the impression that the Duce was constantly working (Musiedlak 1991: 134).

4. The image of youth was already gaining prominence during the Italian Risorgimento; in fact, Mazzini's political organization was called Giovane Italia (Young Italy). Later, just before the unification of Italy (1861), Piedmont chose to celebrate the special detachment of La Marmora's Bersaglieri, which gave statement to the idea of juvenile ardor through their uniform, their way of marching at a run, and their feathers floating in the wind (Oliva 1996: 395).

5. Much has been said about Mussolini's love for his first-born, Edda, and even Pierre Milza, one of the last to write about him, returns to the topic frequently (1999: 462–477, 496–503, 850–854). This father-daughter relation, which ends dramatically on 9 January 1944—as in a Greek tragedy—with Edda's flight to Switzerland, when she understood that her father was not going to commute her husband's death sentence, is one of the events in Mussolini's life capable of highlighting his genitor choice. Lynn Hunt's *The Family Romance of the French Revolution* (1993) sheds light on the use of "familial" relations in politics, and my analysis of the Franca Viola case (Di Bella 1983) underlines the importance of the father's role through this much talked about rape case in Sicily.

6. On the contrary, the father and the mother of Mafarka, the hero, are present in the novel, as is his brother, Magamal. In fact, the plot of the novel turns around the death of Magamal and Mafarka's sadness for being deprived of his beloved presence. This is how Mafarka arrives at the idea of begetting an immortal son, a mechanical huge bird (a forerunner of the fascist eagle?), without a female's participation, to whom he gives

life by sacrificing his own through a kiss. For our comparison between Marinetti and Mussolini, it is worth noting that both men had a cult of their surname's first letter, "M," and reproduced it constantly: Marinetti in his novel ("M" being used for the majority of names in it) and Mussolini in all types of Fascist rituals (along with "Dux").

7. For the anthropological discussion of the pater/genitor dichotomy, see E. R. Leach (1969).

8. Pierre Milza, in his recent Mussolini biography (1999: 478ff.) reminds us that we do not have to take the memories of Quinto Navarra, Mussolini's chamberlain, for granted; possibly the Duce did not make love with the different women that came to see him daily. But, as Milza himself stresses, Mussolini did nothing to contradict this legend and preferred this type of rumor to persist rather than deny them.

9. "Balilla" is the nickname attributed by local tradition to a young boy, Giovan Battista Perasso, who, on 5 December 1746, started an insurrection in Genoa against the Austrian invaders by throwing a stone on an imperial officer. Later, he became a national hero for the Risorgimento elites (mid nineteenth century). He was also very popular in school books after the Italian unity (1861), and with Fascism he became an identity icon for youth (Oliva 1996: 393–397). After 1926, the youth organizations were unified under an institution called Opera Nazionale Balilla (ONB) which was a division of the Ministry of National Education. The ONB comprised the *balilla* (boys from eight to eleven years old), the *balilla moschettieri* (twelve- to thirteen-year-olds), the *avanguardisti* (fourteen- to fifteen-year-olds), and the *avanguardisti moschettieri* (sixteen- to seventeen-year-olds). Girls were divided into *piccole italiane* (eight- to fourteen-year-olds) and *giovani italiane* (fifteen- to seventeen-year-olds). From the ages of six to eight, boys and girls were joined as *figli della lupa*. In 1927, parents were obliged to enroll their children at the ONB (ibid.: 397–398; see also De Grazia 1992; Passerini 1996). The Italian verses of the Balilla's song go "L'occhio del Duce brilla/fisso sui suoi Balilla/siam la scintilla d'amor che un dì/dal suo gran cuore uscì sì sì" (Cervi 1992: 165).

10. Already in 1926, after the attempt on Mussolini's life by Violet Gibson, fourteen-year-old Clara Petacci sent a letter to Mussolini, saying: "Why could I not strangle that murderous woman that wounded you, Divine Being? Why could I not snatch her away, forever, from Italian land, stained by your pure blood, your great, good, sincere Romagnese blood! Duce, my life is for you!" (Luzzatto 1998: 20). Unless otherwise noted, all translations are my own.

11. Once Claretta was firmly established as Mussolini's *favorita*, rumors of a "Petacci's clan" became persistent, but they seem to stem mainly from her brother's self-interested presence beside the Duce. Marcello Petacci was shot in Dongo, along with the other party leaders, on 28 April 1945.

12. As reported by G. B. Guerri (1995: 19), the first mention of Mussolini's syphilis (which was refuted by the autopsy of 1945) was in June 1919, when he was thirty-six years old, by a police captain named Giovanni Casti.

13. In 1941, the Italian army opened new fronts in Greece, the Balkans (which Hitler wanted instead to preserve, to aid his future expansion into Russia), and Russia. Mussolini did not accept Hitler's idea that Italian troops should be confined to North Africa. He insisted, for ideological reasons, on sending them also to Russia, for he wanted to be known as one of the Fascist leaders who had expelled communism from Europe (Colarizi 1991: 352).

14. In this speech, well analyzed by Imbriani (1992), the Duce accused Italians of being poor soldiers because their hatred for their enemies, essentially the British, was not strong enough to motivate them to fight properly.

15. The northern part of Italy was in fact ruled by Albert Kesserling, chief of the German army; Karl Wolff, chief of the SS; and by the German ambassador, Rahn (Guerri 1995: 268).

16. The other four who are executed are: Emilio De Bono, Luciano Gottardi, Giovanni Marinelli, and Carlo Pareschi.

17. In fact, it seems that Mussolini's first comment was "With all the difficulties we have to overcome and all we're going through just now, there are still people who bother

with this tittle-tattle." This was understood by Vittorio—a little hastily according to us—as "that he didn't attach overriding importance to his affair with Clara Petacci." So he went on to say to his father, "if this was the case, it wouldn't be too great a sacrifice to send her away" (V. Mussolini 1973: 52).

18. On 8 August 1944, fifteen hostages were shot in Piazzale Loreto (Milan) by the Fascist Guardia Nazionale Repubblicana and the German army. The shock among the population was astounding, and for almost one year the square was called Piazza dei XV Martiri (Piazza of the fifteen Martyrs) (Dondi 1996: 489). In the autumn of 1944, when Rachele visited Claretta, she had just received an anonymous poem whose refrain was "We will take them all to Piazzale Loreto" (R. Mussolini 1958: 249).

19. The question of Claretta's execution has not been discussed much by Italian historiography, nor has there been an inquiry into the fact that her corpse did not undergo an autopsy, though she was not wearing panties while exhibited in Piazzale Loreto. In fact, when her body was strung up by the feet from the iron roofwork there, somebody put a belt around her skirt to prevent it from falling and showing her nudity. According to Pisanò (1996), the articles in L'Unità (November 1945) relate how Claretta searched for her panties before leaving the house of the De Maria, while "Colonel Valerio" (W. Audisio) pressed her to join them. Unfortunately, I was unable to see these articles and check Pisanò's assertion. On the other hand, this particular event cannot be found in the book published by Audisio a few years later (1975: 375–393). Indeed, only an autopsy would have foreclosed the suspicion that, possibly, Claretta was raped before her death.

20. On 29 April 1945, seven bodies were strung up by the feet from the iron roofwork of a filling station in Milan's Piazzale Loreto. These were the bodies of Mussolini, Petacci, and the party leaders A. Pavolini, F. Barracu, P. Zerbino, R. Romano, A. Siveroni (De Felice and Goglia 1983: 32). Achille Starace, who happened to be in Milan on that day, was arrested and shot in front of them (Guerri 1995: 193–194).

21. For a long time, the Fascist period was omitted from history courses in Italian schools. Only members of the generation that is now in its forties were able to study Fascism in high school. For the popular memory of the Fascist cultural experience among Turin's working classes, see Passerini 1987.

22. Nowadays, the De Maria house, on Como Lake, is hardly visited, whereas before it was one of the main stations in the Fascists' via crucis. But Mussolini's birthplace, Predappio, is annually visited by young neofascists. The noisy presence of "Alalà" or "A noi!" disturbs Mussolini's popular granddaughter, Alessandra, as it disturbed her grandmother, Rachele. Alessandra Mussolini—daughter of Romano, a major Italian jazz pianist, and Maria Scicolone, sister of Sophia Loren, the well-known Italian movie star—portrays, for many Italians, a pleasant syncretism of their past.

23. I have worked extensively not only on the problem of compelling today's culprits into denouncing others (Di Bella 1987–88), but also on "repenting" and confessing the "truth" (Di Bella 1999a and 1999b), and on "lies" (Di Bella 1991) in Sicily (sixteenth through the twentieth century).

# References

Audisio, Walter. 1975. *In nome del popolo italiano*. Milan: Teti Editore.
Baioni, Massimo. 1996. "Predappio." In *I Luoghi della memoria. Simboli e miti dell'Italia unita*, ed. Mario Isnenghi, pp. 501–511. Rome and Bari: Laterza.
Bandini, Franco. 1968 [1963]. *Le ultime 95 ore di Mussolini*. Milan: Mondadori.
Belli, Gabriella. 1996. *Fortunato Depero futuriste. De Rome à Paris 1915–1925*. Paris: Musées.
Bellini delle Stelle, Pier Luigi, and Urbano Lazzaro. 1975 [1962]. *Dongo, la fine di Mussolini*. Milan: Mondadori.
Beltramelli, Antonio. 1923. *L'Uomo nuovo, Benito Mussolini*. Milan: Mondadori.
Berezin, Mabel. 1997. *Making the Fascist Self: The Political Culture of Interwar Italy*. Ithaca: Cornell University Press.
Bidussa, David. 1994. *Il Mito del bravo italiano*. Milan: Il Saggiatore.
Boatti, Giorgio, ed. 1989. *Caro Duce. Lettere di donne italiane a Mussolini 1922–1943*. Preface by C. Cederna. Milan: Rizzoli.
Bodin, Jean. 1986 [1593]. *Les Six Livres de La République*. 6 vols. Paris: Fayard.
Bollati, Giulio. 1984. *L'Italiano. Il carattere nazionale come storia e come invenzione*. Turin: Einaudi.
Carocci, Giampiero. 1975. *Storia d'Italia dall'Unità ad oggi*. Milan: Feltrinelli.
Cervi, Mario, ed. 1992. *Mussolini. Album di una vita*. Milan: Rizzoli.
Colarizi, Simona. 1991. *L'Opinione degli Italiani sotto il regime, 1929–1943*. Rome and Bari: Laterza.
———. 1996. *Biografia della Prima Republica*. Rome and Bari: Laterza.
De Begnac, Ivon. 1934. *Trent'anni di Mussolini, 1883–1915*. Preface by F. T. Marinetti. Rome: Arti Grafiche Menaglia.
———. 1936. *Vita di Benito Mussolini. I. Alla scuola della rivoluzione antica: vita dei Mussolini dalle origini al dicembre 1904*. Milan: Mondadori.
De Felice, Renzo. 1988. *Le Fascisme. Un totalitarisme à l'italienne?* Paris: Presses de la Fondation Nationale des Sciences Politiques.
———. 1995 [1969]. *Le Interpretazioni del fascismo*. Rome and Bari, Laterza.
De Felice, Renzo, and Luigi Goglia. 1983. *Mussolini il mito*. Rome and Bari: Laterza.
De Grazia, Victoria. 1992. *How Fascism Ruled Women: Italy, 1922–1945*. Berkeley: University of California Press.
Della Porta, Donatella. 1997. "Il terrorismo." In *Storia d'Italia. Annali 12: La criminalità*. ed. Luciano Violante, pp. 373–420. Turin: Einaudi.
Di Bella, Maria Pia. 1983. "Mythe et histoire dans l'élaboration du fait divers: le cas Franca Viola." *Annales ESC* 4:827–842.
———. 1987–1988. "Manquer de parole: omertà et dénonciation en Sicile." *Le Genre humain* 16–17:229–242.
———. 1991. "Témoignage et justice: un épisode sicilien." *Annales ESC* 1:45–51.
———. 1999a. *La Pura verità. Discarichi di coscienza intesi dai Bianchi (Palermo, 1541–1820)*. Palermo: Sellerio Editore.
———. 1999b. "L'omertà pietosa dei condannati a morte in Sicilia." *Prometeo* 68:98–104.
Di Cori, Paola. 1996. "Le leggi razziali." In *I Luoghi della memoria. Simboli e miti dell'Italia unita*, ed. Mario Isnenghi, pp. 461–476. Rome and Bari: Laterza.
Dondi, Mirco. 1996. "Piazzale Loreto." In *I Luoghi della memoria. Simboli e miti dell'Italia unita*, ed. Mario Isnenghi, pp. 487–499. Rome and Bari: Laterza.
Freedberg, David. 1989. *The Power of Images: Studies in the History and Theory of Response*. Chicago: University of Chicago Press.
Gadda, Carlo Emilio. 1957. *Quer pasticciaccio brutto de via Merulana*. Milan: Garzanti.
———. 1967 [1955]. *Eros e Priapo. (Da furore a cenere)*. Milan: Garzanti.
———. 1976 [1952]. *Il primo libro delle favole*. Milan: Garzanti.
Gilmore, David D. 1990. *Manhood in the Making: Cultural Concepts of Masculinity*. New Haven: Yale University Press.

Gruzinski, Serge. 1990. *La Guerre des images de Christophe Colomb à "Blade Runner" (1492–2019)*. Paris: Fayard.

Guerri, Giordano Bruno. 1995. *Fascisti. Gli Italiani di Mussolini. Il regime degli Italiani*. Milan: Mondadori.

Hulten, Karl Gunnar Pontus, org. 1986. *Futurismo/Futurism. Esposizione a Palazzo Grassi*. New York: Abbeville Press.

Hunt, Lynn. 1993. *The Family Romance of the French Revolution*. Berkeley: University of California Press.

Imbriani, Angelo Michele. 1992. *Gli Italiani e il Duce. Il mito e l'immagine di Mussolini negli ultimi anni del fascismo (1938–1943)*. Foreword by A. Lepre. Naples: Liguori Editore.

Kantorowicz, Ernst H. 1957. *The King's Two Bodies: A Study in Mediaeval Political Theology*. Princeton: Princeton University Press.

Lacey, Walter K. 1986. "Patria potestas." In *The Family in Ancient Rome*, ed. Beryl Rawson, pp. 121–144. Ithaca: Cornell University Press.

Leach, Edmund R. 1969. "Virgin Birth." In *Genesis as Myth and other Essays*, ed. Edmund R. Leach, pp. 85–124. London: J. Cape.

Lemaire, Gérard-Georges. 1995. *Futurisme*. Paris: Editions du Regard.

Lepre, Aurelio. 1995. *Mussolini l'Italiano. Il Duce nel mito e nella realtà*. Milan: Mondadori.

Loy, Rosetta. 1997. *La Parola ebreo*. Turin: Einaudi.

Luzzatto, Sergio. 1998. *Il Corpo del Duce. Un cadavere tra immaginazione, storia e memoria*. Turin: Einaudi.

———. 2001. *L'Immagine del Duce: Mussolini nelle fotografie dell'Istituto Luce*. Rome: Editori Riuniti.

Malaparte, Curzio. 1963 [1928]. *L'Arcitaliano e tutte le altre poesie*. Florence: Vallecchi Editore.

———. 1949. *La Pelle. Storia e racconto*. Rome: Aria d'Italia.

Malvano, Laura. 1996. "Le mythe de la jeunesse à travers l'image. Le fascisme italien." In *Histoire des jeunes en Occident*, ed. G. Levi and J-Cl. Schmitt, pp. 277–308. Paris: Plon.

Marinetti, Filippo Tommaso. 1910. *Mafarka le futuriste, roman africain*. Paris: Sansot.

———. 1924. *Futurismo e fascismo*. Foligno: Campitelli Editore.

———. 1983. *Scritti francesi*. Introduction, texts, and notes by Pasquale A. Jannini. Milan: Mondadori Editore.

Marshall, J. 1970. *The Castle's Keep: The Villa Serbelloni in History*. Bellagio: Rockefeller Center.

Milza, Pierre. 1999. *Mussolini*. Paris: Fayard.

Milza, Pierre, and Serge Berstein. 1980. *Le Fascisme italien, 1919–1945*. Paris: Seuil.

Montanelli, Indro. 1947. *Il Buonomo Mussolini*. Milan: Edizioni Riunite.

Mosse, George L. 1996. *The Image of Man: The Creation of Modern Masculinity*. New York: Oxford University Press.

Murialdi, Paolo. 1986. *La Stampa del regime fascista*. Rome and Bari: Laterza.

Musiedlak, Didier. 1991. "Le Duce, le balcon et la foule." In *Rome, 1920–1945. Le modèle fasciste, son Duce, sa mythologie*, ed. Françoise Liffran, pp. 133–138. Paris: Editions Autrement.

Mussolini, Rachele. 1958. *Benito il mio uomo*. Milan: Rizzoli.

Mussolini, Vittorio. 1973. *Mussolini: The Tragic Women in His Life*. New York: The Dial Press.

Oliva, Gianni. 1996. "Balilla." In *I Luoghi della memoria. Simboli e miti dell'Italia unita*, ed. Mario Isnenghi, pp. 391–401. Rome and Bari: Laterza.

Ortalli, Gherardo. 1994. *La Peinture infamante du XIIIe au XVIe siècle: "Pingatur in Palatio."* Paris: Monfort.

Palla, Marco. 1994. *Mussolini e il fascismo*. Florence: Giunti-Casterman.

Paris, Robert. 1968. *Les Origines du fascisme*. Paris: Flammarion.

Passerini, Luisa. 1987. *Fascism in Popular Memory: The Cultural Experience of the Turin Working Class* [*Torino operaia e Fascismo*. Laterza, 1984]. Cambridge and Paris: Cambridge University Press and Editions de la Maison des Sciences de l'Homme.

———. 1991. *Mussolini immaginario. Storia di una biografia 1915–1939*. Rome and Bari: Laterza.

———. 1996. "La jeunesse comme métaphore du changement social. Deux débats sur les jeunes: l'Italie fasciste, l'Amérique des années 1950." In *Histoire des jeunes en Occident*, ed. Giovanni Levi and Jean-Claude Schmitt, pp. 339–408. Paris: Plon.

Pensotti, Anita. 1983. *Rachele. Settant'anni con Mussolini nel bene e nel male*. Milan: Bompiani.

Pisanò, Giorgio. 1996. *Gli Ultimi cinque secondi di Mussolini*. Milan: Il Saggiatore.

Porta, Gianfranco. 1996. "Il confino." In *I Luoghi della memoria. Simboli e miti dell'Italia unita*, ed. Mario Isnenghi, pp. 439–460. Rome and Bari: Laterza.

Rafanelli, Leda. 1975 [1946]. *Una Donna e Mussolini*. Introduction by Pier Carlo Masini. Milan: Rizzoli Editore.

Rousset, Jean. 1978. *Le Mythe de Don Juan*. Paris: A. Colin.

Sarfatti, Margherita G. 1926. *Dux*. Milan: Mondadori.

Setta, Sandro. 1993. *Benito Mussolini*. Teramo: Lisciani & Giunti Editori.

Sulis, Edgardo. 1934 [1932]. *Imitazione di Mussolini*. Milan: Novecentesca.

Theweleit, Klaus. 1987–1989. *Male Fantasies*. 2 vols. Minneapolis: University of Minnesota Press [*Männerphantasien*. Verlag Roter Stern, 1977–1978].

Thomas, Yan. 1986. "A Rome, pères citoyens et cité des pères (IIe siècle avant J.-C.-IIe siècle après J.-C.)." In *Histoire de la famille, I. Mondes lointains, mondes anciens*, ed. André Bourguière, Christiane Klapisch-Zuber, Martine Segalen, and Françoise Zonabend, pp. 194–229. Paris: Colin.

Valeri, Nino. 1962. *La Lotta politica in Italia dall'Unità al 1925. Idee e documenti*. Florence: Le Monnier.

Zangrandi, Ruggero. 1963. *Il Lungo viaggio attraverso il fascismo. Contributo alla storia di una generazione*. Milan: Feltrinelli Editore.

# Gottvater, Landesvater, Familienvater: Identification and Authority in Germany

*John Borneman*

## Hitler's Death and the Afterlife of His Image

After months of heavy fighting outside the city, the Russian army finally surrounded Berlin, where Adolf Hitler was sheltered in the bunker of the Reichskanzlei. Sometime during the day of 29 April 1945, Hitler had been informed about Mussolini's fate: shot along with his mistress and hung by their feet in a gas station in central Milan where crowds kicked and spit at the bodies. Rather than face such humiliation, he ordered two hundred liters of gasoline to be brought to the bunker and to be used, following his suicide, to burn his body and make it unrecognizable. In preparation, Hitler summoned a civil servant to wed him to Eva Braun, his longtime companion, in order to take her, as he explained in his personal testament, "as my spouse with me into death" (cited in Fest 1973: 1015). During his twelve-year rule, he had refused to marry, claiming that his dedication to the life of the *Volk* precluded such a personal bond. With his death impending, marriage appeared in a new light, as a personal completion, a final closure and legitimation of life. Hitler's doctor had provided him with cyanide tablets, but fearing they might not work, he first tried them on Blondi, his beloved German shepherd, who died within an hour. Shortly before 3:30 A.M. on 30 April, Hitler followed his bride and swallowed cyanide tablets, after which the two bodies were burned and buried in a granite grave.

On the following day, Hitler's successor, Admiral Doenitz, announced on German radio that Hitler "had fallen at his command post," but he insisted that the Germans should fight on. A short excerpt from Bruckner's Seventh Symphony preceded the announcement; a selection from

Wagner's *Twilight of the Gods* followed. Two days later, Hitler's trusted head of propaganda, Joseph Goebbels, along with his wife and six children, also took cyanide. After another month and hundreds of thousands of deaths, on 5 June, Doenitz signed an unconditional surrender to the Allied forces.

By the time Soviet soldiers arrived at the Reichskanzlei, Hitler's burned body had been removed to another floor, casting some doubt on the exact identity of the bodies found. Under the extraordinary situation of preparing to administer the occupation of Germany, the Soviet army moved the remains of the body they presumed to be Hitler's, reportedly first to the city of Magdeburg southwest of Berlin, before finally transporting it to Moscow. Soviet secrecy about these circumstances, and the extreme concern of Allied authorities with the entrancing effects of Hitler and Nazi symbolism over the German people, contributed to the mystery around Hitler's death and the disposition of his body. Hitler had been the Führer, the personification of the Third Reich, central source of meaning and power for the Volk. Was he dead, or wasn't he?

Written and oral descriptions of this death scenario circulated widely and immediately, but the only material representations or images were a photo of a burned corpse vaguely resembling Hitler and one of his teeth circulated by the Soviet occupiers. A Soviet doctor present at the autopsy first made these photos widely available in a 1969 American publication, which was reprinted in Russian in 1986, and translated and published in German in 1990 (Bezymenskij 1990). Throughout the Cold War, rumors circulated in Germany and abroad that Hitler had indeed escaped and even been sighted in the New World. The myth of Nazi survival found support in the alleged sightings of other Nazi leaders, such as Hitler's private secretary and second most powerful man in the Third Reich, Martin Bormann, most of whom were never apprehended by legal authorities.[1]

Because the Allied occupiers enforced an immediate ban on the representation of Hitler or the use of Nazi paraphernalia, the German people were spared a public discussion of the power and appeals of Hitler and Nazi symbolism. Both the Federal Republic of Germany (FRG) in the West and the German Democratic Republic (GDR) in the East, though motivated by different pedagogical and political theories, repressed parts of this past by reinforcing the initially Allied-imposed taboo on Hitler's images and writings. Nazi symbology was also removed—eagles and swastikas chopped off building entrances, Hitler's *Mein Kampf* and other documents of Nazi ideology removed from libraries, pictures and posters burned, monuments blown up. The two Germanys were probably the only European countries where one could grow up during the Cold War and not see a swastika in public space. This repression was intended to prevent the creation of a Hitler cult, and in that it was successful. But it also worked, predictably, to assert the importance of Hitler's absence (see Knopp 1979). Since the charred body in question was found not in the basement bunker with Eva but on the next floor of the Reichskanzlei, and since it had been moved around subsequently, skeptics questioned whether the body in the photo by Bezymenskij was actually Hitler's.

In 1990, the year of German reunification, there was again an extended public discussion in Germany about the circumstances of Hitler's death—and about his remains. In the debate about what to do with the acre of land on which the old Reichskanzlei had been located on Potsdamer Platz, it was decided (much as in 1945) that the exact place of the bunker and Hitler's death would remain unmarked.

This chapter examines the effects of Hitler's suicide and of the enforced silence about him. It addresses a series of questions. What is the significance of suicide as a mode of social death and the efficacy of a policy of official silencing? What were the dynamics of identification in regime transformations in Germany, and what is its relation to the changing nature of German national identification? My primary concern is to contribute to theorizing the end of Nazi authority in 1945. How did a society depart from a form of political authority that was totalizing and patricentric? How did this regime end, and how is authority transformed through this end? Any analysis of regime change assumes a before and an after, but the cause of this transformation is never reducible to a single factor at a single moment in time. The weight given to these various factors depends on the questions and perspective of the analyst. This essay is intended as an analytics of symbolic forms of German authority and not as a history or causal account of German authority. It begins with knowledge in the ethnographic present before tracking it through memories and memorials back to various beginnings. The Nazi regime, then, is situated in the context of memories of prior regime transformations in Germany and memorialization of dead leaders. Such an analytics, it is hoped, will yield new perspectives on transformations authority, specifically on changes in Germany the "order of the father"—*Gottvater, Landesvater, Familienvater* (God-the-Father, father of the country, father of the family)

## Death Cults, Mourning Practices, and the Identificatory Father

Hitler's suicide was followed by the unconditional surrender ending World War II. This surrender severely undermined and destabilized forms of authority in Germany, producing a general "sovereignty crisis" at all levels—transcendent, territorial, political, economic, and domestic. Four occupation armies, each with its own policies, occupied different zones, administered a divided capital, held hundreds of thousands of male prisoners of war, and created a massive market for sex with German women. The economy had been thoroughly destroyed, and the Reichsmark thoroughly devalued, so that in many areas cigarettes and chocolate became the most stable currencies of exchange. The Allied occupation not only devalued and destabilized, however, it also provided a framework and a temporal reprieve that enabled a radical transformation in relations of authority. An essential element in legitimizing the Allied power over the Germans (in this respect the Western powers were much more successful than the Soviets) was that the unconditional surrender of sovereignty was followed by an extensive and long-term nonpunitive occupation. The occupation forces clearly situated themselves as the pater—the source of discipline and order, while they competed with each other for the role of identificatory father. Only Japan (see Han, this volume) has experienced an occupation of similar scope and manner. The German occupation was unique, as I will discuss later, in its dual, oppositional order: with the dominant U.S. occupiers setting up an "economy of exchange," while the Soviets set up an "economy of extraction."

The crisis in German sovereignty led to key modifications in mourning practices, particularly in the memorialization of leaders and in the state's role in remembering the dead. The Allies prompted and encouraged but did not directly cause these modifications. Their fear of a Hitler or Nazi cult led them to impose an initial taboo on public discussion of Hitler's self-immolation and the sources of his power. Any sign of mourning for Hitler or the Third Reich was strictly forbidden, vigorously enforced with the threat of imprisonment by both local authorities and, in West Germany, by the Constitutional Police. Hence, the Allies left unmarked the place of Hitler's death and disallowed any association of his bodily remains with a burial site that could later be used to commemorate him. This taboo on the leader's image was then followed in both East and West Germany by a policy, mentioned above, of systematic elimination of signs of the major symbols associated with the Third Reich. The demilitarization prescribed by the Potsdam Accords also included the disbanding of the many traditional fraternities that had propagated a self-image linking the German to honor, chivalry, and militarism. Finally, the Allies attempted to prevent an honoring of fallen soldiers and dead leaders that might resemble the cultivation of death cults that characterized German society following World War I (Koselleck 1994; Mosse 1990). The day of 15 November, which had been set aside in 1922 as a national holiday to honor the victims of World War I, was reconsecrated as Day of National Mourning *(Volkstrauertag)* in 1952, and rededicated to principles of atonement, understanding, and peace. I personally experienced that day five times in Berlin in the decades of the 1980s and 1990s. Each time, I had the sense of a frozen time—streets were still and empty, individuals withdrew from the public sphere—there were no signs of any *collective* remembrance.

These bans on honoring the dead made it difficult for Germans to mourn their own losses. For they, too, had suffered personally—millions of injuries and casualties in the war, immense displacement and coerced population relocation from the eastern territories. All Germans were not exactly "unable to mourn," as in the famous description by the Mitscherlichs (1967) description, their bereavement was privatized and denied the public ceremony that usually accompanies departure from the dead. This privatization was due both to the inability of existent German public figures, in particular those tied to political authority and the state, to initiate mourning practices and to the new international regime of guilt in which Germans were held responsible for the war and the Holocaust. Unlike in Italy, where the Italians cheered the arrival of the American Allies because they had already broken with Mussolini, Germans did not always welcome the invading Allies. The several German attempts to assassinate Hitler had failed, so that ultimately his break with "the people" was one he had effected through his suicide. Hence even people who themselves had been persecuted under Hitler's rule often feared an Allied policy of revenge that would make no discrimination as to degrees of complicity among the Germans.

A major effect of this sequence of events is that in German society since 1945 there has been an aversion to death cults, with limited or nonexistent public mourning for national leaders. The lack of death cults of national figures suggests a shift in the status of current identification with German leaders who might occupy the symbolic space of the national Father. There has been no space for a national Landesvater. During the course of fieldwork between 1986 and 1996, I visited the graves of German leaders often. In the summer of 1996, I selected for revisit graves of the five leaders who people had mentioned most often as national leaders: the Prussian king Frederick II; Otto von Bismarck, the first chancellor of the united German Reich; Walter Ulbricht, the GDR head of State and Party who most strongly shaped the East German state; Willy Brandt, the first postwar Social Democratic Party chancellor, and Franz Josef Strauss, remembered fondly as the Bavarian Landesvater and national patriot. The men in this partial list of leaders with pan-German stature suggest alternative identificatory possibilities with political authority.

Of these men, only the remains of King Frederick II (known as the Great) now lie in a prominent place, making his grave easy to visit. It is no coincidence that he is the only political leader deemed worthy of national honor by the three postwar German states: the former East Germany (after 1987), the former West Germany, and the united Germany. His prestige is sufficiently large so that his statue (the sovereign leader riding a horse) graces the center boulevard on Unter den Linden in Berlin. During World War II, his body had been relocated from his summer palace, Sanssouci, in Potsdam near Berlin, to rest in relative safety along with that of his father (known as the Soldier-King) in the Hohenzollern estate in Baden-Württemberg. In 1995, the remains of both Frederick II and his father were returned on a flatbed train to Sanssouci in an officially private ceremony. Chancellor Helmut Kohl and other prominent persons attended, but, significantly, as private persons and not as representatives of their offices. Mourning even for Frederick the Great remained a private affair in which participating public figures had to disclaim their public personas. The corpses were greeted by thousands of well-wishers, including conservative nationalists waving the old Reich's flag, and gay and lesbian groups who passed out leaflets heralding Frederick II as "our gay King." Members of the latter group dressed in period costumes with wigs and gowns and staged a separate ceremonial walk up the long steps of Sanssouci. Frederick's remains were placed in a grave with his beloved hounds, as he wished in his last testament. The grave itself is in a poorly marked and unassuming spot on the top of a terrace. Only the name of Frederick II on a small cement plaque identifies the site as a burial spot; the names of the hounds on their seven cement plaques have disappeared over the years. A marble statue of a nude woman holding a baby positioned slightly in front of and between Frederick's tomb and that of his dogs creates a strange juxtaposition, for during his lifetime, Frederick had little to do with women (much less with a nude one), and he fathered no children. Unmarked Roman busts of learned men perched on stands in a semi-circle hedge surrounding the grave create a third context, that of Frederick's admiration for the Enlightenment (omitting, of course, any reference to the French, with whom he particularly identified).

Bismarck's grave in the family estate in Fredericksruh near Hamburg situates him within his Junker class origins and Prussian heritage, drawing little attention to his pan-German legacy. His body lies in a tomb next to his wife's in a chapel on the estate. Bodies of his children and heirs, along with their spouses, rest just outside the chapel. The friend accompanying me was most concerned with his present heirs, wondering if they lived in the estate, what part they took in its maintenance. Caretakers could not answer her questions. Part of the estate does in fact serve as a tourist attraction, and we walked among the large collection of exotic, living butterflies, initially bred by Bismarck's wife, and viewed the museum where Bismarck memorabilia documents his extraordinary place in history. Later, I realized that I also enjoyed the memory of the former *Reichskanzler* on a daily basis by drinking the popular Bismarck mineral water, and I've tried Bismarck schnapps, as well as Bismarck herring, available in stores throughout Germany.

Of those local provincial leaders who retain the prenational tradition of being honored as Landesvater, Bavaria's Franz Josef Strauss represents perhaps the strongest figure. Given the historical rivalry between Catholic Bavaria and a dominant Protestant Prussia, Bavaria still stands out among German provinces for its strong assertion of regional political identification over the national. A friend from the former East who moved to Bavaria in 1989 drove with me in search of Strauss's grave. His body is buried next to his wife's in a modest crypt just outside of Munich. The modesty seems at odds with Strauss's partisan, often belligerent, role in German politics. Following local Catholic tradition, his corpse rests in a crypt that belongs to his wife's family. Although it is well known that Strauss had a mistress, the grave bears no sign of this relationship. Moreover, for the outsider, the burial site offers no clues as to the political status and stature of Strauss. "Perhaps his memorialization is better represented in another site," I thought as I flew out of Munich the next day: Strauss's status has been preserved by renaming Munich's airport after him.

There is some indication of a postwar revival of the provincial Landesvater tradition. Immediately after World War II, local leaders in many of the German provinces, such as Hessen and Bremen, reasserted the authority of the local father, a tradition that seemed to ebb some in the 1960s, but then had another revival in the 1970s. One can trace such a history through Hans Filbinger, for example, the former Nazi judge and minister-president of Baden-Württemberg in the West, who was deigned Landesvater in the 1950s; his replacement in the 1980s, Minister-President Lothar Späth, inherited the appellation. In the 1990s, three other ruling minister-presidents, Johannes Rau of Nordheim-Westphalen in the West, Kurt Biedenkopf of Saxony, and Manfred Stolpe of Brandenburg in the East, were referred to as Landesväter. But even here, the affective ties to these figures are limited when compared to their meaning before the twentieth century. Most *Länder* do not even have such authority figures, and more competitive democratic elections make it possible and likely that the top leaders will be replaced frequently. Perhaps the greatest change in the term Landesvater is that it now stands on its own as a limited form of identification, no longer deriving its authority from either the domestic or transcendent father. Even at the pragmatic level, office is strongly separated from person, so that unlike in Great Britain or the United States today, or in Wilhelminian or Nazi Germany, leaders' sex lives and domestic affairs, as well as their religious affiliations, are largely irrelevant for political identification. Only at the level of the symbolization of the physical body—former Chancellor Kohl's height and bulk, for example—does the personal stand for the social body.

No consideration of the types of postwar political leaders is adequate without comparing East and West, for competition between the two Germanys largely shaped leaders' careers. There were chancellors in the West (Konrad Adenauer, Ludwig Erhardt, Kurt-Georg Kiesinger, Willy Brandt, Helmut Schmidt, Helmut Kohl), heads of Party and State in the East (Wilhelm Pieck, Otto Grotewohl,[2] Walter Ulbricht, Erich Honecker, Egon Krenz). Brandt, Pieck, Grotewohl, Ulbricht, and Honecker had all lived in exile during the Third Reich and were active in resistance movements. After World War II, all of the above leaders defined themselves as anti-fascist. Although leaders in the 1950s cultivated a paternalistic authority and worked toward restoration of what were understood as familial traditions (especially in the West), as I discuss later, they were unable to reassert the old order of the father, largely because of the need for women's labor. In the West, where there existed a strong tendency in and out of the government to reassert patriarchy, generational youth rebellions constantly challenged this old order. As well, a proliferation of social movements worked toward democratization and the creation of a public sphere. Partly in reaction to empirical changes in German kinship organization, and to the 1968 student and feminist movements, the government enacted major reforms in kinship laws in the 1970s. As West German society became more prosperous within a European Community it had co-initiated with its former enemy, France, more citizens began to travel abroad, creating possibilities for (Western) European, if not international identifications.

Leaders in the East had a more difficult struggle for legitimacy since their authority was increasingly dependent on repressive law—a pater that resembled and brought forth the specter of Soviet authoritarianism. The most charismatic Communist leaders had died or were killed before the end of the war, leaving few possibilities for identificatory figures. It did not help that Ulbricht, who monopolized national leadership for over two decades, was a mediocre man who lacked charisma of any sort. My friends in the East in the 1980s always mentioned his appearance. His shape: like a pear. His voice: high-pitched and squeaky, with a Saxon dialect easy to mock. His most convincing source of masculine identification, one man told me, was his goatee, which suggested to some that he was mimicking Lenin, another sign of subservience to Soviet rulers. Ulbricht's successor, Honecker, cultivated the role of the party and state functionary and dissolved his person into the office to the point of total self-effacement. After Honecker helped vote himself out of office in October 1989, he underwent a series of humiliations. First he was forced out of his home and could find refuge only with a Lutheran minister (who had himself been persecuted by Honecker's government). Then he escaped to Moscow to avoid trial, hid in the Chilean embassy before being eventually released (against his will) to German authorities, and sat several months in the Berlin-Moabit prison awaiting trial. He was finally freed (on humanitarian grounds because of deteriorating health) to join his wife and daughter in Chile. When he died in Chile there was hardly a word uttered in Germany. No mourning work was necessary since he generated no loyalty or identification.[3] If Ulbricht or Honecker symbolize anything today (they are rarely talked about), they have come to represent national trauma: the nightmare of a would-be Communist dictatorship, the pathetic normalizing vision of the *Kleinbürger*, and national division.

Helmut Kohl, Honecker's Western counterpart, has come to be known as the Chancellor of National Unity. His mythical stature grew following unification in 1990, though his reputation has since been damaged by revelations of his involvement in the "Kohl finance affair" (he, along with the Christian Democratic Union [CDU], had resorted systematically to illegal means of raising money in order to stay in power). During his sixteen years as chancellor, Kohl dominated within his own political party, the CDU, which ruled in coalition with the Bavarian Christian-Social Union (CSU) and the Free Democrats (FDP), by systematically eliminating his potential rivals (Späth, Biedenkopf, Geissler, Sussmuth) by assigning them to marginal or peripheral posts. This elimination resembles one possible outcome of the Freudian primal scene of the "brother-horde," where, in the struggle for succession among the brothers, they conspire to kill the father, who, in turn, kills them. It was always clear, however, that eventually someone would succeed Kohl through a formal election.

On the larger national political scene, however, the analogy to an Oedipal complex is no longer appropriate. Before unity, Kohl had already situated himself as the *Enkelsohn*, grandson, of Adenauer (much as his frequent opponent, Lafontaine in the Social Democratic Party, situated himself as "grandson" of Willy Brandt). It appears that Adenauer stands to Kohl not as an "actual" but as a "substitute father." The difference between this substitute father and such figures in "simple structures" is that in Germany today there is no "actual father" who is being replaced. Since German political identification has omitted the actual father altogether, the only potential substitute is the grandfather. Therefore, when Kohl situated himself as the creator of national unity and a direct descendent of Bismarck, he was in line to move from Enkelsohn to the next national grandfather. In the 1998 election, which Kohl lost, the winning candidate of the opposition Social Democrats, Gerhard Schroeder, positioned himself as a replica of the former Kohl, saying, in effect, that he was a substitute for Kohl, the youthful version of Kohl, and that Kohl was no longer himself but already a grandfather.

The leapfrogging of "father" and immediate elevation of Kohl to "grandfather" suggests that there is no longer an identificatory father to kill since he has already been removed from the lineage. Kohl not only lacked identity with the pater in an Oedipal structure, he also lacked any of the functions of the genitor, any expectation that he would physically reproduce his own successor. Hence not the father's sons but the grandfather's sons—or daughters, perhaps—are positioned to become the new father/leader. As source of identification, the German parliamentary system sets up the mortal chancellor who has heirs to share the space of the "king's two bodies" with the immortal federal president (*Bundespräsident*) who has no heirs. The chancellor is the actual executive involved in politics, whereas the President is the leader responsible for symbolic functions. (The first federal president, Theodor Heuss, was in fact fondly called "Papa Heuss.") The federal president is the "good daddy," charged with standing above political factions, and he is expected to deliver speeches about ethics and morality, which reconcile national and supranational divisions. Unlike the chancellor, the federal president is part of a symbolic conjugal couple. His wife plays a prominent symbolic role in the public sphere, usually in good samaritan functions. (For example, the last president's wife, Frau Herzog, had her own televised cooking show.)

Today the pater, or disciplinary figure, is most frequently associated with either the Constitutional Court or the Bundesbank. Both institutions are represented neither by the individuals who sit on them nor by the sum of their members but as collective moral bodies. The Court and the Federal Bank act as transcendent bodies, independent of both the national executive and domestic authority, and capable of disciplining other branches of government because they are thought to apply general and universal principles (of law and economics) to concrete issues. Willing submission to the Court is an instantiation of what the philosopher Jürgen Habermas lauds as *Verfassungspatriotismus* (constitutional patriotism), which he identifies as a West German legacy. But when Habermas criticized the East Germans' motivation for unification as being submission/identification with money *(D-Mark Nationalismus)*, he seemed to oppose subordinating the pater to the economic principles of the Federal Bank. Let me defer, for now, a further discussion of this East/West divide. The Federal Bank's function—to represent issues of household and "domestic budgets," of the traditional private domain—locates it as a mater or feminine-disciplinary authority. The fact is that only the Constitutional Court and Federal Bank, and not national political leaders such as the chancellor, are in a position to provide a bridge between transcendent and domestic authority. In short, the status of national leaders, as well as the fate of the people they represent, appears independent of the old order of the father. This split between the Constitutional Court and Federal Bank (as collective paters), on the one hand, and the federal president/national executive (as identificatory leaders), on the other, dissolves the Oedipal problem, explicated in the introduction, of having to identify with the father who disciplines.

To return to my initial point, the inability of the state to initiate and organize mourning in the two postwar Germanys resulted in a privatization of mourning practices and in extremely modest and non-state directed memorialization of dead leaders.[4] This withdrawal of the state, above all, of the national executive, from mourning practices has been accompanied by a displacement of the symbolic positions of the Father. The identificatory father remains the powerless federal president (Bundespräsident), shared to some degree by the national executive *(Kanzler)*, but the pater function has been moved to institutions with claims to universal norms—the Court and the Bank, and the genitor function, as I will argue later, has been assumed by women alone. Postwar West German Christian Democratic chancellors, Adenauer, Erhard, and Kiesinger, rest in nondescript graves near their places of birth in western Germany. Social Democratic Chancellor Brandt's grave is in an inconspicuous cemetery in Berlin, notably not in the center alongside other famous Berliners. The place of the grave of the GDR's Ulbricht is not common knowledge among Berliners, but it can be found in a cemetery in Berlin-Lichtenberg, marked by a small plaque alongside those of other GDR-prominents in a semicircle surrounding a phallic-shaped rock. Many well-known leftists from the early part of this century are also buried in this cemetery, including, for example, the anti-Nazi artist Käthe Kollwitz. The corpse of Ulbricht's replacement, Honecker, has not (yet) been returned to Germany.

This present identificatory scheme is part of a history of the "order of the father." In the interests of historicizing this present, I want to take the reader back to the Middle Ages and offer a summary sketch and model for transformations in this order.

## Transformations in German Authority from the Middle Ages to the Third Reich

At least since the late Middle Ages, in German-speaking areas a principle of phallic authority operated in the name-of-the-father as a structuring metaphor to anchor all other metaphors. The father functioned as a general equivalent in the symbolic economy in which political and domestic authority were exercised. There existed an idea of the universal commensurability of fathers. Up until the unification of Germany in 1871, paternal authority was located in different, competing, proliferating sources. The phallic principle fostered homologies between the (transcendent) Christian authority of the stern *Gottvater* (God the Father), who blessed and punished; the economic-social structure of the *Herbergsvater*, the warden who taught the journeyman; the *Landesvater*, who dominated the political structure of the various Länder (provinces); and the *Hausvater* (head of the household). Even the academy created its own homology through the structure of the *Doktorvater*. There was, in other words, a chain of substitutable, hierarchically ranked fathers, with no single empirical father who served as the measure of all the others. This configuration is confirmed by etymological studies, which reveal that the concept of father in German speech has historically been defined in terms of power and political authority of the heavenly and earthly fathers, having little to do with the contemporary associations of either biology and sentiment or the bureaucratic state (Trier 1947: 232–260).

Which father came first is a kind of chicken-and-egg question, for the relation is not temporal but dialectical. The historical evidence weighs against the thesis arguing the chronological primacy of the authority of the *leiblichen Vater* (biological father). For Germans in the Middle Ages, the genesis of the authority of Gottvater and Familienvater can more readily be traced to the primacy of economic relations of production and work. The crafts and guilds structure was built upon a model of apprenticeship. An apprentice was "taught to fear God and obey his *Meister* (master) as he would his own father" (cited in Mitterauer and Sieder 1983: 105). The link between God, master, and "his own father" was realized through the household (*Haus*, or *ganzes Haus* [entire house]), which remained the basic kinship unit in Germany well into the eighteenth century.[5]

The hierarchy of the Haus was traditionally organized around the Meister, who headed a household of dependents (including wife, children, servants, domestic laborers). Ties between household members were neither sentimental, nor biological, nor racial, but based primarily on hierarchies of work and residence. Luther's Reformation in the early sixteenth century strengthened the Meister's authority, thereafter presumed to have been derived from a sacred transcendent in accordance with a coherent doctrine of the general order of things. Throughout the feudal period, the "biological father" appears most frequently as the last, residual chain in structures of authority. During the territorial consolidation of German

Länder (provinces) in the seventeenth century, the terms used to organize collective belonging were *Stammbaum* (clan) and *Hausgenossenschaft* (household), the former based on the genealogical unit, the latter on place of work. Although *Geschlecht* (lineage) was not foreign to German thought, only during the Third Reich did Nazi ideologues reduce the concept explicitly to *Erbgut* (inheritance through shared blood). Whether "descent was real or fictitious," write Mitterauer and Sieder (1983: 10), "seems to have made no difference to the lineage as a social unit." The term used in the late fifteenth century by Luther, for example, in the first chapter of the Gospel of Matthew was *Geschlechtsregister* (genealogy), referring to inheritance though the *pater familias* (authority of the household father, or the Lacanian "name-of-the-father"). Genealogy was not limited (or extended) to biological parenthood, as women were not even listed in the register. To the extent that "the woman" in this period took on symbolic importance, it was in her role as mother, in a traditional way as mother of the collective, as in *Muttersprache* (mother tongue). The relation between men and women was significantly refigured again in the late nineteenth century, with the expansion of the bourgeois family form and increased importance attached to a single identificatory father. In sum, neither Geschlechtsregister nor Hausgenossenschaft were organized around principles of consanguinity and affinity, though German-speaking peoples also utilized such kinship principles. Rather, a Geschlechtsregister was generated by tracing dependency relationships based on a principle of descent in the name-of-the-father, a Hausgenossenschaft by relations to residence and work; both were organized around a conceptual pater.

With the dissolution of the feudal system in the sixteenth century, political and religious authorities increasingly competed for control over transcendents. This feudal crisis reached its apogee in a wave of intensive religious, ethnic, and political conflicts—brutal even by twentieth-century standards—now called the Thirty Years' War, which ended in the Peace of Westphalia in 1648. The treaties signed at Westphalia set up the modern system of territorial states, though for the most part these states remained absolutist regimes or empires claiming divine authority. In Germany, the period of intensive state building that followed is most directly associated with the enlightened rule of King Frederick II of Prussia (1712–1786).[6]

Following the French Revolution, Germany developed a peculiar mimetic relation to France, whose nation form served as a model for organizing people's identifications throughout Europe (Anderson 1983, Balibar 1991: 622–633). Compared to its European rivals, Germany lacked not only a politically influential intellectual class (Frederick II spoke French in his court), but also the unifying force of colonialism, which was integral to forming modern nation-states such as Spain, Portugal, England, The Netherlands, France, and Belgium. Germany did not partake in the early colonizations of Asia and the New World, and it came late to the colonization of Africa. At the end of the eighteenth century, then, Germans did not share the clear sense of mission, based on assumed racial unity and superiority, the racial imperative behind political imperialism, which developed elsewhere in Europe. This condition led many German intellectuals, when they compared their situation to the coherent mission of their cosmopolitan French counterparts, where political unification and cultural imperialism were combined in one project, to think of themselves as clearly provincial and trapped in small states *(Kleinstaaterei)*. They were clearly a Volk, but they did not approximate the nation form. To the extent that any collective sense of protonational sentiment existed in Germany, it was through elite propagation of the notion of the Kulturnation, a cultural elite that did not see itself as involved in economics or politics (see Elias 1989). This sense of lack of political mission intensified through the nineteenth century as German intellectuals—the carriers of the Kulturnation tradition—increasingly lost faith in the Christian transcendent as the source of all Being and authority. The decisive Prussian defeat of the French in the war of 1870–1871 (frequently interpreted among Germans as atonement for Napoleon Bonaparte's defeat and occupation in the first part of the century) was quickly followed by the unification of German provinces under one government in 1871. Both events served to arrest the general sense of insufficient political development in Germany. And they seemed to provide the impetus needed to begin turning the various German-speaking peoples into a nation.

The triumph of the nation-state model as political norm of European order coincided with a new ideological hegemony of the nuclear family form and a legal codification of patriarchy, which both secularized authority and put legal limits on the taking of life. We might call this symbolic form "modernism." Introduction of the family into Germany, approximately a century later than in France and the Latin countries, replaced eighteenth century domestic forms organized around the household and master. Those premodern forms prized romantic, homosocial, and sentimental relations, while the modern ones prized patriarchal, rational, and heterosexual relations with distinct male and female domains (Flandrin 1979; Mitterauer and Sieder 1983: 5–13). A reproductive ideology emerged around the conjugal couple; private property and the norms of bourgeois respectability became dominant forces in these changes (Mosse 1985).

In Germany, the law mirrored, initiated, and reinforced these changes, providing a new impetus for the replacement of household by family. In 1791–1794, with the passage of the Prussian State Justice Code, for example, a distinction between family as a distinct group of blood relatives *(Blutsverwandschaft)* and the *Hausgemeinschaft* (household) entered German legal codes. With the embracing of an idea of the German *Rechtsstaat* (rule under law), there was an assumption of an inherent worth for each life, making it difficult to take life without legal cause. Hence, the Prussian state's 1794 reform of criminal law shortened the list of capital crimes and secularized the execution ceremonies in the carrying out of capital punishment. The legal status granted to the nuclear family bolstered other social processes involving the rigidification of oppositional gender identities, the creation of separate public and private domains, and the growth of private property and its regulation. This rigidification in turn reached its apogee in the second half of the nineteenth century, with increased demands for absolute obedience of children to the father, a devaluation of the authority of the mother within the family, and a general refiguring of women's status, with the female embodying morality, feeling, and emotion as against male reason and order (Hausen 1983; Weber-Kellermann 1974: 73–90, 118).

Up to the end of the nineteenth century, the "paternal authority" of the master was generally considered equal to the authority of the domestic father (Mitterauer and Sieder 1983: 108), with both being subordinate to Gottvater. Accordingly, the religious confessions—Catholic and Protestant, or, in some places, Jewish—regulated entry into, or membership in, one of the provincial communities of the German empire, resulting in a coerced confessionalization of German-speaking peoples. This confessionalization was one of the key effects of the 1648 Treaty of Westphalia. Moreover, for adult immigrants, a change of faith was most often accompanied by marriage to a member of the community, which made marriage the primary performative ritual and initiatory rite marking conversion. Following political unification in 1871, the Prussian state began to appropriate this powerful form of ritual conversion for its own quasi-religious purposes. Among the earliest acts intended to introduce pan-national standards for membership, civil marriage was introduced in 1875. Intellectuals, especially in the discipline of *Volkskunde* (the study of German folklore and culture), provided the ideological justification for this act by linking theoretically the bourgeois family form and the authority of the father to the concept of the nation.[7] Thereafter, the state and church shared control over rules for membership in the Reich, rules that no longer centered around dependency through work or in a household but around affinal ties and ascribed marriage, and later including rules of consanguinity and inheritance.

In 1896, with the enactment of the *Bürgerliches Gesetzbuch* (comprehensive civil law), the state codified the complex set of marital and property relations that centered around patrilineal inheritance. Finally, in 1913 the government passed an amendment to the 1870 *Reichs-* and *Staatsangehörigkeitsgesetz*, which introduced into law the principle of jus sanguinis, blood or descent-based, as the basis for membership in the pan-German state. These two final acts of legal codification, in 1896 and 1913, basically completed the long process of replacement of feudal identifications and household hierarchies with bourgeois family norms and a racial Volk. Marriage then increasingly served as the primary symbolic and legal link between the nuclear family and the racialized nation. In sum, by the end of the century, the patriarchal Hausvater had been displaced by a bourgeois model of the family, and confessional control over transcendent authority had been challenged by, and in part transformed into, identification with a universal national-territorial mission of the people.

The increased power of marriage and familial ideology did not, however, produce stable nuclear family units. Households had to respond to increased pressures resulting from the breakup of large estates, mass migration from the country to cities, and the increased autonomy of sons as they became the new urban proletariat. In fact, the increased centrality of marriage seems to have been quickly followed by a decline in the authority of the family father as pater and a focalization of his authority as genitor, now defined solely as biological paternity. As Di Bella (this volume) indicates, by the turn of the century in Austria and elsewhere in Europe, dramatic changes in the role the father and his "death" had already become a theme in literature and the arts. But in contrast to the eroding power within the Austro-Hungarian Empire, Wilhelminian Germany and the *Kaiserreich* were becoming more powerful as they underwent major internal social and economic changes, accrued colonies, and militarized authority structures generally. Consequently, the felt lack of an authoritarian, repressive father/leader to represent the newly united Volk grew in importance in Wilhelminian Germany even as the "biological father" was less able to exercise his power in a changed social environment.

The eighty years between German unification and the end of World War II were a period of intense nation-building. Much has been made of the "lateness" of German national unification when compared with its European neighbors (Plessner 1959). But rather than assume this particular trajectory, from provincial *Völker* to the fullness of a German nation, it may be worth asking what positing the absent and late nation has meant to Germans. Many provincial leaders historically resisted unification because they were grateful that German loyalty to *Heimat* (native land/ home) did not extend beyond the local. Even the official political "unification" of 1871 had to be realized sequentially, in a series of contested policies, national symbols, and practices. For example, Germany had no national flag until 1892 and no national hymn until after World War I.[8] Indeed, the greatest push for national monuments and other symbolic embodiments of unification came around the turn of the century, and then again, after the loss of World War I (see Koselleck 1994). This mythification quickly became contentious as it entered into the social and class divisions of Weimar. Therefore, such symbols of the nation arguably never achieved a wide social consensus until the Third Reich. The one symbol that might have been reconstructed as embodying this nation form was the Chancellor of Unity, Otto von Bismarck.

For thirty years Bismarck had imposed his will upon the king, on the crown prince, on German political parties, and he dominated European politics by "saber rattling" or actually making war—against Denmark, Austria, and France—at the slightest indication of opposition. Officially Bismarck was merely chancellor and he served the emperor, but theses titles are misleading. The emperor himself was uninterested in politics. Kaiser Wilhelm I expressed their relationship most succinctly: "It is difficult to be Kaiser under Bismarck."[9] But during his lifetime, Bismarck was regarded as contentious for usurping the power of the local Länder and taking advantage of the flux in other levels of patriarchal authority. Many provincial leaders, along with foreign states, bestowed awards on him immediately after unification, though positive popular identifications were less immediate. They required a myth around Bismarck, the German nation, and German sovereignty within Europe.[10] The development of a myth of Bismarck as a national father/leader, a kind of national Landesvater, was uneven, and no figure of comparable national political stature or authority reappeared until Hitler.

Bismarck's "successor," Kaiser Wilhelm II (1888–1919), fired or ignored much of the old guard who had capably served Bismarck, and his court was continually threatened by scandal, especially by scandals concerning homosexual activities. When he made his closest confidant, Philipp von Eulenburg, a prince and a Serene Highness, the old guard and the daily presses had a field day widening the circle of friends involved in the scandal to include prominent members of the military. United on this issue, they tried to force the Kaiser to abdicate (Sombart 1991: 31–53; Steakley 1988). Why did homosexual desire at this time pose this kind of threat? What made it the kind of scandal that could nearly bring down the crown and impugn the reputation of the highly respected military? The scandal posed, as Mosse (1985) and Steakley (1988) maintain, what appeared an obvious threat to this kind of political authority because nationalism and bourgeois (familial) respectability were in alliance. Much as the bourgeois family father makes the pater role subservient to the genitor, the national leader's enlarged pater role was increasingly linked to the idea of the national reproduction. Accordingly, at the end of the nineteenth century, the "nation" called forth the "population sciences," whose analytical units were based on an assumed reproductive heterosexuality, on rational, statistical calculations of national health, fertility, and stability. The Kaiser's lack of commitment to this model of identification (he was coerced into marrying) made him a suspect leader, not only in Germany but also among the growing bourgeoisie throughout Europe. Moreover, in the years leading to World War I, the Kaiser lost control of the government to leaders in and around the military (Röhl 1994; Wehler 1985). The foolhardy entrance into World War I and the defeat that followed led to his abdication and exile in 1918. (The Kaiser did first try to turn the German Reich into a parliamentary monarchy, but his effort came too late.)

The men who grew into adulthood during Wilhelminian Germany were "transitional people," as Martin Doerry (1986: 98–116) has called them, caught between the *Haushalt* structure and bourgeois familial norms, still holding on to an absolutist patriarchal political authority that was unable to deal with a rapidly changing social world (e.g., the introduction of the car, the telephone, the airplane). They loved war but had not fought in any. Perhaps because of this they developed a social Darwinist model of manliness, which devalued as "untimely weaknesses" all of the attributes of their own fathers and their eighteenth century Enlightenment forefathers: reflection, reason, sensibility, sensitivity. Intellectuals frequently use the Wilheminians to stereotype the Germans as authoritarian, aggressive, conformist, worshippers of authority. Although patterns of kinship varied by region and class, the kinship of this generation was standardized into a strict patriarchal child-care style characterized by corporal punishment, coldness, a taboo on sexual discourse (especially strong among women), and the withholding of love. This pedagogical style was, in turn, carried over from the family to the school.

Going into World War I, the men of this generation controlled most of the important positions in Germany, and their most significant act was to send their sons into the trenches to fight that senseless war. The losses of the war—foreign occupation, Weimar reparations, demilitarization, lost foreign colonies, a reduced territorial Reich—burdened them with a double guilt. In a single act, they had sacrificed the lives of their own sons and gambled away the inheritance of their fathers (Doerry 1986: 178–179). One way of dealing with this guilt was to further mythify Bismarck and his era, *die Gründerzeit*, as the apogee of German life, with the world since in decline. For them, the loss of the war marked the end of regional loyalties ("German particularism") and a new era requiring national identification. Those sons who survived the war and returned to their Heimat subsequently doubted their father's authority, while, at the same time, they inherited from their fathers a lack of commitment to the democratic structures of the Weimar Republic (Theweleit 1987).

Hence, the parliamentary democracy called the Weimar Republic also failed, for a multitude of reasons: the Great Depression, the perception that it was considered an artificial construction governed by traitors, that it lacked a great leader. Many of its liberal reforms, such as restricting the penalty of capital punishment to homicide, were rolled back by the Nazis. Returning soldiers were frequently maimed, always humiliated, and most could find no work during the Great Depression. The hyperinflation of the 1920s made the Reichsmark, symbol of national unity, nearly worthless. Under these conditions where Money, God, and Government had lost their supreme authority, fathers experienced a loss of authority in families. The general crisis in male identity was deepened by contradictions in the conditions necessary to reproduce the recently constructed male ego ideal. A healthy male identity required the abjection of emotions and feelings (assumed to be feminine) that might have helped men deal with the trauma of the lost war and an exaggeration of martial behaviors. Artists such as Otto Dix, Max Beckmann, and Georg Grosz popularized scenes of the new positions of men and women following the catastrophic experiences of men in the trenches during the war. An oft-repeated joke during Weimar was that even whores despised the war invalids. Indeed, their invalidity became symbolic of the Weimar Republic generally. The last *Reichspräsident,* before Hitler eliminated the office in 1934, was Field Marshall Paul von Hindenburg, who was known at the time as "Savior of the Weimar Republic." He was never able to overcome the effects of the loss of World War I on group pride.

## Identification and Authority under the National Socialists

In 1933, Field Marshall von Hindenburg handed power over to Hitler. In 1934, less than a year after Hindenburg's death, legal theorists of the Third Reich forumulated a new conception of state power and sovereignty. Hitler abolished the title Reichspräsident, designated himself Führer and Reichskanzler, and called the new basis of his authority *Führergewalt* (Führer power). "The Führer unites in himself the whole sovereign power of the Reich," wrote legal theorist Ernst Hüber in 1939, "all public power in the state as in movement stems from the Führer's power. We must speak, not of state power, but of Führergewalt if we want to describe political power in the Völkisches Reich correctly. For it is not the State as an impersonal unity that is the carrier of political power, but rather the Führer as executor of the whole people's will. The Führergewalt is comprehensive and total" (cited in Craig: 1978: 590). With the theoretical displacement of power from state to leader, and with the *Gleichschaltung* (synchronization) of daily life in the Third Reich, all sacred and profane authority was collapsed and concentrated in one source: the Führergewalt. Hitler's power, then, was not based on a direct appeal to the order of the father. Indeed, being a fatherless Austrian, his own position with respect to German authority was as illegitimate son. Nazi authority referenced Vater only as something abstract: an imperial, expansive *Vaterland* (fatherland), which Hitler merely served. Hitler as Führer did, however, rework the identification and authority invested in the concept of Father: He functioned as both pater (source and locus of meaning) and genitor— "transcendent genitor" of the reproducing Volk. Moreover, in a very Modern sense, he sought to make himself into the identificatory father.

The historiography of official Nazi proposals and programs and of life and death in the Third Reich is rich and extensive, and need not be repeated here. I will focus solely on the socio-logic of displacements of authority and identification that were required to realize fascist authority. The ideology, as always, was explicit and unambiguous, unlike the practice. In the words of Wilhelm Stuckart and Hans Globke,[11] authors of the official commentary on Nazi citizenship laws: "In Germanic community thinking, the state consists of a system of communities—family, clan, an organized body of a hundred men, Volk community—each of which may encompass a number of more closely knit communities. The entire life of the individual comrade unfolds within these communities. Outside of these communities no human life exists in the legal sense, but only a biological, vegetative existence.... Thus the state is not something 'other' in contradistinction to the comrade nor something 'above' the comrade. Rather, the comrades of the community in their totality constitute the state" (Stuckart and Globke in Mosse 1966: 327).

Following this line of thought, the *Volksstaat* (state of people, opposed to *Rechtsstaat* or state of law) was composed of men who stood for the Volk and women who stood for its foundation, the family. Himmler, founder and head of the SS, put this in even more radical terms, calling the Nazi state a *Männerstaat* (state based on the comradeship of men). The family, in turn, was a "religious-moral" unit in the service of a national eugenics project, composed of the "twin pillars of 'premarital chastity' and 'conjugal fidelity.'" Marital monogamy served the crucial bourgeois function of "the fettering of the male Eros out of the depths of the purely animal instincts" (Paul in Mosse 1966: 36–37). To achieve this, people, especially men, required constant policing against wayward desires, a redirection of desire away from "animal instincts"—specifically away from sibling rivalry—to camaraderie and eugenic mating. Alongside the family were the schools and the youth groups, HJ (Hitler Jugend: Hitler Youth) for boys, BDM (Bund Deutscher Mädels: League of German Girls) for girls, whose jobs were to prepare and educate the sexes for their proper roles. In short, the state was to engage in a vigilant policing of desire, leading from premarital chastity to conjugal fidelity in domestic life, from same-sex comradeship to ultimate unity in the "German Spirit," the national community, in public life.

Outside of this community, it was not necessary to acknowledge other "human life." Hence all humans who might be considered a challenge to the eugenic spirit were placed outside the group, reduced to "vegetative existence," and perhaps killed. As both internal to the German spirit and yet often marked by a difference, Jews at the time symbolized the most significant threat to German reproduction, to the genitor function. Their persecution and annihilation represents a paradigmatic acting out of the externalization of an internal identification revolving around reproduction of the group. Justification for this killing was the ancient doctrine of sovereignty, the right to treat people as objects without value. But threats to the pater, to discipline and order, also appeared from sources other than Jews.

National Socialist authority embraced a heterosexual procreative ideal but rejected some key aspects of the ideal of bourgeois normality from which that ideal came. The regnant bourgeois ideal would have meant an attempt to unite the repressive father and the biological father into a single identificatory father, with his genitor role superior to the pater role, and to create a universe of families as replicable Oedipal units with no higher instance of transcendence. Born out of an Oedipal dilemma of sibling rivalry and a perceived need for gender differentiation, the bourgeois man unites within himself pater and genitor, and he stands in an oppositional yet complementary relation to the woman. Ideally he becomes "normal" by enacting sibling rivalry, disidentifying with his mother, breaking with or rebelling against his father, uniting and completing himself with a wife in sexual union, and founding his *own* family. The spheres of activity between formally equal and married men and women are then further divided into public and domestic activities (Foucault 1980; Habermas 1991; Lacqueur 1992; Mosse 1985: 1–47).

As against this bourgeois family model, the model Nazi family pandered to an ego ideal of a racialized homosociality—an Aryan *Männerbund*. This Nazi ego ideal subordinated bourgeois heterosexuality to a national model of identification—a national eugenics project—whose telos was not bourgeois normality but comradeship, strength in community, union in a procreative Volk (cf. Oosterhuis 1991). Comradeship made unthinkable not only sibling rivalry but also Oedipal feelings of any sort. It made unthinkable what the father asks from the son—in this case, death as soldier-warrior—unthinkable. Above all, it made sex itself unthinkable. All of these unthinkables were placed in the unconscious, so that when sex or death appeared, in particular when homosexual desire appeared, which it did in and outside the Männerbund, it served as a reminder of that which had been repressed, as a misrecognized sign of an Oedipal problem that was unthinkable. In sum, any threat to Hitler as pater was displaced into a problem of homosexual seduction, which, in turn, signaled a threat similar to the Jews, yet one capable of being "disciplined."[12]

With the promised elimination of Jews, the threat of racial purity was to be enormously reduced. Thereafter, as Mosse (1985) has shown, the Nazis relied on the bourgeois norm of respectability to enforce internal standards of behavior within the community. This focus on Nazi use of the categories of normality/abnormality understates, however, key aspects of the ideal of bourgeois respectability that the Nazi movement had rejected: namely, sibling rivalry, rebellion against the father, Oedipal familial completeness. Instead of making the pater subservient to the genitor but contained within one person, Nazi ideology proposed an unusual splitting of the pater from the genitor, with the pater superior to a transcendent genitor. By racializing the Volk concept, biological reproduction for the Volk was elevated into a new transcendent. For that reason, the identity of the biological father in reproduction remained irrelevant to the Nazis provided he was of superior Aryan racial qualities. The identificatory father was in any case embodied by the person of Hitler and symbolized by the collective Männerbund. To be sure, the Nazis encouraged marital monogamy as the heterosexual norm. But since women were reduced to mere mothers and symbols of national virtue (much as, after the Middle Ages, they had been relegated to the foundation of Germanness, Muttersprache, home and hearth), they served as conduits for male authority, as vessels to reproduce the whole Männerstaat and the collective. Accordingly, the Nazis forumulated an idea of the Aryan as the key feature of the racial whole. The Aryan was also a transcendent category, tied not to the individual German male but to the collective German Volk and the Vaterland, a point explicated by Dumont (1992) in his study of Nazi ideology.

Hitler served as identificatory figure for and symbolic embodiment of this Volk, in whose name people were to experience a oneness.

In suppressing sibling rivalry, Nazi ideology also elevated *Kamerad-schaft* (comradeship) and male bonding (Männerbund), over and against the heterosexual completeness of the conjugal couple, into an expression of the transcendent racialized nation. This kind of ego ideal created a particular identificatory dilemma: with women relegated to the role of mothers and men reaching fulfillment in same-sex comradeship and mutual identification there was a constant threat, as Mosse (1985: 66–89; 153–180) emphasizes, of the homosocial spilling over into and exciting not warrior solidarity but homosexual activity. To restate my argument: because the homosocial activity of the Männerbund threatened to become homosexual, Nazi leaders were constantly reminded of and involved in negating the very thing whose existence they had denied—homosexuality, which, in turn, they misrecognized as a sign of the unthinkable Oedipal problem.

The much-discussed misogyny of Nazi leaders expresses the other face of the comrade ideal. It was motivated both by a rejection of certain bourgeois norms (as effeminate, cowardly) and by fears that the bourgeois family might assert itself as a transcendent form. The danger therein was that men would be taken out of circles of comradeship and allowed to retain individual authority as the unified pater/genitors in the nuclear family. Women who were identified as racially inferior were forced to abort, or even forcibly sterilized. But women identified as eugenically fit symbolized the continuity and immutability of the nation. They in turn were pressured to have babies for Hitler, who embodied this nation, and to fulfill this duty, if not married, to breed with any generic German Aryan (Bock 1986; Kaufmann 1988: 34–43; Koonz 1993: S8–S1; Mühlfeld and Schönweiss 1989). Hence, Hitler could remain an asexual character yet be the spirit behind sex, for women and men were having sex in the presence of and for the Führer, in the-name-of-the-Father. Identification with Hitler was also encouraged by a huge propaganda effort to portray him as loving of children, and children as loyal to him as they would be to "father and mother."[13] Many of his subjects, men and women, clearly developed romantic and eroticized relations with him. Indeed, Hitler worked to portray himself as a figure for a particular kind of mass identification: a man of action and author and source of the truth, loving of children (with whom he was frequently photographed), yet willing to give up family life, to sacrifice everything, for the Volk. Two kinds of evidence reveal the peculiar kind of identification with Hitler: love letters[14] and dreams.

Even before Hitler actually became head of state, he had entered into people's dreams. Throughout the 1930s Charlotte Beradt, who later fled Germany, collected these dreams. In them, we find that most Germans seemed to share a version of the seduction theory held onto by Nazi leaders. These dreams reveal a consistent wish to be the object of the Führer's desire, and they often portrayed Hitler as a literal seducer. But it is a peculiar sort of seduction, not as literal genitor as in the case of Mussolini, but as pater and *Verführer*/Führer (seducer/leader), what I have been calling "transcendent genitor." For one, people dreamt about identification with repressive law.[15] For another, Beradt reports dozens of identical dreams of the desire to be wanted or seduced by Hitler, Goebbels, or Göring.[16]

In sum, the Nazi regime appealed to a mix of ancient, premodern, and modern forms of sovereignty as well as a demand for subjective identification with the Father. The ultimate base of Nazi power was the ancient doctrine of sovereignty: that they could transform the existence of their subjects into *homo sacer*, "naked life"; they could reduce individuals— Jews, Slavs, homosexuals—to objects without intrinsic value, agency, or rights. Impurity of the Volk was the threat that motivated the exercise of this doctrine. Preservation of the "transcendent genitor" function, which Hitler embodied, was rationalized through a people's eugenics. The attempted annihilation of the Jews and the mass killing of other groups identified as external and impure served this purpose. Nazi authority was also modern, however, in that the killing was justified legally, not in the terms of religious authority as in the medieval period but in the name-of-the-people. In redefining the Rechtsstaat as a Volksstaat, Nazi ideologues extended the use of capital punishment, to serve in the proper and rationally administered life of the people. To amend Foucault, the old power of death was not supplanted but supplemented by the administration of bodies and the calculated management of life. Hitler and other Nazi leaders incorporated another key element of the modernist doctrine of sovereignty: the killing of the Father. Hitler the illegitimate son could only be leader and never become father, and therefore never think of any sons, of any successors. Finally, Nazi authority was also premised on an inescapable and subjective identification with the leader, an equation of the identificatory Father with the pater who disciplines. Hence the death of Hitler was also necessarily the death of the entire Reich.

## Cold War Authority

Following the war, people viewed all transcendents with great skepticism—whether God, Volk, or species. The various Allied-initiated trials of German war criminals, symbolized in the Nuremberg Trials, were initially generally dismissed as "victor's justice" but grudgingly accepted, though they came to be interpreted as a positive legacy a couple decades after the war. Public opinion polls of Germans in the 1950s indicated a staunch unwillingness to believe in any authority figure or regime, which led one of the leading German sociologists at the time to describe working-age adults of this period as "the skeptical generation" (Schelsky 1957). Elsewhere I have traced the changes in East and West Berlin in authority patterns and everyday life (Borneman 1992a: 119–154, 202–236), and I will not repeat this chronicle here except as it relates specifically to changes in political authority. More than seventeen million German men were armed participants in the Nazi war effort. Six million of these did not survive the war, and by war's end over ten million were prisoners of war in twenty different countries. Fathers returning from the front or from prisoner-of-war camps, called *Heimkehrer* (those returning home) reported nobody listened to them or wanted to hear their war stories (Lehmann 1986). Their traumatic experiences remained unaddressed, and were accordingly passed on—especially in the form of guilt and speechlessness—to their children. Subsequently, adult women accrued a great deal of practical power to bring about order within families, establishing a new relation with phallic authority, often in the actual father's absence. Many women in fact explicitly took over a domestic pater function. Near the end of the war and in the several years after, many youths with the aid of their mothers or other female relatives resorted to covert action to secure food or coal, by stealing or trading on the black market, rather than submit to the distribution regime of local authorities or engage in self-sacrifice (Borneman 1992a: 156–161).

When the Allied occupation began, German family life for youths was marked by reversal and inversion of authority. Bourgeois distinctions between public and private, home and working world, male and female, broke down. The streets where mothers cleaned up rubble became a playground, the kitchen often a bedroom. The "comradeship and egalitarianism" to which the Nazis appealed in their Volk ideology was now experienced as what Arnold Van Gennep called a liminal state. To the extent that "pleasure" was to be located, it was in theft and criminality, not in obeying the law. Adults reported that their children were in constant "trouble with the law"—breaking both old laws and the new edicts of the Allies and their German proxies.[17]

Whereas the United States pursued an "economy of exchange" in its relations with the Germans, the Soviet Union pursued an "economy of extraction." The former relied on "money" (the deutsche mark) as the new phallic authority and means of discipline; the latter on police and "meritocratic" hierarchies. Both strategies initially had similar effects: they stemmed youth crime (which peaked in both parts of Berlin in 1949), organized work, and enforced the law. Significantly, Article 102 of the West German Basic Law of 1949 abolished the death penalty. The remilitarization of both Germanys in the course of the Cold War did not reverse the major epistemic shift in identifications of the 1950s: a departure from a warrior and a production/reproduction identification model to one based on consumption and an affirmation of pleasurable desires. In West Berlin, legitimate political authority was tied to a federal constitution and democratic political form *(Verfassungsstaat)*, and to the ability to revive the economy, now reorganized around the principle of a "social market economy." Efforts in the 1950s and 1960s to restore the death penalty failed. In East Berlin a new totemic pater figure, an anti-fascist and socialist state, tried to organize an alternative collective basis for the Volk. The death penalty was carried over into the GDR's constitution, though severely limited in the scope of crimes to which it applied. But as its social welfare and economic policies failed to keep up with the Marshall Plan-supported West, the GDR increasingly resorted to repression and the intensive use of fear to enforce public authority. West Germans came to occupy the word "German," leaving for the East Germans the acronym of their state: the GDR. When asked, Are you a German citizen? East Germans would answer, "No, I am a citizen of the GDR."

In strictly carrying out the Potsdam Accords (denazification, democratization, demonopolization, demilitarization), Soviet authorities were engaged in constant extraction. The East German regime reached regularly into domestic life to restructure hierarchies in relations of class, inheritance, gender, and work. By representing itself as a revolutionary authority that broke radically with the Nazis, it hoped to preempt resistance to its goal of restructuring the domestic domain. In addition to radical land and industrial reform ("Junker Land in Farmer's Hands") which destroyed the class base of the *Adel* (aristocracy) and the Junker, GDR authorities destroyed many symbols of the propertied classes (such as castles), and they neglected the churches that had survived the war. While land reform enjoyed much popularity, other forms of expropriation as well as the neglect or purposeful destruction of symbols of the past did not create widespread support for the regime. The dependence of the GDR on Soviet authority also militated against its legitimacy, for the Soviet occupiers were associated with a Bolshevik past, which Germans had mythified shortly after the Russian Revolution into a brutal anti-Christ movement. Moreover, the widespread rape of German women by Soviet soldiers was one of the first experiences of "extraction" by the Occupiers; later, when the Americans came, intercourse with German women was experienced as "exchange"—sex for material goods and comforts the wealthier American soldiers were in a position to offer.

Progressive East German reforms in the area of family policy and gender equality proved more popular among some, though their effects were delayed and not usually what was intended. Moreover, people always evaluated these effects by comparing them with the effects of West German policy, where after the 1960s, the social welfare state had more money to distribute. The large and steady migrations of skilled labor from East to West, along with a strong-state industrial policy, quickly eliminated unemployment in East Germany, so that the economy was marked by a labor shortage, requiring importation of contract labor from allies such as North Vietnam and Cuba. After the revolt of 1952, the East German state's problems with several generations of "dissidents" were primarily conflicts with the new state's repressive authority and not dissatisfaction with many of its policies. Under pressure from West Germany, in 1987 it abolished the death penalty, though it had not been applied for more than two decades. By 1989, the GDR was ruled by an aging, increasingly inept, and increasingly illegitimate gerontocracy, which held onto power by dramatically increasing its debt to the West and expanding its police state functions. Under these circumstances, it collapsed from within and reformed itself out of existence through free elections in March 1990.

In West Germany, occupation by, above all, the United States, and identification with America—its prosperity and culture—was legitimated through an economy of exchange. With more people to absorb into the economy in the West, and with more reliance on slow market-driven processes, unemployment remained high in West Germany through the late 1950s, and then declined for two decades before rising substantially again in the 1980s. The early criminal gangs in the West were soon succeeded by working-class toughs, such as the Halbstarke, who, though less "criminally" oriented, still posed a challenge to bourgeois forms of respectability.

A series of youth social movements—first, the working-class-based Halbstarke in the mid 1950s, then the student-based "68ers" after 1968, followed by the environmental and Green party movements in the 1970s and 1980s—began reorganizing the relation to public authority. The urban, anticonsumer, antibusiness terrorism of the Baader-Meinhof gang and the Red Army Faction of the 1960s and 1970s should be viewed as merely one reaction of some members of the postwar generation to the older one, one violent response, symptomatic of generational reaction to silencing and to widespread social repression. In the political domain, of most significance is Chancellor Willy Brandt's 1970 visit to the Warsaw ghetto to commemorate Jewish and Polish victims of Nazi aggression. His image of spontaneously falling to his knees quickly became the key symbol of German atonement and of a changed German authority.[18] In the artistic domain, there was a "softening" of forms of expression, in particular male expression, which began in the 1960s and extended through the 1970s. This was best exemplified by the influential Joseph Beuys and the Fluxus movement; Beuys insisted on working only with soft materials, primarily fat and felt, but also honey, wood, water.

Much of this generational conflict was organized around expressions of sexuality and alternative partnerships, both considered threats to the reassertion of the bourgeois model of family life. Sexuality, nudity, eroticism, abstraction and expressionism in art and life—all were affirmed with a vengeance by a postwar generation that came of age in the 1960s as a reaction to the Nazi period and to the repressive atmosphere of the 1950s. In the 1970s even marriage lost its public monopoly on fulfilling emotional needs, with alternative *Lebensgemeinschaften* (living-together arrangements) and new child-care patterns practiced, especially in large cities. Child custody law, which had traditionally given total control to the father, was reinterpreted in courts in both the East and West as granting nearly total control to the mother. Granting such legal authority to the mother frequently had the effect of positioning her with respect to the children as the pater. The long-term effect has been a refiguring of kinship, with a relativizing of marriage and the bourgeois family form—literally, a death of the "traditional" Familienvater. A large number of adults in East and West now consider marriage a voluntary stage in life for youth, much like military service used to be. Especially in the West and in large cities, a liberal ideology of toleration of distinct difference is now regnant, so that issues surrounding sexuality and marriage are considered largely irrelevant to public life. This does not preclude the promulgation of norms of either gender correctness or sexuality in legal codes and organizational forms for social life. It does mean, however, that the vast majority of people act, or conceive of themselves as acting, as if these norms were private matters alone.

## German Fathers: Transformed Authority in Edgar Reitz's *Die zweite Heimat*

Let me situate the reader at this crucial moment of transformation by examining a filmic representation of German society made in the 1980s. I will focus on two scenes from Edgar Reitz's two-part, ethnographically inspired epic film *Heimat*. These scenes are taken from the twenty-three hour second part, *Die zweite Heimat*, which portrays the attempt by a postwar generation to deal with the sovereignty crisis that I introduced at the beginning of this chapter, and to transform West German authority between 1960 and 1970. Films are significant not because they represent typical histories but because they expose in a highly condensed form the dominant ways of reading, viewing, and experiencing of the particular period in which they are made. They are reflexively symptomatic of the symbolic forms of that period.

The major character, Hermann Simon, moves from the fictive village Schabbach in Rheinland-Palatinate to the city of Munich in Bavaria to study music composition. Inspired by Schönberg's atonal music, he and his peers attempt to break radically with the classical notions of harmony, rhythm, continuity, and beauty. Throughout much of the film, Hermann is torn between the comfort of village tradition and the spontaneity of the student movement. For several years, Hermann enjoys the sensual and intellectual pleasures of student life. Eventually disillusioned with his student friends, he succumbs to the charms of a girl from his village, ignores his ambivalence and enters into a conventional marriage with her—thus immersing himself in the traditional, the rural, the naïve— what Hermann initially fled from. In one scene, Hermann and his wife join another married couple for dinner. The other wife, Clarissa—a talented musician and Hermann's real love—has bought a fish to serve.[19] The fish is collectively unwrapped. "What kind of fish is it?" they ask. They search to match the catch with photos of fish types. Then the fish must be beheaded. But who will perform this decapitation? The two wives look on in embarrassment; Hermann's wife holds her hand to her throat. After this awkward collective hesitation, Hermann steps forth with a knife and we hear the rasping sound of the head being sawed off. Immediately after, the couples accidentally discover an article in the newspaper in which the fish was wrapped, which announces that Hermann had won an award for his music; he is about to become famous. In other words, decapitating the fish—the symbolic murder of the son as would-be Father—is a precondition for success.

Later in the *Heimat* series, Hermann has been picked to be the inheritor of a fortune by a childless couple, Herr Theobald Konsul and his wife. We do not know exactly what Herr Konsul, who produces Hermann's music, did during World War II, but for members of Hermann's generation, any man of that age was implicated in Nazi crimes. The scene, which I have shortened some, goes as follows:

*[Hermann enters the house of Herr Konsul, greeted by Frau Konsul.]*
FRAU KONSUL: My husband is not feeling well. He was only acting at the Oktoberfest yesterday. Did you know that?
*[We enter the bedroom, where Herr Konsul, sweating and looking ill, is still in bed.]*
HERR KONSUL: May I call you Hermann? Have you shown him our house?
FRAU KONSUL: Later, Theobald, later.
HERR KONSUL: As you perhaps know, we've remained childless. For many years, it was our greatest wish. But as you'll see, our house is made for children. Even a children's room. To cry for!
FRAU KONSUL: Don't be sentimental.
HERR KONSUL: But I would like Hermann to get to know us.
FRAU KONSUL: Come, I'll show you.
*[Frau Konsul takes Hermann to the abandoned child's room, cluttered with toys, pillows, and other baby things. Hermann looks on from the doorway while Frau Konsul rocks the cradle awaiting a baby. Hermann suddenly sneezes.]*
FRAU KONSUL: You staying for supper?
*[The scene shifts to the downstairs, with Herr Konsul showing Hermann his large music and movie studio which overlooks a lake.]*
HERR KONSUL: I'm stricken by inheritance-hunters. My employees, they all suspect that they'll inherit my company if I have an accident. They're all after me.
HERMANN: But that's pleasant.
HERR KONSUL: Naturally, it's pleasant, but also dumb. Have you already seen? A small secret. I would have liked a son, one like you. I'm serious. What does your father do, Hermann?
HERMANN: I saw him once in my life, when I was four years old. My stepfather lives in America. Electrical engineer. I grew up with my mother.
HERR KONSUL: Have you ever wanted a father?
HERMANN: Yes, often, one I could hate.
HERR KONSUL: I want to say something, Hermann. If you want to stay with me, engaged, with body and soul. For all of me, you can hate me! Then you'll inherit my entire firm.
HERMANN: But I'm a musician!
HERR KONSUL: I know.
HERMANN: Do I have to decide right away?
HERR KONSUL: No, but soon.

*[The two men move to the dining room and, as night has fallen, Reitz switches the shooting from black and white to color. (Color appears only at night in Germany.) Frau Konsul enters with a platter of baked, golden fish. Hermann looks uncomfortable as the married couple watches him expectantly. Frau Konsul goes to her husband and begins crying; he comforts her.]*

This scene depicts several characteristics of the postwar German pattern of identification and generational transmission of authority:

1. The biological father, or genitor, is absent and his replacement (stepfather) escaped abroad, to America; only a grandfather (in the person of Herr Konsul) is present, standing in as a potential identificatory father and pater, or, as Hermann puts it, "one I could hate"—inheritance, law, repressive authority; in other words, there has been a pointed disruption in phallic identification in the bourgeois family.

2. Generational authority exhibits radical discontinuity; even the authority of the grandfather is rejected by the grandson during an evening meal where fish (signifying Hermann, the wished-for son and would-be Father) is served, an embarrassing and hugely ambivalent scene.

3. The location of the transfer is at home, in a politicized domestic sphere (i.e., not an innocent, private domain) where the transmission of authority from the grandfather (father-substitute) occurs with the absence of the father. The son can now choose to accept or reject the inheritance. If he accepts, his hate for the Father would turn into love and redeem Herr Konsul. In this transfer, Herr Konsul's wife, the grandmother, cries, but for whom? She, too, is childless and therefore has failed, much as her husband has failed, to pass on her authority.

4. How the fish is caught is not shown, but who cuts the head off and how it is served is the key. In the first scene, Hermann cuts off the head, an act symbolizing the son's self-castration—the real love between Hermann and Clarissa must be denied. In the second scene, Hermann is served fish by his substitute grandfather (Herr Konsul), symbolizing the potential sacrifice of the son to the future; but the grandfather has no automatic authority, as Herman can self-consciously choose to accept or refuse Herr Konsul's authority, which itself is bound to (Nazi) history. Since 1945, all authority in Germany has a taint of illegitimacy. Hermann eventually decides not to take the inheritance and he rejects Herr Konsul's offer. By the end of the film, Hermann has left his wife and daughter and returns alone to his hated birthplace, Schabbach, to reexamine the history of his putative break with his past. In short, Hermann has rejected both having a father (or father-substitute) and being one, both inheritance of the past through the pater and responsibility for the future defined in terms of physical reproduction in the role of genitor. Hermann's character suggests a new kind of German male subjectivity as well as a new relation to German culture and political authority, to the sovereign.

## Post–Cold War Authority

As the character of Hermann Simon in *Die zweite Heimat* attests, one of the major goals of members of the first post–World War II generation in West Germany was to formalize this break in identification and in lifecourse design with their fathers.[20] This break holds for East Germans also. In both Germanys, Familienvater has been largely deconstructed in ideology, and the conjugal couple and nuclear family are merely one frequent form of intimate practice among many alternatives. Germany, like most other European countries, has experienced a steady increase in the number of singles (people who do not marry or have divorced) and in the number of people who do not have children. Today between 30 and 40 percent of German families with children have a woman as sole domestic authority, as pater, perhaps shared with the state, the teacher, or other male or female acquaintances—meaning authority is no longer necessarily phallic; there is no single measure and often no identificatory father. The genitor function in those families is largely in the hands of women. The name of the actual father is sometimes even omitted altogether from the birth certificate. In terms of lineage, the most meaningful membership code is having a German or European passport, meaning one's relation to the state or the European Union and not proof of descent, of being the product of a particular father of a particular race or Volk.

At the national level, East and West Germans differ substantively most in their relation to the pater. Both Cold War states occupied this position of discipline and order totemically. But whereas the East German state had tried to occupy this role literally through its security apparatus, in West Germany the legal system and prosperity, symbolized in the strong D-Mark, have gradually become totemic authorities. From this perspective, to which I alluded earlier, Habermas criticized East Germans in 1990 for their *D-Mark Nationalismus*, loyalty to the mark, and appealed instead to a *Verfassungspatriotismus*, constitutional patriotism, as a West German achievement and that which should bind all Germans to German authority. East Germans tend to experience Habermas's critique of their identification with money as hypocrisy, since he is asking them to give up something his West German compatriots would not. For his part, Habermas's critique is equally directed toward the economy of exchange introduced by the American occupiers and further developed by the FRG.

Since 1990, the popularity of the Constitutional Court, and the legal system generally, has increased greatly in both East and West in comparison to other institutions. This is significant in that, despite the inability, a decade after formal unification, of the political leadership to unify or to produce the same life-chances in East and West (as initially promised by Chancellor Kohl, for example), there has been no significant search for any form of Führergewalt. The wave of right-wing violence directed primarily against foreigners that reached its apogee in 1992 was stopped largely by a tightening of immigration law and by public demonstrations of solidarity with the victims. In addition, a major police crackdown seems to have taken away, imprisoned, or frightened the leadership of such groups (Borneman 1998). Today the "68ers" hold many positions of authority in the united Germany. Their working through of the social death of the Father has resulted in a form of contemporary political authority marked by desire for personal authority but ambivalence about its exercise—a kind of narcissism fundamentally different from the relation to authority before 1945.

Rather than a reethnicization or nationalization of Germans as a whole, which would posit the German Volk as an essence different from other European ethnic groups, East and West residents have discovered and frequently emphasized their embarrassing differences. A noticeable re-regionalization of German identities suggests a return to the heterogeneity of forms that existed prior to the ordered nationalism of the Nazi era. It is also, of course, an articulation of new class difference along lines determined by the world market and of the effects of a costly unification at a moment of relative economic stagnation. In any case, the return home of Hermann in the *Heimat* film, much like the cultivation of East German *Ostalgie* (nostalgia for the old East) among some people in the eastern part of the new Germany, should not be read as a nostalgic search and return to the roots, for the place to which they are returning is fundamentally different from the one from which they had departed.

Many analysts within Germany decry the lack of unifying personalities and leaders, often pointing to Helmut Kohl as the only present figure who stands for both East and West. Especially members of an older generation, such as the conservative pollster and celebrated demographer Elisabeth Noelle-Naumann (1987), lament that the Germans are a "wounded nation" that needs to recover its pride. But this lack at the national level is not and never has been felt by everyone. It must be understood in the context of a strengthened identification to the provincial Landesvater, and to a general skepticism about strong leaders. There is still no established festival at the federal level with consensual symbols and meanings where Germans celebrate national unity and national authority. There is, in fact, little sense of nationalism at national events other than sports contests.

Among such potential festivals is the anniversary marking unification, called *Tag der deutschen Einheit* (Day of German Unity). I attended the fifth anniversary on 3 October 1995, in Berlin. What struck me was the solemn atmosphere and lack of celebration. Most West Germans look at unity with some resentment, especially at the annual "solidarity surcharge" tacked on to taxes that are said to finance the East's development. Most East Germans resent the West German "takeover" or elimination of their industries, and they are still making the transition (some of the older generations unsuccessfully) to West German rules, norms, and life-structures. What ultimately made unification of the East and West in 1990 possible and acceptable to other European countries was the assertion that Germans were no longer the same nation that had begun two world wars. Hence, the creation of descriptive terms such as "posttraditional identity" (Habermas 1987) and "postnational nation" (Jarausch 1995). At this unification celebration of 1995, the evening's performances were topped off by the indomitable British pop singer Elton John, who sang not one word about German unification. Instead, his lyrics celebrated love and "Philadelphia dreaming," international peace and AIDS education. Imagine the scandal if Elton John had been invited to sing for a festival celebrated by Kaiser Wilhelm II! Indeed, the common knowledge that Elton John is openly homosexual was nowhere discussed.

Perhaps the two most significant Volk celebrations in Berlin in the last decade have been European affairs: Christo and Jean-Claude's wrapping of the old Reichstag building (where the federal parliament moved in 1999) in July 1985, and the Love Parade (an annual event started in 1989; see Borneman and Senders 2000). The former event attracted well over a million people of all ages and classes over the course of a week; the latter began with 750 people and grew to more than a million within a decade. Both events, initially scoffed at as non-events, were sources for post-national identifications for Generation III, Germans youths who have experienced neither war nor the 1968 rebellion and who were too young (or too far removed from Berlin or the GDR) to take part in the demonstrations of the fall of 1989. They were, in effect, first exercises in mass identification for these youths. Both events were organized around an ostensive de-politicization—Christo's event around "astonishment" at watching a virtuoso overcoming bureaucratic obstacles to wrap a mammoth overdetermined historical monument, the Love Parade around a public performance of the fiction of "We are one family" through solipsistic dance to techno-music, pointless fun, and play.[21] These events were attended by men and women from all over Europe, were inclusive of all generations, and were difficult to oppose or criticize since they stood for nothing in particular. German politicians of all ilk— who tend to appropriate nearly every issue and event for political party competition—were peculiarly silent during the Love Parade, not knowing how to position themselves to it. This universalist-oriented display of a new German Zeitgeist represents a formal de-politicization of the Volk, and it stands in sharp contradistinction to most sporting events or other national folk festivals in Europe.

In addition to this de-politicization, the German nation has been largely demilitarized, with military action constrained by pan-European organizations (such as NATO) and subject to constant Supreme or Constitutional Court approval. In Dumézil's (1970) terms, the jural-political— the Rechtsstaat—is completely dominant over the warrior function. As a consequence of losing both world wars, those elites in both German states who would have liked to link defense of the nation to male soldiering (sacrifice for the Vaterland) have faced considerable opposition. Despite some success in building standing armies during the Cold War, the argument for disarmament—for a very limited and circumscribed military—has gained the stronger hand over time. Germany ranked sixth among world states in disarming from 1985–1994, following Nicaragua, Iraq, Bulgaria, Ethiopia, and Hungary. In this period, the number of soldiers decreased by five hundred thousand, and the length of compulsory military service was shortened (Steiner et al. 1996: 1). A majority of German men now personally opt for a longer period of civil service rather than fulfill military duty.

Minimally since the 1960s, transcendence in Germany is no longer tied to either a traditional Christian religiosity or the Volk. A reproductive anxiety about the Volk is reiterated periodically across the political spectrum, but this is most often expressed as fear that the declining number of working people in the population will be unable to pay retirement pensions. The decline in traditional Christian religious authority was again demonstrated during the 23 June 1996, visit to Berlin of the pope, who still refers to himself as the Holy Father. He was met by provocative demonstrations, spearheaded by gay and lesbian groups. Berlin's two entertainment weeklies organized a "Pope-Free Zone," where they then showed the anti-Catholic Pasolini film *Teorema*, and read from Karlheinz Deschner's four-volume *The Criminal History of Christianity*. While the pope spoke under the Brandenburg Gate, one woman stripped and hurled her naked body at the pope's vehicle (undoubtedly, as Maria Pia Di Bella said to me, forcing him to cover his eyes). Other demonstrators threw tomatoes and eggs, and yelled obscenities.

Today transcendence among Germans is identified with different projects involving protection (*Schutz*) of life.[22] This embrace of "protection" assimilates a feminine model of co-dependency and a rejection of any premodern notion of sovereignty that might assume the right to kill into a new activism. It is manifested in the protection of human life as in human rights, environmental care, or of what are understood to be "European legacies." These are domains where the Constitutional and the Supreme Court also have been very active. For example, individuals engage in extreme acts of self-sacrifice by tying themselves to trees designated to be cut down, or by devoting themselves to campaigns to protect endangered species, and in international forums, Germans are some of the strongest defenders of universal human rights. These are sacred domains expressive of a rationality of ultimate principles, *Wertrationalität*, contrasted with the equally constitutive profane domain of consumption. Consumption is, in turn, expressive of an instrumental rationality, *Zweckrationalität*, possible only through money and largely associated with America—signs that evoke great ambivalence. These new sacred and profane domains have only tenuous relations to the nineteenth-century united Volk or to the religiosity of official confessions.[23] Berlin, reconstructed as the new German capital city, is merely one site in this decentralized federal authority structure that is fully embedded in European unification processes.[24] The D-Mark, formerly identified with the Bundesbank in Frankfurt, has been replaced by the euro (over which the German bank still has disproportionate influence); environmental protection and human rights are fought over in Brussels, Strasbourg, and Luxembourg (the European Union parliament, court, and executive council); and the Constitutional Court (the Bundesverfassungsgericht) in Karlsruhe must now make rulings consistent with those of the European court in Strasbourg.

In the near future, any German identification with a national leader/ father will not be structured around the father/son hierarchy but around a relation of co-dependency between the grandfather/grandson. German identification at present has little to do with filling in the "national void" that culminated in the Nazi regime. The opening of the Berlin Wall in 1989 demonstrated the chimerical nature of this void: Germans needed the excuse of cultural unity to justify political unification, but unification could no longer be thought of as a process of producing a complete, full, bounded People. Above all, any German leader derives authority from a German Volk not above, but within, Europe, an authority that acknowledges the needs of other peoples as a condition of its own legitimacy. Nonetheless, many European political leaders still fear that Germany will dominate Europe, especially through Germany's economic power. This perspective rests upon a view of national political power as subservient to national economic power, as discrete and unchanging in (imperialistic) form, and of German authority structures as unchanged— all dubious propositions. Among Europeans, the British are especially fond of projecting onto Germans their worst nightmare of a specter that will take away their treasured national sovereignty. In the words of the learned Noel Annan in the *New York Review of Books* (1996: 27): "Fifty years since Stauffenberg died, Germany holds sway in Europe. Her Chancellor looks to a time when the bankers of Frankfurt will mastermind the economics of other European countries and their defense and foreign policies will be controlled by an unchallengeable European bureaucracy." If there is any truth in what Annan says, then the question becomes not how to stop German domination or to reform German authority, but how to question the sovereignty of money more generally and to make bureaucracies more ethically responsive and accountable to local and global needs. These authority problems are not primarily derived from the order of the father and death, and their solutions are imaginable neither at the German nor the European level, but only in articulation with global and local authority structures.

"What Remains"

Segment of Hitler's upper teeth brought, along with other remains, by the Russians back to Moscow. They were concealed until the period of perestroika in the early 1990s, when the Moscow Archive was opened to scholars.

Source: Unknown

"Something for the Home"

A customer in a German art shop chooses a portrait of Hitler for a special Christmas gift.

Source: Süddeutscher Verlag Bilderdienst, Munich

# Notes

Many people have given me ideas for this essay, and I thank collectively the members of the Bellagio team workshop. Inspiration for the linkage between the three levels of *Vater* in the title comes from Baber Johansen; my gratitude to Mia Pia Di Bella for alerting me to the importance of the pater/genitor distinction; Nicholas Dirks for comments on Lacan, colonialism, and race; Dieter Haller for asking me why boys must learn to fish so frequently in U.S. films; Uli Linke for bringing Backfisch to my attention; Michael Meeker for reminding me of the relation of sibling rivalry to paternal authority; Karin Wieland for comments on Weimar; Michael Minkenberg for many historical details and a discussion on religiosity; and Konrad Jarausch for a general critique. I also benefited from discussions with Thomas Hauschild and Bernd Jürgen Warneken following a presentation before ethnologists at Karl-Ludwig University, Tübingen.

1. Not until 1997 were the rumors about Bormann's escape and life in exile put to rest, as DNA testing of bodily remains, found in 1972 at a construction site in Berlin, matched samples of those of an 83-year-old relative of Bormann. It is assumed that he took his own life on 2 May 1945, two days after Hitler had done so.
2. Wilhelm Pieck was first state-president of the GDR, Otto Grotewohl the first minister-president. Walter Ulbricht, as secretary of the Central Committee of the Socialist Unity Party (SED), actually had the most power, and after the death of Grotewhol and Pieck, Ulbricht assumed control of the party and state.
3. After the collapse of the GDR, the attitude toward Honecker turned immediately ironic. For the first five years after unification, the restaurant in the building of the Party of Democratic Socialism, the successor party to the former ruling socialist party, hung kitsch representations of Honecker on the walls, including a portrait of him imprinted on a white bear's pelt that he had received as a state gift on a visit to Siberia.
4. In the famous 1985 visit to the German military cemetery in Bitburg, Kohl did try to initiate a mourning ceremony by inviting then-U.S. President Ronald Reagan to a site that included corpses identified as both victims and perpetrators of the Nazi regime. This attempt to initiate memorialization of German dead caused a national scandal, and led to scheduling a second visit on the same day to the Bergen-Belsen concentration camp. Unification provided another occasion where buildings and sites had to be rememorialized. In 1993, the rededication of the Neue Wache, Karl Friedrich Schinkel's first major commission on Unter den Linden in Berlin, became such an occasion. Initially used to house the king's guards, it stood empty from the end of the Kaiserreich until 1931, when the Weimar Republic turned it into a memorial honoring fallen soldiers from World War I. In 1960, the GDR rededicated it to "victims of fascism and militarism." It again stood empty from 1990 until 1993, when it was reopened, amid much controversy and under Kohl's direct intervention, to honor victims of "war and tyranny" (different perspectives are presented in Akademie der Künste 1993; English language summary in Ladd 1998: 217–224).
5. Some of this genealogy is drawn from an article in which I trace this sequence of conceptual shifts from the perspective of collective membership categories (see Borneman 1992b; longer version 1997a). For a detailed social history of changes in the patriarchal family in Germany, see Weber-Kellermann 1974.
6. The relation between Frederick II's rule and person is exemplary for the growing cleft at that time between an empire *(Reich)*, a political form that increasingly centralized and militarized society, and social forms of civility that valued sentiment, learning, and freedom. Because Frederick's tyrannical father wanted his son to be a soldier, he feared that the son's love for books—for what was called a "French disease"—would make him effeminate. Hence, the young Frederick's father subjected him to the harshest of disciplinary measures, including physical abuse. After an attempt to escape his brutal father and flee to England at the age of seventeen, the crown prince was forced

to watch the execution of his closest male companion, who had tried to help him escape. His father eventually forced Frederick to marry (he reportedly slept with his wife one hour), but he fathered no children, explicitly rejecting the role of genitor (claiming that he need not reproduce since royalty could always find an heir).

Frederick did manage to combine in an "innovative" way his own love for learning and his father's love for the military: he fostered the development of German *Bildung* (education/learning) and became a master at war strategies. He both embraced the intellectual project of the French Enlightenment and pushed Prussia toward an extreme militarization. This apparently contradictory combination has led subsequent biographers to assess him in radically different ways, using his character and career for antithetical purposes: as the destroyer of the Reich, the founder of the Reich, a great Enlightenment man, a revolutionary, a militarist, a demi-God, an evil troll, a traitor, a national hero (Dollinger 1986). Whatever identificatory possibilities Frederick II offered—which were many—they remained more Prussian than pan-German.

7. Intellectuals active in Volkskunde, such as Wilhelm Heinrich Riehl, seem to have been the first to foreground the linkage between family, Volk, and nation. Riehl's 1855 book, *Die Familie* (subtitle: The natural history of the people as the foundation of a German social policy), went through seventeen editions.

8. There was at this time, in fact, a Kaiser hymn, to the tune of "My country, 'Tis of Thee,'" but the Kaiser, as I am arguing, was not a figure of strong national identification.

9. After the 1871 unification, people in Germany practiced several kinds of translocal identification, with the Kaiser, the local Landesvater, and the national Kanzler being the most prominent political identifications, which competed with confessional ones (e.g., Catholic, Protestant, Jewish). The creation of class identifications at this time introduced other variations of translocal identification. For example, the Socialist leader August Bebel was called the "Kaiser of the Working Class," while much of the bourgeoisie identified with the Vaterland were in search of a post-Bismarck national leader. This working-class identification collapsed famously when Socialist leaders joined the German national effort in World War I. Also, from 1908 to the Nazi seizure of power in 1932, the *Graf Zeppelin* was referred to as *Volkskaiser*. Vigorously courted by the Social Democratic Party, the Graf and his Zeppelin became symbols of the unity of the Volk, initially upstaging Wilhelm II and later presenting a potential challenge to Hitler (see Warneken 1988: 52–55, 1984: 59–80).

10. This myth attributes to Bismarck a role in German nationalism that he never played. He was not a nationalist by conviction, nor did he intend national unification—unification was a by-product of his goal to unite the Prussian Reich.

11. Globke had a stellar career in West Germany after the war, despite his role during the Nazi period, even climbing to the post of state secretary to the chancellor.

12. Hitler himself was remarkably clear and consistent about the significance of comradeship, but he did not initially exploit public prejudices about the same-sex desire fostered by comradeship. Shortly before the 1934 purge of Ernst Röhm and other homosexuals in the SA, Hitler declared that the SA was "a gathering of men with a political aim, an association of raucous warriors … [and not a] moral institution for the education of daughters from the better classes." Rejecting bourgeois virtues, he argued: "We are the vanguard of the nation's power … the power of its loins" (cited in Oosterhuis 1994: 252). Two weeks after the Röhm purge, Hitler pragmatically reversed himself, declaring homosexuality to be a "poison" that required special penalties. Soon the regime extended paragraph 175 of the Criminal Code, which outlawed anal intercourse between men, to include other activities between men such as fondling, nude bathing, and kissing. Historians have pointed to the Röhm purge as "a decisive date of the National Socialist take-over" (Fest 1973: 642), without, however, analytically taking into account the specific nature of the threat posed by Röhm. In his justification for the purge, which involved the summary execution of approximately two hundred SA leaders from all parts of the country, Hitler made no mention of the reasons initially discussed for the executions: an attempted putsch by Röhm and his followers, of rebellion

against the Führer. Instead, Hitler stressed the threat to "millions of respectable *(anständiger)* people" posed by a *krankhafte Veranlagung* (sick disposition), *Gegensätze* (oppositional activity), and *schwerste Verfehlungen* (serious transgressions)—threats that present homosexuality as a misrecognized sign of the unthinkable challenge of sons to the father (Fest 1973: 637, 643).

According to Nazi theories of desire, homosexuality was not innate but in most cases spread through seduction, where it worked like an infection and could have an "epidemic effect" in the Männerbund. Male bonding, nonetheless, was viewed as necessary, and was celebrated by such popular writers as Ernst Jünger in his depictions of the soldiers' experiences in World War I. Yet such bonding had to be contained. Sex, like life, was meaningful only with reference to a collective, procreative, transcendent—the Führer, the Volk, the race, the community. Heinrich Himmler, the Reich's chief of the SS, stated openly his fear that Hitler Youth and the SS could become infected with homosexuality. Because he believed a lack of female contact could also cause homosexuality, Himmler even encouraged—contrary to official Nazi policy—sex with female prostitutes for the men under his command. His own position for a strengthening of penalties against homosexual activity eventually predominated. As chief of police, he argued for deportation to concentration camps of all convicted homosexuals who had "seduced" more than one partner. If, after release from confinement, men continued to engage in "unnatural lewdness," they were to be shot. In 1941 Hitler issued a decree to keep the SS and the police free from homosexuality: those men who committed "lewdness" with another man or permitted themselves to be "seduced" were given the death sentence. Prior to 1942, most "seduced" men were returned to the army after a period of imprisonment. After 1942, they also were subject to confinement in concentration camps. Estimates of the number of men thus accused who died in those camps range from five thousand to fifteen thousand (Plant 1986).

13. In addressing Hitler in fables, folktales, and pictures, a common refrain, for example, went, "My leader, I know you well and love you, like father and mother."

14. In love letters held by an American military officer for fifty years before being published in 1994, women addressed Hitler as *höchster Mensch* (highest human), *herzlieber Mensch* (cherished human), *Süßes Adilie* (sweet Adilie), *Lieber Adi* (dear Adi), *Verehrte Majestät* (honored majesty), *Lieber, guter Führer* (dear, good leader), *Lieber Adolf* (dear Adolf), *Mein heißgeliebtes Herzelchen* (my hotly loved little heart), *Mein Süßer* (my sweet), *Mein lieber zuckersüßer Adolf* (my dear, sugar-sweet Adolf), *Führer! Lieber! Sieg! jubelt in allen Herzen! Einzug in Paris!* (Leader! Dear! Victory! Joy in all of my heart! Invasion of Paris!). Throughout these letters to Adolf, women assumed a tone of familiarity and intimacy; Hitler was already known and part of them, as they were both symbols of the immutable Volk. A transference of love and authority onto Hitler was therefore no alienation of, but an identification with, an eviscerated self, a point made by the Mitscherlichs (1967). The men closest to Hitler also identified closely with him, as revealed, for example, in Goebbels's and Speer's diaries. Although love—in the sense of identification with and sacrifice for the whole, fulfillment in a transcendent union—for Hitler was by no means universal, it was nonetheless widespread and intensified in the late 1930s.

15. A thirty-year-old woman, listed as having no profession, said in 1933: "In the place of street signs which had been abolished, posters had been set up on every corner, proclaiming in white letters on a black background the twenty words people were not allowed to say. The first was 'Lord'—to be on the safe side I must have dreamt it in English ... the last was 'I'" (Beradt 1968: 23–24). Clearly a parable form, the removal of signs indicates loss of orientation, with repression the new alternative. The relation to the transcendent ("Lord," which cannot be spoken in German) and to the "I" are unspeakable. In a second example of the same kind of identification, a man dreamt that he heard on the radio, especially following days when Hitler's speeches were broadcast, a repetition of the phrases "In the name of the Führer, in the name of the Führer" (Beradt 1968: 40). Other familiar political slogans reappeared in his dreams in unusual forms, such as

seeing *Kritikaster und Päderaster* (fault-finders and pederasts) splashed across the front page of the *Völkischer Beobachter*, the leading Nazi daily (Beradt 1968: 41).

16. A twenty-six-year-old transport worker said: "I was marching in a column of Storm Troopers but wasn't in uniform. They wanted to beat me up. Along came Hitler and said, 'Let him be—this one we want'" (Beradt 1968: 123–124). An elderly woman, who insists she was "against Hitler and all that is erotic," reports: "I often dream of Hitler or Göring. He wants to do something with me, and instead of saying that, after all, I'm a respectable woman, I tell him: 'But I'm not a Nazi'—and that makes him like me all the more" (Beradt 1968: 124–125). A young salesgirl relates: "Göring wanted to feel me up at the movies. I told him, 'But I'm not even in the party.' He said 'So what?'" (Beradt 1968: 125).

   A housewife said, "On my way home from shopping I noticed there was going to be a street dance like on Bastille Day in France, because it was a holiday to commemorate the Reichstag Fire.… All of a sudden someone with strong hands grabbed me from behind and pulled me through the ropes onto the dance area. As we began to dance I discovered it was Hitler, and I liked it very much" (Beradt 1968: 126). Another housewife told of being at a cafe with Hitler: "With one hand he gave me a leaflet, while with the other hand he began caressing me, starting with my hair and then on down my back" (Beradt 1968: 126). In both of these dreams, we see a peculiar fusing of the ideological (the leaflet) and the erotic (caressing) in a seduction scene.

17. Youth gangs proliferated during the first decade after the war, the most renowned of which were two Berlin groups: the Gladow-Bande and the Fliegenpastetenbande. A court doctor described gang leader Gladow, known as the "Al Capone of Prenzlauer Berg," after his arrest as "having a psychopathological drive for freedom and unboundedness." In line with the draconian penalties Allied authorities gave to members of youth gangs—frequently ten years imprisonment for burglary—Gladow was executed in 1950. Girls also joined these gangs, and many also engaged in crime, mostly prostitution with the Allied soldiers and petty theft. A 1947 report of the Evangelical Church talked of "unrestrained voluptuousness as a typical postwar phenomenon." The inability of organized religions to deal discursively with sexuality contributed to a new sense of postwar religiosity in both German states, one that "repressed" talk about sexual practices, which in turn affirmed sex as something private.

18. Brandt's symbolic gesture, along with other substantive measures initiated by subsequent German statesmen, has virtually eliminated historic animosities between the two peoples. The Polish minister of foreign affairs and historian, Bronislaw Geremek, recently characterized the reconciliation between Germany and Poland and their relations as "a miracle" (cited in Jane Perlez, "Trying to Make the Twain of East and West Meet," *New York Times*, 17 April 1998, A4).

19. Connections between fish symbolism and male initiation are certainly not unique to Germans. What I find intriguing is that regimes represented as discontinuous in political authority are more likely to be concerned with the preparation and eating of fish, whereas those represented as continuous, such as the United States or the precolonial Baruya of New Guinea (see Godelier 1986), are more concerned with the catching of fish. The relation between German fish symbolism, authority, and gender is also a dynamic one. In early Christian symbolism, the letters of the Greek word for fish were understood as an acronym of "Jesus Christ, Son of God, Savior," and the fish represented the host served to the congregation. Likewise, there is a long history of associating women with fish. Fish in Germany, particularly *Backfisch* (literally, a young fish too small to cook but ready to bake), are equated with "ready-to-be-baked" girls—basically, girls between the ages of fourteen and seventeen. In public at age fourteen, girls are to be addressed legally no longer with the informal *Du* but with the formal *Sie*. (In fact, schoolteachers are required to change the form of address at this age.) To this day in certain parts of Germany, when girls turn fourteen their mothers present them with a jewelry fish, which can be bought in a store, and they recite the phrase of mixed metaphors: "With fourteen years and seven weeks the Backfisch comes out of its shell

[*ist ausgekrochen*]." In the last decade, I am told, some Germans have begun using the term "Backfisch" for both boys and girls, indicating a tendency toward gender equality in social-sexual initiation (personal communication, Uli Linke).

20. Using survey data, German sociologists tend to confirm that authority patterns remained relatively constant after the war, and then radically changed between the years 1965 and 1975. Hondrich (1992: 236–242) notes that children experience greater individual freedom within families because parents are less authoritarian, that hierarchical authority based on status has largely been replaced by functional authority based on competence, and that citizens have become more willing to criticize institutions.

21. The Love Parade has been organized under such banal slogans as "One Love, One World," "Peace on Earth," "Planet Love," "We Are One Family," *Friede Freude Eierkuchen* (Peace Joy Pancakes), and "Let the Sun Shine in Your Heart."

22. Trier (1947: 236) argues that the Germanic root of the word for father has a primary reference to *Zaun* (fence) and the idea of encircling rather than to the idea of "protection." This linkage becomes interesting again in the late twentieth century with the death of the father, the proliferation of nonterritorial sources of authority, and the inability of national states to police territorial borders.

23. These trends are to some degree pan-European. German scholars in the sociology of religion describe them in terms of a "de-institutionalization of religion," a "de-Christianization," a process of "religious individualization," and a "privatization of belief" (see Daiber 1989; Kerkhofs 1992: 167–171). See Minkenberg (1997: 63–82) for a discussion of appeals to religion and religiosity following unification.

24. My gratitude to Parvis Ghassem-Fachandi for his insights on German religiosity.

# References

Akademie der Künste. 1993. *Streit um die Neue Wache zur Gestaltung einer zentralen Gedenkstätte.* Berlin: Akademie der Künste.

Anderson, Benedict. 1983. *Imagined Communities.* London: Verso Press.

Annan, Noel. 1996. "The Abominable Emperor." *New York Review of Books* 433 (10): 20–27.

Balibar, Etienne. 1991. "The Nation Form: History and Ideology." In *Race, Nation, Class: Ambiguous Identities,* ed. Etienne Balibar and Immanuel Wallerstein, pp. 86–106. New York: Routledge.

Beradt, Charlotte. 1968. *The Third Reich of Dreams.* Trans. Adriane Gottwald. Chicago: Quadrangle.

Bezymenskij, Lev. 1990. *Der Tod des Adolf Hitlers. Die Endphase der Zweiten Weltkriegs aus sowjetischer Sicht. Unbekannte Dokumente aus Moskauer Archiven.* Frankfurt am Main: Ullstein. [In English, *The Death of Adolf Hitler: Unknown Documents from the Soviet Archives.* New York: Pyramid Books, 1969.]

Bock, Gisela. 1986. *Zwangssterilisation im Nationalsozialismus. Studien zur Rassen- und Frauen-politik.* Opladen: Leske u. Budrich.

Borneman, John. 1992a. *Belonging in the Two Berlins: Kin, State, Nation.* Cambridge: Cambridge University Press.

———. 1992b. "State, Territory, and Identity Formation in the Postwar Berlins." *Cultural Anthropology* 7 (1): 44–61.

———. 1997a. "State, Territory, and National Identity Formation in the Two Berlins, 1945–1989/95." In *Culture, Power, Place: Explorations in Critical Anthropology,* ed. Akhil Gupta and James Ferguson, pp. 93–118. Durham: Duke University Press.

———. 1998. "Education after the Cold War: Remembrance, Repetition, and Right-Wing Violence." In idem, *Subversions of International Order: Studies in the Political Anthropology of Culture.* Albany: State University of New York Press.

Borneman, John, and Stefan Senders. 2000. "Is the Love Parade a New Form of Political Identification?" *Cultural Anthropology* 15 (2): 294–317.

Craig, Gordon. 1978. *Germany, 1866–1945.* New York: Oxford University Press.

Dollinger, Hans. 1986. *Friedrich II. von Preußen. Sein Bild im Wandel von zwei Jahrhunderten.* Munich: Gondrom.

Daiber, Karl-Fritz, ed. 1989. *Religion und Konfession. Studien zu politischen, ethischen und religiösen Einstellungen von Katholiken, Protestanten und Konfessionslosen in der Bundesrepublik Deutschland und in den Niederlanden.* Hanover: Lutherisches Verlaghaus.

Doerry, Martin. 1986. *Übergangsmenschen. Die Mentalität der Wilhelminer und die Krise des Kaiserreichs.* Munich: Juventa Verlag.

Dumézil, George. 1970. *The Destiny of the Warrior.* Chicago: University of Chicago Press.

Dumont, Louis. 1992. *German Ideology: From France to Germany and Back.* Chicago: University of Chicago Press.

Elias, Norbert. 1989. *Studien über die Deutschen: Machtkämpfe und Habitusentwicklung im 19. und 20. Jahrhundert.* Frankfurt am Main: Suhrkamp.

Fest, Joachim C. 1973. *Hitler. Eine Biographie.* Frankfurt: Propyläen.

Flandrin, Jean-Louis. 1979. *Families in Former Times: Kinship, Household, and Sexuality.* Cambridge: Cambridge University Press.

Foucault, Michel. 1980. *The History of Sexuality.* Vol. 1, *An Introduction.* New York: Vintage.

Godelier, Maurice. 1986. *The Making of Great Men.* Cambridge: Cambridge University Press.

Habermas, Jürgen. 1987. *Eine Art Schadensabwicklung.* Frankfurt am Main: Suhrkamp.

———. 1991. "Der DM-Nationalismus." *Die Zeit,* 30 March, p. 8.

Hausen, Karin, ed. 1983. *Frauen suchen ihre Geschichte. Historische Studien zum 19. und 20. Jahrhundert.* Munich: C.H. Beck.

Hondrich, Karl Otto. 1992. "Authority." In *Recent Social Trends in West Germany 1960–1990,* ed. Wolfgang Glatzer, Karl-Otto Hondrich, Heinz-Herbert Noll, Karin Stiehr, and Barbara Wörndl, pp. 236–242. McGill: Queen's University Press.

Jarausch, Konrad. 1995. "Die Postnationale Nation: Zum Identitätswandel der Deutschen 1945–1995." *Historicum* (Spring): 30–35.

Kaufmann, Franz-Xaver. 1988. "Sozialpolitik und Familie." *Politik und Zeitgeschichte* B 13/88: 34–43.

Kerkhofs, J. 1992. "Wie religios ist Europea?" *Concilium* 28:165–171.

Koonz, Claudia. 1993. "Ethical Dilemmas and Nazi Eugenics: Single-Issue Dissent in Religious Contexts." *Journal of Modern History* 64:S8–S31.

Koselleck, Reinhart. 1994 "Einleitung." In *Der Politische Totenkult: Kriegerdenkmaeler in der Moderne,* ed. Reinhart Koselleck and Michael Jeismann, pp. 9–20. Munich: Wilhelm Fink Verlag.

Knopp, Guido. 1979. *Hitler Heute. Gespräche über ein deutsches Trauma.* Aschaffenburg: Paul Pattloch Verlag.

Lacqueur, Thomas. 1990. *Making Sex: Body and Gender from the Greeks to Freud.* Cambridge: Harvard University Press.

Ladd, Brian. 1998. *The Ghosts of Berlin: Confronting German History in the Urban Landscape.* Chicago: University of Chicago Press.

Lehmann, Albrecht. 1986. *Gefangenschaft und Heimkehr. Deutsche Kriegsgefangene in der Sowjetunion.* Munich: C.H. Beck.

Minkenberg, Michael. 1997. "Civil Religion and German Unification." *German Studies Review* 20 (1) (February): 63–82

Mitscherlich, Alexander, and Margarete Mitscherlich. 1975 [1967]. *The Inability to Mourn: Principles of Collective Behavior.* New York: Grove Press.

Mitterauer, Michael, and Reinhard Sieder. 1983. *The European Family.* Chicago: University of Chicago Press.

Mosse, George, ed. 1966. *Nazi Culture.* New York: Schocken.

———. 1985. *Nationalism and Sexuality: Middle-Class Morality and Sexual Norms in Modern Europe.* Madison: University of Wisconsin Press.

————. 1990. *Fallen Soldiers: Reshaping the Memory of the World Wars.* Oxford: Oxford University Press.

Mühlfeld, Claus, and Frederick Schönweiss. 1989. *Nationalsozialistische Familienpolitik.* Stuttgart: Enke.

Noelle-Naumann, Elisabeth. 1987. *Die Verletzte Nation. Über den Versuch der Deutschen, ihren Charakter zu ändern.* Stuttgart: Deutsche-Verlags-Anstalt.

Oosterhuis, Harry. 1991. "Male Bonding and Homosexuality in German Nationalism." *Journal of Homosexuality* 22 (1/2): 241–264.

Plant, Richard. 1986. *The Pink Triangle: The Nazi War against Homosexuals.* New York: H. Holt.

Plessner, Helmut. 1959. *Die Verspätete Nation.* Stuttgart: W. Kohlhammer.

Riehl, Wilhelm Heinrich. 1855. *Die Familie: Die Naturgeschichte des Volkes als Grundlage einer Deutschen Social-Politik.* Stuttgart: Cotta'scher Verlag.

Röhl, John C. G. 1994. *The Kaiser and His Court: Wilhelm II and the Government of Germany.* Cambridge: Cambridge University Press.

Schelsky, Helmut. 1957. *Die skeptische Generation; eine Soziologie der deutschen Jugend.* Düsseldorf: E. Diederich

Sombart, Nicholaus. 1991. *Die deutschen Männer und ihre Feinde.* Munich: Carl Hanser Verlag

Steakley, James. 1983. "Iconograpy of a Scandal: Political Cartoons and the Eulenburg Affair." *Studies in Visual Communication* 9 (2) (Spring): 2–51.

Steiner, Susan, David Lazar, and Edward Karst, eds. 1996. "Survey: Germany Among Leading Nations During 'Decade of Disarmament,'" *This Week in Germany,* 19 April, p. 2.

Trier, Jost. 1947. *Vater: Versuch einer Etymologie. Zeitschrift der Savigny-Stiftung fuer Rechtsgeschichte 65,* ed. Hermann Böhlans, pp. 232–260. Weimar: R. Wagner Sohn.

Theweleit, Klaus. 1987. *Male Fantasies.* Vol. 1, *Women, Floods, Bodies, History.* Minneapolis: University of Minnesota Press.

Warneken, Bernd Jürgen. 1984. "Zeppelinkult und Arbeiterbewegung." *Zeitschrift für Volkskunde* 80:59–80.

————. 1988 "Entfesselung der Zeppelinkult als Volksbewegung." *Baden-Württemberg* 4:52–55.

Weber-Kellermann, Ingeborg. 1974. *Die deutsche Familie.* Frankfurt am Main: Suhrkamp.

Wehler, Hans-Ulrich. 1985. *The German Empire, 1871–1918.* New York: Berg.

CHAPTER 3

# Two Deaths of Hirohito in Japan

*Kyung-Koo Han*

This chapter examines the two deaths of Hirohito: one in 1945/1946, and the other in 1988/1989. In it, I will focus on three themes.

First, the emperor system, and perhaps the emperor's life, was saved by the negation of the Emperor-Father's divine nature and his Father-hood of the Japanese nation after Japan's defeat in 1945. Discarding his strong father image, Hirohito transformed himself into a gentle, friendly, and vulnerable figure. This elimination of the strong father at the national level was paralleled by the decline of the father's authority and margin-alization of the father in the postwar Japanese family.

Second, through the juggling of the boundary between the secular and the religious by the Japanese government, Hirohito's funeral became a state affair attended by representatives from all over the world, and the emperor system was fully legitimated as the ancient and unique tradition of the Japanese nation. The continuity and unity of the Japanese nation was affirmed publicly and solemnly. The tremendous success of Japanese capitalism was fully displayed. Through Hirohito's second death, the emperor system again became the very identity of, and the symbol for, the unity of the Japanese people.

Third, in this effort to legitimate the emperor system, the timing of Hirohito's death was very important. Through his incredibly timely death on the first Saturday of 1989, possible inconvenience and conflicts were minimized. Indeed, it effectively deprived many critical groups of a chance to voice their opposition to the emperor system. It also effec-tively decreased disruptions in the everyday lives of ordinary Japanese, thus preventing them from reflecting seriously upon the nature of the emperor system.

# Hirohito's First Death: The Strong Father-Emperor Dies

The image of the strong father was eliminated with the end of the war. The strong father died and a new form of father was born. This was, in a sense, necessary for the survival of the emperor system. It is important to note, however, that prewar Japanese emperor's strong father image was carefully nourished in the early Meiji period for political purposes, and does not conform to the traditional image of the emperor throughout Japanese history.

At the end of World War II, the majority of the American people, not to mention those of Korea, China, Australia, New Zealand, The Netherlands, and Britain, were in favor of punishing the emperor of Japan as a war criminal. However, with the task of occupying and disarming Japan ahead, the United States decided to preserve the emperor system. If the United States had executed the emperor, he might have been regarded as a martyr, and the Allied forces might have had enormous trouble in keeping peace and order in occupied Japan. There might have been great confusion in Japan. Indeed, Japan might have become a communist country, as many conservatives had worried. With the start of the Cold War, the emperor's usefulness in keeping Japan from communist influence grew.

## Invention of the Father-Emperor

Although the emperor appeared in the seventh century for the first time in Japan, the foundation of the contemporary emperor system is quite modern. Many late Tokugawa thinkers deplored the absence of a native belief system in Japan equivalent to Christian religion in the West, which they understood, somewhat mistakenly, as the source of superior Western power. Some of them "found" that Japan had a unique emperor system and that emperor worship could play a role equivalent to what the Christian religion supposedly did in the West (Wakabayashi 1986). In other words, the emperor was to be used as a rallying point for national unity in order to modernize and produce a "rich state and strong army."[1] It was a classic case of what Hobsbawm has called the "invention of tradition."

During the early days of the Tokugawa period, the emperors were kept "above the clouds." They were under surveillance and closely guarded by the officials sent by the shogun in Edo. They were dissociated from any direct political action and they had no military function. It was the shogun who was the head of the warriors. In this way, the shoguns appropriated for themselves the symbols of virile masculinity while the effeminate emperors lived in a secluded world surrounded by court ladies (Fujitani 1996). The shogun, while spending enormous financial resources to build palaces for the emperor, enforced regulations limiting the imperial court's contact with warriors and saw to it that the role of the emperor was limited to rituals and study of literature.

This changed with the Meiji Restoration. The emperor began to practice, in theory, "direct imperial rule," as had the emperors of ancient Japan. As the emperor became the central actor in the state, it was no longer possible to have an effeminate or an ambiguously gendered emperor as head of state; the ruling emperor had to become a ruling father.

Moreover, simply because the new emperor's image was modeled on that of the male monarchs then reigning in Europe, the Meiji emperor "had to be masculinized with military uniforms, medals, and facial hair" (Fujitani 1996: 172). It was important to have a virile and mature image through which Japan could assert its right to independence.

Hence, the emperor's physical appearance changed dramatically after the Restoration. In 1871, it was declared that the dress style of the court would be reformed. It was changed from the Tang style, which "gave the impression of weakness," to active and militaristic Western style. The emperor in his splendid military uniform reminded the people that Japan had originally been ruled militarily, and that the emperor had been the commander in chief. In this way, the emperor discarded the effeminate image and recovered the masculine and warrior image from the shogun.

To create a look appropriate for an emperor practicing "direct imperial rule," the photograph, which produced a naturalistic representation of the emperor, was left much to be desired. Therefore, the official portrait distributed in the second half of the Meiji period was not a photograph of the emperor himself, but "rather a copy of a copy of a representation of the emperor" (Fujitani 1996: 177). This copy was the photographic work of an Italian artist who had been originally employed by Japan's Mint Bureau. According to Fujitani (1996), this artist first sketched the emperor, and then drew a seated portrait of him based on the sketches. A Japanese photographer then took a picture of the Italian artist's drawing. Such a "simulacrum three steps removed" was necessary to give the desired effect of the emperor as a dignified, militarized and masculinized man.

At the same time, the invention of a masculinized, militarized and dynamic emperor as political actor had created "a new public image for the women of the imperial household as serving and nurturing, as representations of the "good wife, wise mother" ideal (Fujitani 1996). As the imperial household was supposed to be the "head family" of all the other branch families in Japan, and thus serve as the model for the Japanese people, "good-wife-wise-mother-ism" became the official policy on education for girls in the 1890s.

Up until the end of World War II the Japanese people were claimed to be the children of the emperor and Japan was regarded as a "family-state" (Ito 1982). Meiji Japan's rapid industrialization and urbanization created a state of anomie; individuals lost the sense of security in the process of the disintegration of the traditional village community and the extended family. They did not know where to turn for help and guidance in times of crisis. Individuals increasingly felt the need for protection and security as these large family networks dissolved. A new family-state ideology developed to replace the extended family as the provider of this sense of security. A modern nation state was proclaimed to be "one big family" in which the relation between its constituent members was not one of class antagonism and competition but of harmony and cooperation.

In preparing the Imperial Household Law, serious efforts were made to adjust the rules governing Japan's royal court to approximate those of the Western monarchies. One result of these efforts was the writing of a provision concerning the relation of descent and affinity to succession, implicitly mandating that the mother of the heir to the throne should be the wife of the sovereign (Packard 1988). This meant a major change in the rules since so many emperors in Japanese history had been born to women who were not the legal wives of the sovereign. It seems that the Japanese were most concerned with how these matters would be perceived by foreigners. As a result, there arose the critical problem of ensuring reproduction within the conjugal couple: the candidate for marriage to the crown prince had to be able to conceive and deliver a male child.

According to a court gossip (Bergamini 1971; Packard 1988), Hirohito's mother (Sadako) was impregnated by Crown Prince Yoshihito (Emperor Taisho) before the marriage (at the age of fifteen). The reason was because it was decided that the critical element of her fertility should not be left to fate or luck but must be tested in advance.[2] She gave birth to a son on the evening of 29 April, 1900. Having passed her test indisputably in this way, the baby's mother and father were married eleven days later.

As far as the outside world was concerned, Hirohito was born a year after his parents' marriage. This arrangement of chronological time was a happy solution for everybody. No Japanese custom was seriously breached; Western rules of propriety were observed; and most important, the Imperial House of Japan was guaranteed an heir in advance (Packard 1988).

In the "family-state" of the Japanese Empire, the relationship between the emperor and the people was construed as identical to that between the father and his children.[3] This idea was based on *ie*, a family form legally established by Japan's new civil code. This ie was modeled upon the samurai class family of the Tokugawa period (Kawashima 1957). The ancestor worship within the family was interpreted as identical, by extension, to the emperor worship of the state. Moreover, when the imperial household is declared to be the main house of all the other households in Japan, the relationship between the imperial family and people's families was construed as identical to that between the main house and the branch house. In this way, the imperial household came to be regarded as the ancestor of the Japanese people. And the entire Japanese nation became one hierarchically related great family (Ito 1982).

The Meji civil code was initially based on the French civil code promulgated by Napoleon. When the draft code was completed in 1878, however, it ran into serious criticism that it was based on the Western idea of individualism, and that it ignored Japan's traditional institution of the family. As the conservatives were not only concerned with "too rash" Westernization but also interested in the idea of using the traditional family as the bulwark against destabilizing tendencies, an entirely new section on family was prepared, which was based on the idea of regarding ie, not individuals, as the constituent unit of Japanese society (Kawashima 1957)

Within Japan's family-state, loyalty to the state was structured as identical to filial piety. The emperor would love and care for the people much as a father would love his children. A new myth of the imperial family was constructed as the national origin myth (Kawashima 1957). Many people who felt acute anxiety in a rapidly industrializing and urbanizing society could find some comfort and safety in the fictive extended national family, in which they could theoretically rely on the protection and care of the emperor, who was the family head (Kamishima 1961).

The new civil code and the idea of the family-state gave great power to the head of the patriarchal family. Women's inferior status came to be legally stipulated. Moreover, such family ideology was used to control the village by setting up a number of analogies. The unequal relationship between the landowners and tenants was structured as analogous to that between the father and his children, which, in turn, was analogous to that between the head family and the branch families. These formal analogies served to naturalize and justify the class situation within the traditional village. Moral education in primary school was responsible for instilling the ideas of filial piety and loyalty into the children (Hall 1949a, 1949b).

As result, in addition to family and village, paternalistic leaders, whose authority was ultimately drawn from the emperor according to the idea of one great hierarchically organized family-state, would appear in every social situation. These leaders would exercise unlimited power and demand absolute submission from their followers; at the same time, each "little emperor," as they were called, would submit himself to his superiors.

All of the orders of the entire society were constructed as a chain, with the emperor at its apex. The legitimacy of the rule and justification for submission was based on each little emperor's relative distance from the supreme Emperor (Maruyama 1964). An order of authority was rationally constructed, which linked every sector of the society through a chain of analogies with the ultimate source of authority. This order instilled an impulse to identify with the ultimate being who embodied the source of all authority. In this society, everybody was regulating somebody, while he was, at the same time, regulated by somebody else (Maruyama 1964).

The Emperor-Father was at once both the apex of the social hierarchy and above and beyond the specific class divisions and interests. He was the generative source of all the hierarchies, yet he also transcended them. Because he was assumed to transcend the local hierarchies and class structure of the society, the emperor as the Father was considered the ultimate savior of the poor and the oppressed within the empire. When he saw the Japanese people, he would see them with the same benevolent eyes (Imperial Gaze) regardless of their positions in the social hierarchy.

Hence, much as the emperor system was an effective ideological weapon against Western imperialism in the late nineteenth century, he could also be used against the "threat" of Marxism in the 1920s.

Within the family-state, the emperor was declared sacred and inviolable. All the laws and orders were issued in-his-name, but he was not involved in the actual process of making laws. Hirohito appeared in military uniform on horseback as supreme commander of the army and the navy, but he did not actually lead the army and the navy. The importance of cultivating an image of the emperor as the commander in chief is illustrated by the government injunctions to prohibit certain photographs of the emperor from being made public. One of them is a photograph of the emperor riding on his white horse with several other high ranking army officers. The problem with the photo was that the emperor looked smaller in size compared to the officers around him. In another photo, the emperor, in a visit to a naval base, was talking with his officers in a hilarious mood. For officials in charge of ideology and the emperor's image, it was unthinkable to show a photograph of the sacred emperor laughing heartily like ordinary mortals.

## Death by Negation or Metamorphosis of the Father

This strong Father-Emperor image came to an abrupt end with the defeat in the Pacific War. According to Field (1993), some Japanese felt betrayed: "The world changed after that day, but what surprised me more than anything was that the emperor, who, in military uniform, had declared to us, 'I am thy commander in chief' and issued the orders, transformed himself overnight into a suited and hatted figure pictured lovingly with white doves symbolizing peace, attempting thereby to appeal to the people and to the Occupation authorities." "I believed what they told me and prayed earnestly. When the defeat came unexpectedly, I simply could not understand why the emperor and professional soldiers did not slit their bellies and die. Shouldn't the emperor have died by his own hand on the day of surrender?"

The elimination of the stern father involved neither the biological death nor the dethronement of the emperor but a metamorphosis of personhood. Indeed, it might be appropriate to use the term "metamorphosis"; the emperor changed himself from the sacred and inviolable father to a gentle and friendly man. In this way he was portrayed as the prisoner of the prewar system like other Japanese. By declaring on New Year's Day of 1946 that the emperor was not a sacred deity "as has often been *misunderstood*" and that the "relationship between the people and the emperor has always been one of love and trust, not based on some preposterous mythical ideas," it was conveniently denied that Hirohito ever was the strong father of the nation responsible for militarism, fascism, and the atrocities committed during the war in his name. This declaration of the emperor's humanness and denial of his divine character was, of course, strongly suggested, or even required by General MacArthur and his advisors, who wanted to preserve the emperor system in order to use the emperor for pursuing American interests in the Far East.

The proposition that the emperor is politically powerless has a long history. In fact, there were two contrary attitudes in the Tokugawa period regarding the relationship between the emperor and the government. One line of thought was that the emperor had latent secular powers. Some Confucian scholars even suggested that the legitimacy of the shogunate was dependent upon the delegation of these imperial powers to the shogun. The other school maintained that the emperor's function was entirely religious or moral (Webb 1968). Their claim was based on the fact that for the most part throughout Japanese history, the emperor's activities were restricted to rituals and religious matters.

Because the emperor had often been referred to as the personified god *(arahitogami)*, many Japanese found it shocking to hear that the emperor was not divine. But for other Japanese, this was not news, since they had never seriously thought that the emperor was a god in the literal sense. For these people, the emperor simply stated what everybody already knew. In Japan, after all, everybody becomes a god *(kami)* after death, and the Japanese idea of kami, a word applied to mythical figures and some human beings, as well as such natural objects as rocks, trees, mountains, seas, birds, and animals that are regarded as sacred, is quite different from the Western conception of the Christian God.

Hirohito the God-Emperor-Father might have died, but as Hirohito the man was alive, people had no need to mourn. Moreover, neither the Japanese nor their new leaders were involved in the killing of the Emperor-Father image. Officially, Hirohito himself got rid of his deity image, if there was one in the first place. In a sense, the metamorphosis of the father was forced upon the Japanese people by the United States, along with a new constitution. In this way, the unity of the nation was preserved; democracy was not won with blood but given as a present by the Occupation forces.

Because it was *not* the Japanese people that brought the elimination of the Father, there cannot be either any abiding hatred or guilt feelings among the Japanese people concerning the question, Who killed the Father? Many Japanese regard this as luck. However, one consequence of this form of death, or metamorphosis, of the Father was that the Japanese people were deprived of a chance to kill their own Father—deprived of the opportunity to revolt against authority. In other words, the Japanese people did not have a chance for a political "coming of age" into a modern democratic order whereby they could establish their own sovereignty.

When the war ended, only a small number of Japanese killed themselves, and most Japanese calmly obeyed the new order. Some felt betrayed and began to blame the emperor for the start of the war, for the defeat, for the atrocities committed during the war. Some were deeply disappointed because the emperor did not abdicate and cleanse the nation of the war guilt. Some felt betrayed at the emperor's remark that he was not a deity. Many Japanese felt grateful to the Americans that the emperor system was left intact.

To make the new emperor palatable to the postwar Japanese people, many measures were taken. About a month after the "Declaration of Humanness," Hirohito began to travel around the country, visiting many places and showing himself to the people. In this fashion, Hirohito succeeded in changing his identity from the sacred and distant figure in military uniform riding his white horse to a gentle, smiling, friendly figure in tie and suit—and always on foot. This transformation happened during the Tokyo War Trials. Australia, New Zealand, and the Soviet Union complained that such visits might influence the trial and demanded that the emperor should stop visiting the country. But the United States and the emperor prevailed.

After the new constitution was promulgated, the emperor and the royal family kept a low profile until the end of 1958, when they announced the engagement between Akihito and Michiko, the daughter of a commoner. The marriage of the royal couple was carefully orchestrated. For six months the mass media were engaged in what can be called a "Michi-boom." The marriage was a great success in the sense that it could direct the public's attention away from the bitter conflict between the Right and Left ignited by the government's attempt in 1958 to revise the Police Duties Act.[4] The marriage could also persuade the Japanese people that the prince had modernized sufficiently so that he could fall in love with a commoner's daughter (not a "common commoner," of course), whom he had met at a tennis court. Much attention was given to making the royal family look lovely, friendly, and democratic to the people. The new couple were to symbolize the new family value of "my homism" of the new middle class (Irokawa 1994).

## Decline of the Father in the Family

Interestingly, the disappearance of the strong father at the national level was followed by the decline of the father in the postwar Japanese family, although this decline in paternal authority was not evident in other sectors, such as business firms and factories. In the Japanese family, the mother became increasingly responsible for the education of the children. Much of women's role was still restricted to the domestic sphere, but the voice of women became louder and louder. Men began to complain that "women and stockings have become stronger after the war." The role of the mother was increasingly linked to the intensive competition for the college entrance examination, and the image of strong and energetic "education mothers" (*kyo'iku-mama*) appeared.

On the other hand, the father's presence and participation in the postwar family has become marginal in the postwar "company-centered" society. The "salary-man father" has become increasingly absent and aloof; his place in the house was often usurped by children studying for the entrance examination. It is no wonder that some alarmed Japanese parent groups organized *itaka-no-kai* (the Association of "Father! Were you there?").

However, this does not mean that the Father disappeared altogether from all spheres of society. Other less tainted images such as "the community" *(kyoudoutai)* began to be adopted as the new ideological weapon for the managers of business organizations (Han 1991). The stern Father was gone, and the ideal of family or community replaced the Father as the paramount social value. In "my home-ism" *(mai-homu-shugi)* and "my company-ism" *(kaisha-shugi)*, the members of the family or company do not obey or work for the Father; they live for the Family and the Company. Political authority has become softer and more humane, but this does not necessarily mean that it is more democratic.

## Hirohito's Second Death

Hirohito died a "natural" death in 1989, but the timing of his death was too good to be natural. For the conservatives, Hirohito's death was a chance to promote the emperor system.[5] The death of the emperor would be the focus of the mass media throughout the nation and the world. It was a chance to show to the nation and the world the antiquity and uniqueness of Japanese imperial tradition. It was a chance to impress the younger generation with the beautiful and mythical rituals. It was a chance to enhance the national consciousness.

One problem was that Hirohito's death and ritual display had to happen in such a way as not to embarrass the government. Hirohito's death would inevitably bring to surface the old questions concerning his war responsibilities, as well as other controversial questions over the national anthem and the flag. If everything went well for the conservatives, they would have a chance to make a precedent of using the unofficial Japanese national flag *(hinomaru)* and national anthem *(kimigayo)* without being challenged.[6] And the death should happen and be handled in such a way as not to cause too much trouble and inconvenience to the people. At the same time it should not present the opportunity for the old conflicts and divisions to surface.

There were a few minor embarrassing incidents but, in general, the mourning and the funeral were a success. High schools and universities raised flags to half-mast unchallenged for three days. Television commercials were eliminated for three days.

### Timely Death of Hirohito

When Emperor Hirohito took to bed in September 1988, I was doing my dissertation fieldwork at a medium sized printing company in Tokyo. Hirohito was eighty-six years old and there seemed to be no hope of recovery. His impending but uncertain death presented a peculiar problem to the Japanese. At the end of each year, printing companies in Japan would print calendars at the request of their customers, that is, for various business firms, retail stores, restaurants, or politicians. These custom-made calendars are then sent to their business clients and other socially significant people in early December. It is a very important socially established custom. As a medium of ceremonial gift exchange, the image of the sender is embodied in these calendars and they are a powerful statement of the sender's identity.

In 1988, the printers could not start printing calendars in October as they had done before because of the uncertainty with respect to Hirohito's death. The printing companies and their customers were faced with an extraordinary problem because of Japan's use of the *gengo* (name of an era) system. The year 1988 was "Showa 63" in Japan, because it was the sixty-third year of the reign of Emperor Showa (Hirohito). Suppose Emperor Showa died in November, shortly after they finished printing the New Year's calendar with an inscription of "Showa 64." With Emperor Showa gone and a new emperor on the throne, the first year of the new era would start immediately. Thus, the next year would be called the second year of the new emperor's reign. There would be no Showa 64 and they would be left with misprinted calendars. The companies that distributed such calendars would be in a very embarrassing position; it would be a considerable expense to print them again or to correct the mistakes. Therefore, the printers and their customers were still waiting in October.

Sometime in November, however, the workers in the factory where I focused my time during fieldwork began to print out calendars. I asked one of the workers why they were doing this. He shrugged his shoulders and said, "I do not know. But they say that the emperor is not going to die in this year." He added that other printers were doing the same thing.

The emperor was still alive in December 1988. Many Japanese were unhappy to see village festivals, year-end parties and other social functions canceled or scaled down for reasons of "voluntary restraint" *(jishuku)* which, to many cynical eyes, were only "imposed restraint" *(tashuku)*.

The "voluntary restraint" was almost a state affair. To show the spirit of "voluntary restraint," Japan's foreign minister, Uno, stopped attending the General Meeting of the United Nations and canceled the proposed meetings with the foreign ministers of the Soviet Union, the United States, and the Republic of China. Finance Minister Miyazawa also gave up attending the meeting of the G7 countries. Other ministers also followed the example and restrained themselves from visiting foreign countries.

Perhaps essential for the "voluntary restraint" to work was the participation of Japan's mass media, which neither criticized nor raised any questions about its extent or voluntariness. The mass media eagerly reported the nationwide restraint efforts and thus contributed to creating an atmosphere in which it seemed preposterous to ask why.

Tokyo was within two hours' flight from Seoul, and I wanted to visit my parents during the long holidays of the New Year. But since I wanted to witness my informants' responses to the death of the emperor, I was a little worried. I did not want to miss the chance to observe the response of the Japanese people and the mass media to the death of the emperor. As a would-be professional anthropologist, I did not want Hirohito to die during my absence from the field.

When I talked about my problems to one of my informants, he said that I could go home without worrying about missing the emperor's death, because the emperor was not likely to die during the holidays. I was intrigued. He explained that the emperor's death during the holidays would cause a lot of trouble for too many people. The public employees as well as politicians and business leaders would have to cancel their vacation plans and hurry to Tokyo. Employees of leading companies would have to do the same. Therefore, he told me, the emperor was not likely to die during the holidays.

He cautioned me to come back as soon as possible, however, because the emperor was not likely to live long into the New Year. The presence of two years (Showa 64 and "So-so 1") in one year (1989) would be very confusing, and the length of Showa 64 must be as short as possible so that the New Year 1989 would be practically regarded as one single year.[7]

Another informant added that the emperor would most probably die on Friday or Saturday, because that would cause minimal conflicts and disturbances in the life and business of people. This was particularly important because whether the national universities and other schools would have to raise the flag to half-mast to mourn the death of the emperor had been a long-standing issue between the authorities concerned on the one hand, and progressive student and teacher groups on the other. For the latter, Japan's "unofficial" national flag (hinomaru) was nothing but the symbol of Japanese imperialism, militarism, fascism, and all the evils, crimes, and other atrocities of prewar Japan.

Since 1958, Japan's Ministry of Education has repeatedly expressed in the "Principles for Guiding Studies at High Schools" its desire to have hinomaru raised and kimigayo (Japan's "unofficial" national anthem) sung on national holidays and other important occasions. In 1985, the Ministry of Education sent notices asking teachers and school administrators to "make maximum efforts" to guide the flag question in the "correct" direction.[8] This immediately raised opposition on the part of many parents and teachers who saw this as a sign of the resurgence of militarism and conservatism. Another informant told me: "If the emperor dies on Saturday when the campus is almost empty, then the school administrators can raise the flag half-mast without much conflict. When the students return to the campus on Monday, which is the third and last day of the mourning period, the half-mast flag would be a fait accompli." She added that those in power in the Japanese state were so clever as to make a "precedent" without serious confrontation, using Hirohito's death as a chance.

The emperor's death was known publicly in the early morning of 7 January, Tokyo time. It was a Saturday! It was also the last Saturday of the winter vacation. The flag was raised half-mast, and when the students returned to school on Monday, it had already been there for two days.

I was really intrigued at this kind of expected coincidence. It was clear that some people in Japan led their lives and coordinated their schedules with an expectation that certain types of coincidences would actually happen.

Later I checked with some of my acquaintances about the question of the flag. One professor of Kyoto University[9] confided that he and his colleagues were practically "saved by this coincidence." Kyoto is known for its right-wing nationalism *and* Marxist influence. It is the place where the "progressive" parents and teachers filed suit against the City Education Committee and school heads who ordered the students to sing "Kimi-ga-yo," on the ground that such action violated "freedom of thought and conscience guaranteed by the Constitution." This professor said: "My colleagues and I had been discussing the question for the whole year. Most of us were personally against raising the Hi-no-maru on the campus, but we, as professors of a national university, were reluctant to go publicly against the wishes of the Ministry of Education. We were also concerned about what the progressively minded students would say or do about it. Hirohito's timely death on Saturday relieved us of all these problems. I felt grateful to the emperor for his timely death."

The timing of Hirohito's death was critical in the legitimation effort of the emperor system in the sense that it deprived critics of any chance to complain about the inconvenience resulting from the gengo (name of an era) system. No less important was the opportunity presented to the Japanese mass media, which stopped commercials and filled the three days with special programs on the passing of the Showa Era and the life of the emperor.

Later, the timing did become an issue. Leftists and others criticized the decision to stop showing commercials, claiming that it was made at a very high level, contrary to the claims of the management of the television stations. These, in turn, argued that it was the result of a coincidence based on "independent decisions of self restraint" by individual television stations.

When one television network presented the issue at a six hour long discussion, which started at midnight, one discussant (a high ranking official of the publicly owned NHK) flatly denied that there was any prearranged plan to do away with commercials and to show documentary films for three days after the emperor's death. The decision to suspend commercials, he maintained, was the result of an individual and independent decision of each network. As these were Japanese networks, it was only natural that their decisions were the same. Some of those present advanced what amounted to a conspiracy theory. It was simply impossible to believe that commercial television stations, which are known for their shameless profit orientation, voluntarily brought about the financial loss of three days' advertisement revenue.

In this way, the self-restraint was continued for more than six weeks after the death of the emperor. Moreover, a lot of archaic terms were introduced to describe the different rites of the funeral. Most people learned for the first time about the many different rites and names for the imperial funeral.

During the funeral, police forces were positioned in downtown Tokyo and the suburb near the imperial mausoleum. Traffic checkpoints were established and people could see groups of riot policemen in helmets and protective gear armed with long sticks.

The funeral of the emperor has always been a spectacular ceremony. In the case of the Meiji emperor, a grandiose funeral was planned in order to "overcome the regime's greatest symbolic crisis" (Fujitani 1996). Those who were involved in the fashioning of Japan's modern imperial pageants knew too well that it was vital to show the great antiquity of Japan's imperial line through ceremony. Through a spectacular ritual, they intended to create an impression both to the outside world and to the Japanese people. This was the result of a survey of the royal rituals of European countries, especially Austria, Russia, and Prussia. The secret of the royal ritual was in the preservation or, if necessary, invention of archaic ceremonial forms. According to Fujitani (1996), a Japanese observer of the European courts and royal ceremonies found that the most important principle for establishing the Imperial Household's ceremonies was the "preservation" of old precedents. To impress upon the public the age of the Imperial Household, old precedents had to be invented, if necessary.

That is how the funeral ceremony of Emperor Meiji was created. The ceremony was very complicated and spectacular. Ancient costumes and utensils were profusely used to give the desired effect. Especially important was the fact that the funeral rites took Shinto instead of Buddhist forms, even though "Buddhist priests had dominated the performance of imperial death rites" since at least the seventh century (Fujitani 1996). Even the funeral of Emperor Meiji's father (Emperor Komei), who died only about a year before the Restoration, was performed according to Buddhist customs. Such an act of "invention of tradition" is not surprising, given that other ceremonies, such as weddings, were also being invented at that time in Shinto style (Hardacare 1989).

Besides the invented antiquity, another important element in the funeral was the promotion of mass nationalism. The spectacular ceremonies, antiquarian costumes, sacred utensils, and funeral procession attended by ten thousand honor guards constituted a visible testimony to the power and glory of the Japanese Empire. The funeral commissioners allowed public viewing of the ancient style oxcart funeral hearse and other funeral paraphernalia, as well as the internment site. According to Fujitani (1996), "When all the nation's citizens should identify with the imperial and national tradition, it was imperative that the material objects of that tradition be seen by as many people as possible."

The funeral of the emperor, so invented, is a very complex and lengthy ritual consisting of at least sixteen significant different rites. For example, in the case of the funeral of the Taisho emperor, the first rite was performed on 26 December 1926; after many other rites the burial rite of the body was performed from 7 February to 8 February 1927; the last rite, which is the rite of exorcising evil spirits, was performed on 10 February 1928. So the funeral took one year and two months, and included the performance of sixteen major rites, which could be further divided into twenty-eight different rites (Murakami 1989).

## Conclusion

The Father-Emperor was eliminated from the political scene in 1945/1946. It was not a "killing of the father," because Hirohito did not meet a biological death. Instead, the heretofore stern Father proclaimed that the Father had never existed; he dismounted from his white steed and took off his military uniform. He made his love and concern for the Japanese people publicly known, and he denied that he ever was a God. He began to walk around the country, smiling feebly, shaking hands, and asking friendly questions.

But even after the disappearance of the stern father from the public and domestic sphere, the emperor continued to rule Japan's "time" through the name of the emperor's reign (gengo) system. The Japanese had to refer to the emperor whenever they talked and wrote about anything that happened in the past. After the passage of the "Gengo Law" in 1979 it became imperative to date all papers submitted to the courts and government offices in terms of gengo. In everyday life, ordinary Japanese have to think such private matters as their parents' and children's years of birth in terms of the emperor's reign, and, by doing so, they relate their everyday lives to the emperor, who, as the incarnation of Japan's unique history and culture, is now a key figure in the new postwar politics of culture. The Japanese cannot refer to the past or the present without being constantly reminded of the fact that they are different from the rest of the world.

Had the emperor died in June instead of January, it would have caused enormous trouble for Japanese people's lives and may have given ordinary Japanese a chance to question their everyday practice enforced by law. But the emperor died a timely death.

A gentle, weak, friendly figure can serve to fulfill certain political aims just as well as a Father-Emperor in military uniform and on horseback could. When the emperor died, all the television channels stopped running commercials, and almost all day long, they instead showed documentary films about what happened during the reign of the Showa emperor. At the end of these documentary film shows, you could hear repeatedly the message that "One historic period has ended *(hitotsu no jidai ga owatta),"* in spite of the fact that there was no persuasive reason to mark the year 1989 as the end and beginning of historical ages.

The emperor's death provided Japan's right-wing and conservative groups with an ideal opportunity to reassert and advance the hegemony of the emperor ideology in a form that was emotional yet not alarming, precisely because Hirohito had been stripped of the stern father image in 1945/1946.

Hirohito's death brought home to me the paramount importance of belonging to a network of social knowledge among the Japanese. It must be very important to live with certain assumptions on the working of the society as practical guides for decision-making under uncertain circumstances. Those who belong to this social network "knew" that the Emperor would not die in December. Hence, they could afford to take the financial risk of printing calendars.

At the present moment, there is no way to find out whether the timing of the emperor's death was carefully orchestrated. Many people regard this idea as preposterous; it is simply too risky to do anything like that. I, as an anthropologist, was not trained to investigate whether there really was a conspiracy in the power center, and if so, to find out how many were involved and to what degree. But, since conspiracy can happen without conspirators, such planning may not have been necessary at all.

We only know that the printers chose to believe that the emperor would not die in 1988. Many public employees planned their holidays in the belief that the emperor was not going to die during the holidays. Some schools did not make a clear decision on the issue of the flag. Is it preposterous to believe that they may have expected to be spared the trouble by the timely death of the emperor?

As the gods do not laugh, the emperor was expected not to laugh. This photograph was taken on 6 April 1935 at the Tokyo Station where Hirohito was waiting for the arrival of Pu'i, emperor of the puppet state Manchukuo. It was prohibited to print the photograph in the newspaper.

The emperor, as the commander in chief of the military forces, rode a white horse in military uniform. This photograph was taken on 29 April 1934, Tenchousai (Emperor's Birthday), while Hirohito was inspecting troops with his staff officers. Since he looked so diminutive compared to his officers and not grandiose as an emperor should, this photograph was also forbidden for newspaper publication.

The metamorphosis of the emperor after the defeat: Hirohito changed himself from the sacred and inviolable father to a gentle and friendly man. This picture was taken on 27 September 1945 when Hirohito visited General MacArthur who was "intentionally" not wearing his ties.

Source for all photos: *Mainichi Guraphu Kinkyu Zoukan Hougyo Showa Tenno* [Demise of Emperor Showa: Emergency special issue of Mainichi Graph] (Tokyo: Mainichi Shinbunsha, 21 January 1989).

# Notes

1. The emperor system and the myths surrounding it had practical purposes. For example, Fukuzawa Yukichi stated in *Outline of a Theory of Civilization* (1875) that imperial loyalism was valuable mainly because it could mobilize the national effort to develop the country. He added: "[W]e should venerate this union between the empire and our national polity not because it goes back to the origins of Japanese history, but because its preservation will help us maintain Japanese sovereignty and advance our civilization. A thing is not to be valued for itself, but for its function."

2. As Packard (1988: 234) found the hypothesis of Bergamini "logical within the context of the Japanese court's then-existing standards of what constituted international propriety," he decided that "it would be remiss to ignore it." Moreover, Bergamini's "gossip" is supported by other corroborative evidence, such as the diary of Count Yoshinori Furuta.

3. "A state is a family. The government is the father and mother, while the people are children. The people of a backward country such as ours must be regarded as children. In order to raise these children, it is necessary to rely on the care of the parents" (Ito 1982: 198).

4. During the Occupation period, Japan's notorious Home Ministry was dissolved, and the state police, together with the special police units under the ministry's tightly centralized control, was reformed and divided into thousands of mutually autonomous municipal police forces. In 1958, the conservative ruling party and the government tried to revise the Police Duties Act. Intellectuals, laborers, and farmers, who vividly remembered the repression of the prewar police activities, successfully opposed it. This skirmish between the Left and the Right was a prelude to the "security treaty crisis" of 1960.

5. A rumor was widely circulated that contingency plans in the event of Hirohito's death had been in existence for years. In government and mass media circles, the date of Hirohito's death was code-named "X Day," and that of the empress's was code-named "Y Day" (Behr 1989: 387).

6. In September 1994, the Socialist Party made a decision by a vote at its annual congress to reverse course on its basic principle and accepted the long-contested kimigayo as the national anthem and hinomaru as the national flag.

7. Emperor Taisho died on 25 December 1926. The first year in the reign of Showa ("Showa 1") started the next day. As Showa 1 was very short (less than a week), the existence of two differently named years in one year did not become a source of major trouble in the life of the Japanese in general. However, it did cause a "huge upheaval in the publishing and printing trades." "Almost all Japanese "refrained from sending New Year greetings cards," which ruined many small printers who had not anticipated the emperor's death when they printed these cards (Behr 1989).

8. In 1990, Japan's Ministry of Education made it mandatory to display the hinomaru flag and sing kimigayo on national holidays in the school calendar (Large 1997).

9. Kyoto University, formerly Kyoto Imperial University, is one of the highly prestigious "national" universities in Japan. Its professors are public employees and are expected to pay due attention to the words from the Ministry of Education.

# References

Behr, Edward. 1989. *Hirohito behind the Myth*. New York: Vintage.

Bergamini, David. 1971. *Japan's Imperial Conspiracy*. New York: William Morrow.

Field, Norma. 1993. *In the Realm of a Dying Emperor*. New York: Vintage.

Fujitani, Takashi. 1996. *Splendid Monarchy: Power and Pageantry in Modern Japan*. Berkeley and Los Angeles: University of California Press.

Hall, Robert K., ed. 1949a. Kokutai no Hongi: *Cardinal Principles of the National Identity of Japan*. Translated by John O. Gauntlett. Cambridge: Harvard University Press.

———. 1949b. Shushin: *The Ethics of a Defeated Nation*. Cambridge: Harvard University Press.

Han, Kyung-Koo. 1991. "Company as Community: A Processual Approach to the Study of a Medium-Sized Japanese Business Organization, Tokyo Inshokan Co., 1947–1990." Ph.D. diss., Harvard University.

Hardacre, Helen. 1989. *Shinto and the State, 1868–1988*. Princeton: Princeton University Press.

Irokawa, Daikichi. 1994. *Showa-shi Sheso-hen* [The history of Showa: Aspects of life]. Tokyo: Shogakkan

Ito, Mikiharu. 1982. *Kajoku kokkagan no jinruigaku* [Anthropology of the family-state perspective]. Tokyo: Minerva shobo

Kamishima, Jiro. 1961. *Kindainihonno seishinkozo* [Mental structure of modern Japan]. Tokyo: Iwanami shoten.

Kawashima, Takeyoshi. 1957. *Ideorogitoshiteno kazokuseido* [Family system as ideology]. Tokyo: Iwanami shoten.

Large, Stephen S. 1997. *Emperors of the Rising Sun: Three Biographies*. Tokyo, New York, and London: Kodansha International.

Maruyama, Masao. 1964. *Gendai seiji no shiso to kodo*. [Thought and behavior of modern politics]. Tokyo: Mirai-sha.

Murakami, Shigeyoshi. 1989. *Cheonhwanggwa cheonhwangje* [Emperor and the emperor system]. Translated by Jang Jinhan and O Sanghyeon. Seoul: Hanwon.

Packard, Jerrold M. 1988. *Sons of Heaven: A Portrait of the Japanese Monarchy*. London: Queen Anne Press.

Wakabayashi, Bob Tadashi. 1986. *Anti-Foreignism and Western Learning in Early-Modern Japan: The New Theses of 1825*. Cambridge: Harvard University Press.

Webb, Herschel. 1968. *The Japanese Imperial Institution in the Tokugawa Period*. New York and London: Columbia University Press.

# CHAPTER 4

# The Undead: Nicolae Ceauşescu and Paternalist Politics in Romanian Society and Culture

*David A. Kideckel*

One day, to discover what people really thought of him, the Romanian dictator Nicolae Ceauşescu disguised himself as a poor peasant to travel among the masses. At the Bucharest train station he asked an old man his opinion of Ceauşescu. The old man looked to make sure no one was listening. Then he beckoned the disguised Ceauşescu to follow as he led him through labyrinthine twists and turns on Bucharest streets. Arriving at a place far "off the beaten path," and again after making absolutely sure they were alone, the old man whispered in Ceauşescu's ear, "I like him!"

## Death and Rebirth

On Christmas day 1989, Nicolae and Elena Ceauşescu, captured two days earlier fleeing a popular insurrection, were executed by a firing squad of eager Romanian soldiers, abruptly ending their quarter-century domination of Romanian society.[1] Before their execution, they faced a panel of military judges, who accused the Ceauşescus of genocide, among other charges. This indictment was based on the decade of privation that Romania and its citizens had suffered prior to the 1989 Revolution. Throughout the 1980s, attempting to rapidly pay off a ten billion dollar foreign debt, Ceauşescu ordered a massive expansion of exports resulting in widespread food shortages, the rationing of basic commodities, increased forced labor, and vast restrictions on the population's access to heat and electricity. The charge of genocide was also based on the alleged massacre of thousands during the Romanian revolt.

The indictment was especially ironic as the Ceaușescus had legit-imized their rule by use of heroic and parental images of the leader's per-sonality cult that proclaimed them the sources of Romanian vigor and prosperity. Romanians ultimately saw much of this symbol mongering as excessive and comic. Clearly, however, the portrayal of the personality cult also touched something in the Romanian soul. Nicolae Ceaușescu ruled Romania for twenty-five years, the so-called "Golden Epoch." In that time he provoked both intense feelings of devotion and revulsion throughout diverse sectors of Romanian society. I suggest below that Ceaușescu's staying power and both his acceptance and ultimate destruc-tion by the Romanian people is best explained by his use of fatherly images and paternalistic practices grafted on to Romanian cultural con-ceptions and relationships. Furthermore, the end of the regime has not, in any sense, ended paternalism in Romanian politics and society. On the contrary, paternalism's persistence not only explains the longevity of Ceaușescu's rule, but also speaks to Romanian uncertainties about the present and future and their readiness to fall back on time-tested prac-tices and relationships in response.

This essay operates at a number of levels. Ethnographically, I detail the relationship of Nicolae Ceaușescu and wife Elena to Romanian society during his ascendancy, abasement, and execution, and his contemporary and partial resurrection. Thirteen years after his death, Nicolae Ceaușescu still commands loyalty, is mentioned continually in daily discourse, and provokes intense debate among Romanians. However, more than the ethnographic examination of the paternal in Ceaușescu's rule, the essay implicitly explores the sources of paternalist attraction in both socialist and contemporary Romania, and by extension, throughout much of glob-alizing Europe today. As I discuss below, the persistence of paternalist leaders and movements is no fluke. Rather they make perfect sense in the socio-political environment of uncertainty and identity loss born of glob-alization, European integration, and post-socialist economic decline. Such circumstances especially pervade Romania, which perhaps offers an archetypical case that sadly causes us to question the ability of demo-cratic values and relationships to be implanted, sustained, and strength-ened in the contemporary period.

In introducing this volume, John Borneman suggests that twentieth-century political authority has largely rested on embodied fathers in familial, governmental, and transcendent roles whose paternalist power rested on national historical crises of identification. This is only partially so in the case of Ceaușescu. True, his image changed from liberal reformer to stern father in the early 1970s as Romanian society was extraordinarily transformed through massive industrialization and demographic change. However, strong paternalist leanings throughout Romanian history (Benedict 1953) and the family model of the one-party socialist state (Verdery 1996) also facilitated Ceaușescu's paternalist legitimation strat-egy. More significantly, I also do not concur with Borneman's optimism that the end of East-Central Europe's symbolic fathers will necessarily give rise to regional democracy by promoting the "bifurcation at the top integral to the democratic variant of modern sovereignty." As events in Romania and throughout Europe attest, paternalist figures marching at the head of integralist (Holmes 2000), populist movements with strong father figures stalk the continent from LePen in France and Bossi in Italy, to Haider in Austria, Meciar in Slovakia, to the despotic, erratic Lukashenka in Belarus.[2]

The Romanian case is especially equivocal, and suggests the continued vigor of fatherly authority. Leader-centered politics, intensified patron-client economic relations, and, to a lesser extent, romantic nationalism, all hold sway in Romania at the millennium. Many Romanians recognized the failure of paternalist leadership and expressed this by replacing paternalist Ion Iliescu, Ceaușescu's successor, with cerebral Emil Constantinescu as Romanian president in 1996. Constantinescu's four-year presidency was a disaster, however, and Romanians responded by again seeking father figure Iliescu for solace. All told, then, despite the execution of the father-leader and the wholesale transformation of Romania from party-state to market democracy, paternalistic politics and practice are not quickly eradicated by hot lead and parliamentary debate.

## The Ambiguity and Duality of Ceaușescu in Romanian Culture

Like the epigraphic joke, Romanians had and continue to have an ambiguous relationship with their communist dictator. During his rule, he engendered both intense support and revulsion, an ambiguity that intensified after his death. In the past, people gloried at the international renown he brought the country even as they cursed him for their economic privation and reviled his ubiquitous security apparatus. Meanwhile, today Ceaușescu is blamed for many problematic aspects of Romanian life, such as people's poor work ethic and lack of personal responsibility. At the same time, opinion polls show that most Romanians would gladly return him to rule to escape their current economic insecurity and put an end to pervasive corruption.

Such Ceaușescu nostalgia expresses the Romanian longing for stern but fair leaders that ensure social propriety by threatening certain punishment to wrong-doers. Expressing their belief that stern leadership provokes an honest society, many people tell a folktale of how, during the reign of Vlad Țepeș (Vlad the Impaler, the historic Dracula), a traveler mistakenly left a bag of gold at an inn. When he realized his mistake and returned, the traveler found the gold right where he had left it. Similarly, Romanians today say that what their country needs to be put right is "an iron hand" *(o mînă de fier)* or "Hitler, Stalin, and Vlad Țepeș rolled into one." Many expressed this desire again during the 2000 presidential election when they voted in large numbers for the extreme nationalist and former Ceauşescu "court poet" Corneliu Vadim Tudor who promised to rule the country "from the barrel of a gun."

The Romanian yen for strong leaders or the ruthlessness of Ceauşescu's security police *(securitate)*, however, only partially explain the longevity of the dictator's rule (1965–1989). Throughout these years many actively supported him and did so as he was able to both satisfy a range of contradictory Romanian cultural longings even as he reshaped Romanian culture and forced people to live and evaluate their lives according to terms that he established. Ceauşescu's resolution of contradictory cultural longings as well as his defining the context of people's evaluation of self and society is best seen in the debate over the national essence that occupied Romanian society through the 1970s and 1980s. The "internationalist" position lauded Romania's role in world culture and hoped for the country's greater participation in world diplomacy, economics, and scientific and technological development. The other "protochronist" position, as Katherine Verdery (1991) characterizes it, looked inward and emphasized the distinctiveness and originality of Romanian culture, and the need to preserve this cultural originality by isolation from international influence (see also Hann 1996).

Ceauşescu's role in this debate illustrates how he was able both to define a contradictory Romanian culture and to resolve these same contradictions. Though these diverse internationalist and protochronist elements were long present in Romanian culture, Ceauşescu intensified their presence and significance by simultaneously putting into play two separate cultural "campaigns" in the 1970s and equally supporting both. In the first, he promulgated the intensification of Romanian economic and political development by extending ties with the West and with Third World countries,[3] and by demanding that the Romanian people orient themselves to participation in the world scientific, technological revolution. Whenever possible, he positioned himself and Romania as equidistant from and/or as mediator in a number of global political crises such as the 1968 Warsaw Pact invasion of Czechoslovakia, in which Romanian forces did not participate, the Arab-Israeli "Yom Kippur" war of 1973, the 1980 U.S. boycott of the Moscow Olympics, and the return Soviet boycott of the 1984 Los Angeles games.[4]

Even as he extended Romanian diplomatic ties and world trade, and pushed for scientific and technological revolution, however, Ceauşescu also supported and embellished the concept of Romanian ethnic purity, the originality of Romanian culture that allegedly pre-dated contact with the West, and a range of other xenophobic policies and practices. For example, though official state policy affirmed the importance of Romania's "coinhabiting nationalities,"[5] Ceauşescu himself implicitly denied their humanity and cast himself in the role of protecting Romanians from such foreign elements. His anti-Magyar policies, such as termination of Magyar autonomous political zones (Helin 1967), restrictions on the use of the Hungarian language in schools and civic life, and the renaming of Magyar towns and villages, prompted widespread international protest. He even "sold" German ethnics and Romanian Jews to Germany and Israel, respectively, at an estimated $15,000 (USD) per person.

Fear of the alien was also manifested in restrictions on Romanians' ability to travel abroad, on the availability of foreign media (from the Soviet Union, other socialist states, and Western countries alike), and periodic campaigns to limit other aspects of foreign influence. The Official Secrets Act, passed in 1974, the year Ceaușescu was named "President for Life," required that all contact between Romanians and non-Romanians be reported in writing to police within twenty-four hours. The law also prohibited non-Romanians from staying in private Romanian homes while visiting the country. Sometimes the xenophobic campaigns took comic turns, such as Elena Ceaușescu's mid 1980s ban on transcendental meditation groups and contract bridge clubs.

## Shaping and Enforcing Romanian Culture and Cultural Practice

Like the other paternalist leaders/fathers discussed in this volume—Tito, Stalin, Mussolini, Hitler—Ceaușescu both defined the nature of Romanian culture and the terms by which Romanians related to that culture and evaluated themselves and others within it. He did so by constructing, legitimizing, and enforcing his rule by policies and practices that shaped the social, cultural, and biological essences of Romanians even as he enforced standards of behavior within that new regime. In short, Ceaușescu classically acted as both genitor and pater to his people, and, in so doing, totally encapsulated their relationships, thoughts, and actions.

Ceaușescu's comprehensive role in Romanian society and his self-identification as the arbiter of Romanian history were embodied in images purveyed in his personality cult (see Fischer 1989), which was in full swing from 1971 until the last moment of the Communist period. At its height, the adoration of Romania's leader was as extensive as any known in the Communist world and was, in fact, modeled on the cults of Kim Il Sung and Mao Tse-Tung, both of whom Ceaușescu visited in 1971. Images cultivated by the personality cult especially embellished his qualities as creator of Romanian greatness and preserver of Romanian independence. One standard representation showed Nicolae as last in a line, and hence implied legitimate heir, to important Romanian historical personalities, each of whom played critical roles in the unification of Romanians in a single polity and defended the fatherland against foreign elements (see Benedict 1953). For example, in a tapestry given him on the occasion of his birthday, his image was preceded by Decebal (king of the Dacians, the people to whom Romanians trace their ancestry), Vlad Țepeș (who fought against invading Turks), Michael the Brave (who briefly unified the Romanian principalities of Wallachia, Transylvania, and Moldavia in the late sixteenth century), and Avram Iancu (hero of the 1848 Revolution that precipitated the modern Romanian state).

As genitor, Ceauşescu's policies such as extreme pronatalism (Cole and Nydon 1990; Kligman 1992, 1998), or "systematization," which sought to revamp Romanian settlement patterns, housing and architecture, and even quotidian family life (Sampson 1984a), operated simultaneously to biologically remake Romania's population and transform the social and historical contexts in which people lived. As pater, Ceauşescu sought to educate, mobilize, and discipline. He was the guide who tried to shape the unruly Romanian people and orient them to his vision of the "new socialist man." Thus, by linking creation and enforcement, the fatherly Ceauşescu thoroughly circumscribed Romanian thought and action within conditions that he, himself, established. "Father" not only "knew best" but also made all.

Ceauşescu was at his generative best in policies that sought to remake the biological conditions and nature of the Romanian people. There has long been an attraction to eugenics in Romanian science (Bucur 2001). Ceauşescu carried this one step further, however, by seeking to expand the gross numbers of people to serve as raw material for the production of "new men." Pronatalism especially sought to redefine Romanian demography in service to the Ceauşescu vision of the Romanian fatherland (*patria*). The diverse explanations for its excessive practices all speak to this vision. These include fears of and attempts to counter high Roma (Gypsy) birthrates, the desire to better integrate Romania's regions into a unitary state dominated by ethnic Romanians, and even Elena Ceauşescu's megalomaniacal goal that Romania overtake Poland to become the most populous East European state.

Pronatalist "carrots" included maternity benefits and increased tax credits granted to couples for each additional child produced. Women who had five or more children were lauded as socialist heroes. Punitive "sticks" outlawed contraceptives, increased taxes on childless couples regardless the cause of their barrenness, required workplace gynecological exams to ensure that pregnant women carried to term, punished doctors in cases of infant mortality, and restricted abortion to cases of danger to the mother's life. To perform legal abortions, doctors needed permission from political authorities, without which abortion was potentially a capital offense.

Furthermore, in service to pronatalism, state ideological campaigns sought to remake the very structure of the Romanian family by reimposing rigid male-female role separation (Verdery 1996). Thus, in Ceauşescu's Romania, typical socialist policy encouraging female participation in economic production and enacting liberal divorce and other family law was turned on its head. Women no longer were portrayed as rugged Stakhanovite laborers but again became demure, fashion-conscious, family-centered objects of sexuality and fecundity (Gal and Kligman 2000,

Kideckel 1988). Men, by contrast, were to be like Ceaușescu: sober, hard-working, self-effacing providers and wise, but stern authority figures. Sometimes this division reached excessive heights, as among the coal miners of the Jiu Valley in western Romania. The miners were defined as socialist heroes and granted high salaries for their labor that provided coal for the expansion of Romanian industry. Wives of miners were largely deprived of occupational opportunities outside the home and regularly cared for families of five, six, or sometimes seven children.

Pronatalism not only increased Romania's population[6] but also envisioned formation of a new people whose family was to be the state itself and who would relate to that state and its father/leader with single-minded devotion. This population was to especially emerge from the great numbers of children abandoned to state orphanages due to the economic difficulties that pressured large families during the 1980s. Most children born during this period of excessive pronatalism, called *Ceaușistii* (Ceaușescuites) by Romanians even today, remained with their actual natal families. Thousands, however, were destined for state institutions and training as devotees to Ceaușescu and his family and for careers in the security policy *(securitate)*.

The attack on the biological family was also waged by policies designed to enforce collectivist living. Of these, none was more egregious that "systematization" *(sistematizare)*, ostensibly designed to rationalize settlement via a rough kind of "central-place" theory (Sampson 1984a). Among other things, systemization planned the destruction of marginal villages and the remodeling of rural and urban architecture. For example, single-family houses in central areas of villages were to be replaced by multi-family flats and apartments, both of which were anathema to rural families. Systemization-related change was carried out in extremis in Bucharest. There nineteenth-century neighborhoods were razed for a new civic center dominated by huge apartment blocks for party loyalists lining the Boulevard of the Victory of Socialism. At the end of the boulevard sat the mammoth House of the Republic and offices of the National Council of Science and Technology headed by Elena Ceaușescu (Giurescu 1989).[7] Another grim policy begun at the end of the reign was the plan to eliminate family commensality and replace it with collective meal-taking at large, neighborhood dining halls. These massive domed structures began to dot the Bucharest landscape by 1987, though Ceaușescu's execution assured that none were ever completed.[8]

Along with bringing Romanians to life via pronatalism, the Ceaușescus allegedly shaped Romania's biological destinies by causing people's deaths. Thus, Romanians believed that the security apparatus regularly removed people from their homes and workplaces and randomly executed regime enemies (LeBreton 1997: 23–24). Also, there is the myth about loss of life during the revolution, executions that Ceaușescu is said to have personally ordered. Numbers of the alleged dead range from tens of thousands bandied about in the first days after the revolution to fewer than a thousand suggested by an official governmental inquiry instituted in late 1990. The death penalty also remained strongly in force through the years of Ceauşescu's regime.[9]

Along with remaking the biological heritage and social organization of the Romanian people Ceauşescu sought to influence all areas of Romanian comportment through his prodigious, paternal activities and pronouncements. To reinforce his quality as disciplinarian and teacher, he regularly demanded campaigns against corruption, delivered lectures on increasing production and perfecting society at party meetings and during working visits *(vizite de lucru)* to provincial farms and factories, and cultivated his and Elena's images as savants and authors. The campaign to encourage Romanian participation in the world technical and scientific revolution also illustrated his didacticism, as did the great emphasis placed on education during his rule.[10]

Ceauşescu's own encyclopedic knowledge was portrayed in the multivolume set of speeches titled *Romania on the Road to Multilateral Development*. Quotes from his oeuvre were obligatory in nearly every nonfiction book, scholarly article, or general interest periodical published in Romania in the years of his rule. Many of these speeches were first delivered at one or another party meeting and printed in the Romanian press as news. Following Stalin's practice, published accounts indicated parenthetically when the audience stopped the speech for "applause," "powerful applause," or "standing ovation with shouts of hurrah." Many also appeared in a hagiographical French biography (Hamelet 1971), widely available in Romanian translation, and often visible on bureaucrats' bookshelves.

The organization of speeches in this volume speaks to the breadth of his alleged knowledge of history, science, and diplomacy, not to mention his qualities as cultural critic and social visionary. The speech categories include: (1) liberation of Romania from the fascist yoke; (2) the conception of the construction of socialist society; (3) creation of the material-technical base of a new social regime in Romania; (4) perfection of organization, planning, and leadership in the economy (the largest section); (5) watchfulness over living conditions; (6) classes and social forces in socialist Romania; (7) education, science, art, and culture; (8) socialist democracy and its necessity in the creation of a new type of society; (9) the socialist state and its functioning; (10) socialist humanism; (11) the socialist nation; (12) capacity for defending the fatherland; (13) the Romanian Communist Party and the communist and workers movement; (14) Marxist-Leninist thought; (15) national and international roles in the construction of socialism; (16) Romania and other socialist nations; (17) Romania and developing nations; (18) international forces; (19) peaceful coexistence; (20) Romanian and European security; (21) problems of disarmament; (22) extinguishing fires and tensions in the world; and (23) what the future holds.

Paternal wisdom exudes from these essays and speeches that offer original and authorizing language for the reformulation of Romanian qualities, conditions, and behaviors. In most, Ceauşescu first speaks of the progress of state, society, and people under his and the party's watch-ful guidance. He then raises a problematic area about the phenomenon in question, and lastly provides formulae for its resolution. His pronounce-ments on creating the nationwide folk festival/competition, "Song of Romania" *(Cîntarea României)*, particularly illustrate the model speech and the integration of pater and genitor roles. In "Song of Romania" insti-tutions at every level of society were compelled to develop artistic ensem-bles for local, regional, and national-level competitions. Thus thousands of people were mobilized for artificial folkloric expression that sought to homogenize regional Romanian folkloric forms into a national tradition (see Hobsbawm and Ranger 1983), which Ceaușescu felt necessary for the cultural unity of a collectivist society. Speaking at a party meeting in the Black Sea town of Mangalia in 1983, after discussing the role of the party in expanding access to art and art institutions, Ceaușescu says:

> The local Culture and Socialist Education Counsels have the greatest respon-sibility to create many forms of mass cultural artistic activities of all different types beginning with the National Theater, the Romanian Opera, until the last local culture hall in the most out of the way commune or ... village becomes a center of revolutionary patriotic education ... for the formation of the new per-son.... In this direction an important role befalls the national festival, Song of Romania, which has truly become a mass cultural-artistic movement, but which needs to be improved so that all its manifestations may better serve rev-olutionary education and the formation of the new person. It will cultivate the people's sentiment of love for the homeland. It will develop Romanian music and dance, the creations of our people! (Ceaușescu 1983)[11]

## The Family Ceaușescu: Paternal Actualities and Social Modeling

Citizen response to paternal political dominion is best assured when a father's power and control is paired with a mother's love and indul-gence. Consequently, when the Romanian paternalist regime began in full force in the 1970s, Elena (née Petrescu) quickly rose to a status nearly equal to Nicolae's. Manufactured images of the conjugal couple showed them steadfastly and single-mindedly working together on the people's business to move others to similar efforts by their love, commitment, and unity. Nicolae was the "Genius of the Carpathians" the "Brightest Light of Romanian History," "Hero of Heroes," and "Great Son of the Fatherland." Elena was the "Perfect Flower of Romanian Womanhood" and, among other things, celebrated as a world-renowned polymer chemist. Depictions of the first couple heightened their parental identi-ties. On visits to one or another Romanian locale, the couple were typi-cally greeted by children offering bouquets of flowers, whom they kissed and hugged warmly.[12]

The Ceauşescus' familistic behavior and images seem especially designed to articulate with Romanian cultural conceptions and practices. Romanian fathers and mothers are expected to indulge their children and further their interests and those of their immediate and wider families. The bilateral kindred *(rudă)* was especially important in socialist Romania due to its role in securing the necessities of life in the economy of shortage. Thus, in his latter years, Nicolae elevated son Nicolae (Nicu) to heir-apparent and also appointed many of his and Elena's family network from their natal Oltenian communities to strategic positions in national society. The presence of the Ceauşescu-Petrescu clan was so extensive that one observer, parodying Stalin's policy of "socialism in one country," wryly noted that Romania was characterized by "socialism in one family" (de Flers 1984). Ceauşescu also boosted his birthplace, Scorniceşti, which grew from small village to regional urban center during his rule. Though a rabid atheist, he also gained legitimacy by having his father's elaborate Orthodox funeral nationally televised.

Romanians were of two minds about Ceauşescu's familism. They saw something appropriate in the first couple's care and feeding of their own, a practice that modeled their own strategy for survival. However, their own economic privation also gave them a sense of being abandoned by their parental guides in favor of a select few relatives. This sentiment was felt even more intensively due to the excesses of the Ceauşescu kin. For example, youngest son and heir-apparent, Nicu, especially inverted the qualities Nicolae sought to embody: tireless worker, teetotaler, and one who denied the pleasure of the flesh. Nicu, who died of cirrhosis in autumn 1996 at the age of forty-five, was a womanizer and alcoholic whose exploits and conquests, including gymnast Nadia Comaneci, were legendary.[13]

Meanwhile, unlike Nicolae's effective unification of Romanian cultural longings and perceptions, Elena was never able to overcome the contradictions between her image and that of expected identity and practice of Romanian women. Women in Romania, as elsewhere in southeastern Europe and the Balkans, are largely expected to serve their husband's needs in a demure, self-effacing manner. However, Elena was rumored to have had a number of affairs, including incestuous dalliances, and trysts with security guards and cabinet ministers (Pacepa 1987). Her alleged intellectual achievements were also known to be the work of others.[14] Most important, she was thought to be the power behind Nicolae's throne and responsible for many of the most egregious excesses of state policy during the "Golden Epoch." Even today many Romanians say that had it not been for her self-indulgence and capricious demands, Nicolae's rule would have been benign, if not, effective.

Thus, despite the precipitous decline in their lives, Romanians held to the father principle and to Ceauşescu as its embodiment. Paternalism served them as it abrogated their own responsibility for political action and decision-making and justified their own complicity with the regime.

A dominant national ethos during the years of socialist centralism was the so-called run from responsibility *(fugă de răspundere)*, a logical response to the domination of politics by the Communist Party and threats to those taking independent political action. The political apathy of Romanian communities in the Ceauşescu years was profound. People understood the ends to which such capitulation led. Still, they felt satisfied, or at least unthreatened, to remain devoted to the leader, at least in their public lives in farm, factory, or office.

Still, as living conditions declined, and the first couple's lavish lives became ubiquitous in Romanian public discourse, parodies of Ceausescu as martinet and fool became incessant and widespread. Though he offered himself as father and model of an idealized Romanian society, his policies and practices put asunder those same relations. Throughout his ascendancy, Romanian society was in constant turmoil fueled by practices of what he termed "multilateral development" (Gilberg 1975). Family life was roiled by collectivization, industrialization, and the massive labor migrations they entailed. Household disintegration was common. Even where people stayed together, there was often increased distance and alienation between generations (Kideckel 1993).

## The Death of Romania's Father

The Romanian revolution began Friday, 15 December 1989, in the western city of Timişoara.[15] It was sparked when a multiethnic group of protesters tried to prevent security police from removing Calvinist minister Laszlo Tökes from his church to provincial exile. The protest grew as word spread. By the next day, it was a full insurrection as marchers chanted and looted stores. Ceauşescu was enraged that the riots were not put down and on Sunday, the 17th, he ordered Timişoara authorities to shoot all protesters. He then left for a three-day state visit to Iran. At first the army hesitated to comply with the dictator's orders. Ten years of economic privation had weakened Ceauşescu's legitimacy. However, as the rioting continued, police fired on the crowd. Many people, even mothers with babies in their arms, rushed the police, shouting that it was better to die than to go on living as they were.

News of the revolt spread rapidly by telephone and by commuting workers and students returning home from shuttered Timişoara University. The rumored deaths of protesters galvanized the nation and Bucharest was electric with tension on 20 December, when Ceauşescu, oblivious to the gathering storm, returned from Iran. Seeking to calm what he thought was mild unrest, Ceauşescu played on usually reliable nationalist hatreds in a televised speech, claiming that the protesters were hooligans and foreign agents. Then, either from stupidity or arrogance, he decided to demonstrate his control by calling a rally in front of the party's Central Committee building the following day. That gathering, however, was decisive. Then, as Ceauşescu harangued the crowd from a balcony, students began to boo, whistle, and unfurl anti-regime banners. Unaccustomed to protest, the dictator was befuddled and his stammers were televised across the nation.

Demonstration of the father's failing powers emboldened more protest the night of the 21st, when many protestors were allegedly killed by army troops. Rumors of the massacre brought out tens of thousands in mass protest on Friday the 22nd. Ceauşescu again called a rally to sway the hostile crowds, but now his talk was fumbling and barely audible. People now shouted and flung debris, and as crowds surged toward party headquarters, Elena pulled Nicolae to safety in his office. Army units were sent to stop the crowds, but many soldiers defected to the protestors. When tanks with protesters and soldiers in solidarity appeared at the Central Committee, the Ceauşescus and some of their high command tried to flee in a helicopter but were captured later that evening. For two days Nicolae and Elena were held in constantly moving armored vehicles, but on the 25th they were remanded to a military base in the Carpathian foothill town of Tîrgovişte, birthplace of Vlad Ţepeş, where they were tried and executed in a matter of hours.

The successful transfer of intergenerational power, i.e., the replacement of fathers by sons, must be a visible process. Rituals of royal succession in Africa (Gluckman 1963) suggest that whether the death of the father occurs by violence or by natural means, the legitimacy of the son is facilitated by the open and public removal of the father's remains and the celebration of his renewal in the person of the son. "The king is dead. Long live the king!" Thus, more than the usual Romanian penchant for rumor (Sampson 1984b), the uncertainties surrounding the flight, capture, trial, and execution of the Ceauşescus called into question the facts of the dictator's rule, his death, and the legitimacy of those seeking to succeed him.

Rumors about the revolution and about Romania's new leaders spread like wildfire in the first days of 1990, fed by limited disclosure of the Ceauşescus' last days. Though the flight of Nicolae and Elena from power was greeted enthusiastically by most, their hasty trial and execution prompted talk of Soviet conspiracy or coup d'état organized within the party. The new leaders offered counter-claims that the speed of execution was to prevent Ceauşescu's rescue by security forces. They also said that the limited television coverage of Nicolae and Elena's trial was to protect the anonymity of those who judged them. Still it was all too speedy for the Romanian masses. Some saw it as an attempt to silence the Ceauşescus about others' collusion in the exploitation of the people. Others bandied Elvis-like tales of a fake execution, with Ceauşescu spirited away by securitate to live in North Korea or the West.[16] Other rumors implicated the legitimacy of the newly installed National Salvation Front (NSF), implying that Ceauşescu was in the dark about the worst depredations of the last years. The "good king" had been duped by his "bad counselors" (see also Sampson 1984b). With conspiracy theories rampant,

NSF leaders felt it necessary to televise the whole trial to clear the political air, which they did the Sunday after Easter 1990.

Despite the NSF goal of illuminating society and quelling rumors, the rebroadcast of Ceauşescus' trial and execution in its entirety had opposite consequences and even improved the dictator's image. Advanced knowledge that the entire trial would be shown that Sunday produced heightened anticipation throughout the country. People wondered whether it would resolve their questions. I watched the rebroadcast in Bucharest with a family of intelligentsia whose forebears included members of the Romanian Academy. Watching television was an aged grandmother, her middle-aged son, his wife, and their daughter in her thirties. The trial and execution transfixed all of us and we spoke little during the two-hour broadcast.[17] When the broadcast ended, however, all expressed anger at the Ceauşescus being such a focus during Holy Week and agreed that both got what they deserved. Soon, though, alternate opinions about the Ceauşescus' fate emerged.

Agreeing with pre-Easter rumors, the family thought the trial and execution precipitous and designed to keep the Ceauşescus from revealing others' misdeeds. They agreed with the popular thesis that those who judged the first couple also had extensive wrongdoing to hide. There was a split in the family's opinion over the qualities and significance of the two Ceauşescus. The wife was the more forgiving. She felt Nicolae really wanted to improve the country but was diverted by others, especially Elena, whom she greatly condemned. Her husband was slightly less forgiving. He said that Ceauşescu may have wanted to help the country, but he knew what was going on. Their daughter totally dismissed the two as thieves and malefactors while grandma sat silently with red-rimmed eyes.

As this family's opinions illustrate, the rebroadcast only reaffirmed popular uncertainty about and sympathy for Ceauşescu's suffering and antipathy for the way he died. Though views of Elena were more equivocal, there was little joy in watching the puzzled old man, badly in need of a shave, led to a wall and gunned down. The ghoulish horror at the contorted bodies only fueled people's anger at their being deprived of the knowledge the two took to their graves. Above all, the NSF's rebroadcast of the trial provided initial impetus for Ceauşescu's rehabilitation, a process that has steadily advanced as the promises of the revolution have dissipated in economic decline, corruption, and the growing uncertainty of post-socialist identities and social relations.

Post-socialism challenges most Romanians. Aside from the business and political classes, Romanians contend daily with unemployment, inflation, declines in health and standards of living, and stress. Alongside these pressures, new standards of beauty and consumption purveyed by mass media, and the bleeding of Romania's "best and brightest" by massive emigration, contribute to vast senses of uncertainty. Within this context of massive and comprehensive change, Romanians and other peoples experiencing analogous disjunctures of globalization (Appadurai 1996) frequently seek stability by falling back on essential cultural principles (Holton 2000), casting blame at outsiders (Holmes 2000), or seeking solace in strong leaders with simple solutions. Thus, despite Romanians' fervent wish to rid themselves of their dictator in 1989, life after Ceauşescu almost guarantees the return of his specter and the paternalism that animates it.

## Reanimating Ceauşescu and the Paternalist Style

Since the end of Romanian socialism there has been a steady, but noticeable increase in public sympathy for Ceauşescu and a positive reevaluation of his rule. Ceauşescu's reanimation and rehabilitation, however, reflects more an affinity for paternalist practice in Romanian politics and economy than respect for the man himself. Paternalism today manifests in attitudes to the West, to political leaders and political participation in general, and especially in day-to-day socio-economic relationships. We see this especially in the treatment of the dictator's corpse and image.

Ceauşescu's reappearance was evident as early as December 1990, and gathered steam through 1991 and 1992, years of massive inflation, recession, nationalist cant, and unstable politics. In those years, the dictator remained an official nonperson, but the people had other ideas. During fieldwork in Bucharest and southern Transylvanian villages and towns in autumn 1992, people often raised him in conversation and his picture continued to appear in public places. Shopping for a valise in Bucharest's Unirea department store, for example, I happened on a larger-than-life portrait of the leader, under glass at a sales counter. "Why do you have that?" I asked the clerk. "I miss him," she said. "His *murder* [emphasis added] left us without a leader." If anything these sentiments have increased at the millennium. In a 1999 poll sponsored by the Soros Foundation, 75 percent of Romanians said they were better off when Ceauşescu was alive. Făgăraş (south-central Transylvania) factory workers and Jiu Valley coal miners, among whom I have worked since 1999, sprinkle their remarks about the difficult conditions of life today by reference to the security and quality of life "in the time of Ceauşescu."

The treatment of Nicolae's and even Elena's graves also illustrate the renewed respect he garners in society today. Though the two were allegedly placed in unmarked graves after their execution, their burial at Ghencea Cemetery in southwest Bucharest was common knowledge. Their graves are about one hundred meters in from the main gate, on different sides of the cemetery's wide asphalt walk. As early as 1992 Nicolae's grave was well maintained and frequented by mourners. It was first marked by a plain black steel cross about 1.5 meters high with his name and years of birth and death painted on the horizontal. Five bouquets of flowers were on the grave and four people stopped to pay their respects while I was there. Their predominant sentiment seemed that of regret.

One woman, responding to my question of why she had come, spoke of the shame of Ceauşescu's execution. She said others were to blame for the state of the country and his trial and execution were only used to scapegoat him.

For a time in the late 1990s, during a period of significant political polarization, Nicolae's grave was also the focus of a political tug-of-war between his mourners and detractors. On significant dates in the Romanian political calendar, the grave was either defiled or repaired. In May 1996, on the 75th anniversary of the founding of the Romanian Communist Party, activists from the Romanian Workers' Party erected a new cross on Ceauşescu's grave to replace the steel one removed by vandals earlier (Shafir 1996). As recently as early 2001 members of the ultranationalist Greater Romania Party (Partidul România Mare, or PRM) even sought his disinterment. They wanted to investigate rumors that Nicolae had been tortured before he was shot to further discredit newly installed (and former) president, Ion Iliescu who, people assume, had benefited from Ceauşescu's summary execution.

Today, perhaps in testimony to the wistfulness of people about the more secure days of his rule, Nicolae's grave is a proper one, indeed. It is marked by a stone cross and emblazoned with a red star, his name and dates of his birth and death, a bronze portrait, and a statement that the marker was erected in his honor by members of the Romanian Worker's Party. Given Elena's more equivocal role in Romanian society, her grave has been treated with markedly less respect than her husband's. In autumn 1992 her grave was still unmarked, though a column of bricks and slightly raised earth was evidence of her presence. During the hour or so I stayed at the cemetery, aside from my friend and myself, no one but us stopped at her grave. By 2002, however, her grave, too was bordered by a low fence and furnished with a small, permanent marker. There were even flowers placed on the grave by previous visitors. Thus, as the graveyard scene suggests, paternalist sentiments are still powerful in Romania today despite the range of other social institutions and practices developed since the revolution.

## Paternalism in Contemporary Romanian Politics

That, for many in Romania, "father (still) knows best" is not surprising. Notwithstanding the extravagance of the Ceauşescu personality cult, paternalist dependency is still a comfortable pose for Romanians. It provides an anchor in an uncertain world and is a time-tested method for accessing resources in a shortage economy, whether created purposefully by socialist policy or by the large-scale unemployment coincidental to capitalist privatization and industrial restructuring. Above all paternalism excuses one from taking personal responsibility in a messy political environment.

The struggle between paternalism and self-interested democratic politics is especially seen in the nature of Romanian political parties since the revolution. Like elsewhere in the formerly socialist states, political parties mushroomed in 1989–1990 but have lately been winnowed, with most maturing as representatives of a broad spectrum of interests as opposed to individuals. Despite a maturing politics, however, leftover concepts of loyalty to party and leader tend to emphasize the same fatherly principles in effect during socialist one-party rule. Though the belief is declining, party membership in Romania is still assumed to demand absolute fealty to its leadership. Membership in competing parties, then, is not so much accepted democratic practice or considered a non-essential difference between people of goodwill. Instead, it implies antithetical identities circumscribed by a circle of patronage, power, and personalism.

Paternalism in Romanian politics also shows up in a variety of other realms. Romanian labor unions are especially prone to following the whims of the single leader. The most extreme example of this concerns Miron Cozma, the now-imprisoned head of the Jiu Valley Union of Miners. Many miners speak of Cozma as the "Morning Star of the Coalfields" *(Luceafărul Carbunului)*. Under his demagogic leadership, the miners massed six times for actual or threatened marches on Bucharest, where they physically attacked students, intellectuals, and representatives of disfavored political parties (Beck 1990). Cozma's prison sentence relates to his role in the violence that brought down the government of Prime Minister Petre Roman in September 1991. The last miner march in February 1999 was an attempt to bully the government to release him. However, in testimony to the ambiguities of paternalism today, many miners, and even some who took part in this last march where they were gassed and shot at by Romanian police and armed forces, express regret and acknowledge their manipulation by Cozma and his lieutenants. Other beneficiaries of the Romanian penchant for paternalism include Marian Munteanu, head of the national revivalist Movement for Romania (Mişcarea Româneasca), PRM president, senator, and former Ceauşescu court poet Corneliu Vadim Tudor, and President Ion Iliescu himself.

Iliescu was ousted in the 1996 presidential election by Emil Constantinescu, former rector of the University of Bucharest and head of the Democratic Convention (Convenţia Democrata Româna, or CD), a loose alliance of center and center-right parties. However, Iliescu returned to Cotroceni Palace[18] in 2000, after four years of CD corruption, incompetent rule, and personalistic squabbles of center-right candidates. Iliescu's paternal style and fatherly visage were central to his campaigns and mode of governance. This image, in fact, was even mocked by the opposition slogan "Iliescu smiles at us and with love he dupes us" *(Iliescu ne zimbeşte şi cu drag ne păcăleşte).* Constantinescu's 1996 victory showed another possibility for Romanian politics. His lack of fatherly, charismatic qualities was even cited by some commentators as a positive feature for a

Romanian president. In contrast, Iliescu's return suggests a reaffirmation of paternalist leanings. In their voting behavior many Romanians reflect the same nostalgia for forceful leaders and acquiescence to recentraliza- tion found throughout contemporary Central and Eastern Europe, from Serbia, Croatia, and Slovakia, to Belarus and Ukraine. Iliescu's own power, in fact, grows from his policies of protecting jobs and his wide- spread use of patronage in the state sector.

The power of the paternal is also suggested by the reemergence of Romanian nationalism (Tismaneanu 1993), a last line of defense against the growth of a democratic, class-based politics. The nationalist revival is illustrated by various phenomena such as the campaign against the Law on Local Administration, giving minorities the right to conduct civic affairs in their own language, periodic violence between Romanians and Roma, and the growth of support for the PRM and its head Vadim Tudor, who placed second in the 2000 presidential election. There have even been attempts to rehabilitate World War II dictator Marshal Ion Antonescu, the latest effort exemplified in a project to erect a monument to him in the city of Băcău.

As an ultimately essentialist, romantic, and quasi-mystical belief sys- tem, the nationalist program demands obeisance to an ideal cultural homogeneity, often expressed through the person of the leader. It is a short hop, as it were, from the nation as single voice to the leader/father as its chief representative. This is compounded by tendencies to define antithet- ical others as counter to the nation and to scapegoat them for economic difficulty and political unrest (Kideckel 1994). The particular identity of the other is of little consequence. It could be the West, multinational insti- tutions such as the World Bank or International Monetary Fund, Jews, or Russians. What matters, however, is how defining such "others" encour- ages national unity and paternalist leadership.

Contrariwise, antinationalist forces also succumb to the attraction of paternalistic solutions to contemporary Romanian economic problems. The single-minded desire for entry into NATO and the European Union (EU) expressed by many Romanian political leaders, now including Ili- escu himself, especially suggests the hold of paternalist solutions in Romania. The "West" is considered as both panacea and scourge (Kideckel 1994). Most people assume that if and when Romania is accepted by NATO and the EU the economy will be miraculously trans- formed by large infusions of investment handed out willingly by a new father, i.e., the beneficent West. Until that time, however, Western demands for economic and political reform strike Romanians as attempts to emasculate national production capacities, to take over the country's markets, and to threaten the integrity of its culture. Thus, the Western rela- tionship with Romania clearly models the qualities of paternal love. It can be bestowed lavishly and without precondition on the dutiful son, but can be painfully withdrawn for prodigality.[19]

## Paternalism in Local Life and Culture

The confusion of economic life, the rapidity and opacity of privatization processes, the disintegration of social networks, people's fears for their jobs and for securing a modest standard of living have especially preserved paternalism at the local level (Kideckel 1992). Paternalism in local economic relations is defined by the domination of informal paternalistic personal networks of clients, cronies, and kin in the Romanian economy (i.e., what Romanians term "mafia") and on others' clear recognition that such patronage and dependency confer advantage. Mafia-type relationships are especially the case in the wholesale take-over of commercial and industrial enterprises in Romanian privatization (Verdery 1996: 216–220), in the capture and use of foreign assistance for personal purposes (Wedel 1998), and even in the operation of state-run enterprises. In this latter case, with every change of political administration new managers are brought in or old managers retained on the basis of their clientilistic ties to leaders. These same ties operate at every level of the enterprise. An unemployed worker at a Făgăraş machine tool factory described this well:

> After the election [1996] a new director, who was a former section chief, took over the factory and right away favored his former section with the orders that came in. He then said that since our section had no orders it should be closed. So he closed our entire section though he sent some of his friends to the open section to continue working. I knew even earlier that he planned to close our section... when he started to get very attentive about all our tools, to make sure that they were kept closely supervised.

Similarly the mass labor contract buy-out campaign *(disponibilizare)* that began in 1997, where workers were offered a large package of severance pay (in addition to state unemployment compensation) to voluntarily quit their work, was especially characterized by decisions made on a paternalistic, patron-client basis. In Făgăraş region factories at first many workers wanted to quit since they had the possibility to use their severance to finance migration to Italy for better paying jobs. Workers claim today that all those given the right to leave had close relations with the factory bosses while others who didn't were forced to remain at work. Conversely, in Jiu Valley coal mines, miners claim that most wanted to keep their jobs and that those who were let go were mainly on the outs with mine administrators.

Mafia aside, economic enterprises in Romania today are frequently organized on a family basis emphasizing the leadership of a strong father figure, top-down decision making, and the pooling of resources largely controlled by the father/leader (see Wolf 1966 for a comprehensive discussion of patronage). In contrast to socialist bureaucrats, who generally exerted paternal leadership over a single sphere of relations (e.g., a local township and its enterprises), some prominent individuals today hold sway in multiple spheres simultaneously. For example, a small-scale regional entrepreneurial couple that I know is linked to banking, politics, real estate, tourism, with broad ties throughout the country in all these spheres. Though he employs over fifty people, his core employees are his wife, his wife's sister and her husband (who is also the local mayor), their neighbor, his mother-in-law, a nephew, and another couple from his natal village. The grandest of business and political leaders (former tennis impresario turned commercial magnate, Ion Ţiriac, or Roma clan leader, Florin Cioabă, come to mind), have networks of relations that reach the highest levels of politics, economics, culture, and even into the international community.

Paternalism and patronage also persist in rural areas where they are often constructed on the remains of defunct agricultural collectives (see Lampland 2002 for a Hungarian example). One type develops when former officials of local collective farms lease large tracts of lands from villagers who, by dint of privatization, have been left with only unproductive minifundia as their main, if not sole, source of income. Villagers also often lack technology and other inputs for successful farming, and forty years of socialism left them ill prepared for agricultural livelihoods. These former officials often dominate their communities like the landed barons of the pre-socialist past; dispensing favors, baptizing children, controlling their co-villagers by loan arrangements and the like. This is especially so when their lease arrangements encompass entire villages, or at least the largest portion of their arable lands, and the ground rents the patron pays are essentially the only cash income available for participating households. Patrons may also assist clients to find other available employment, in many cases in enterprises owned by the patron himself.

Where it exists, then, the patron-client relationship clearly evokes the dependency of the parent-child bond. This was particularly evidenced by a regional official-cum-entrepreneur from a southern Moldavian county who owns a variety of enterprises, including a wholesale food dealership, a small wine-making enterprise, and a tractor park. Along with his government functions, his economic interests place him in a position to utterly shape the life chances of his employees and their families who, in their response to him, show him great deference. They take their hats off in his presence, stand rapt when he instructs them, and (according to him) out of respect alone, provide him with many personal services beyond their formal labor contract.

## Eroding Paternalism from the Bottom-Up: Change in Romanian Families and Households

Even as paternalism is encouraged in economic relations it is potentially challenged and neutralized by the greater possibilities of individual economic initiative and the development of civil society and its array of nongovernmental organizations. In families and households in cities, towns, and villages, various real-life factors erode the potency of paternalism. Emigration, widespread household dissolution coincidental to the economic downturn, and the growth of a media-driven culture of consumption have, to a certain extent, delegitimized the hierarchy inherent in paternalism and are beginning to shake youth free from the confines of their fathers. Though pre-socialist Romanian communities were noted for the paternalist ethos of the family household and the dependent position of women and the young, this was by no means universal and ideology and reality often diverged regionally and historically. Paternalism particularly gave ground during the widespread dissolution of peasant and worker households in the interwar period coincidental to worldwide depression and the spread of capitalist social relations. It was again challenged in the early years of the socialist state. Even during the heights of Ceauşescu's attempts to remake the Romanian family, paternalism did not fare well in many communities. In some regions where men were absent as commuters in industry, women became the effective social, economic, and often political actors in village communities.

The power of the father is equally challenged in households today. To begin with, it was buffeted by the death of Ceauşescu, a signal social psychological event. His execution especially questioned the appropriateness of blind obedience to fathers. In fact, much of the ensuing discourse about the Romanian "revolution" spoke of the sacrifice of youth and used metaphors of children leading the way for their parents. Such values are especially symbolized in the many crosses erected right after the revolution and that remain on the margins of Bucharest thoroughfares and in main squares. Each marks the spot where a typically "young hero of the revolution" fell. They are vivid reminders of the sacrifice of youth and the failure of their parents.

More than Ceauşescu's death, however, the ensuing transformation of national political economy is also contradictorily responsible for inroads on household paternalism even as it maintains the role of the father in more inclusive levels of social organization. In particular, the greater ease of internal and international migration, and the decline of the factory employment system all contribute to the weakening of paternalism. Rural and urban households both are in active processes of dissolution, comparable to the period between the two world wars. The emigration of many young workers to seek employment in Western Europe also mirrors the process that took place in the years leading up to World War I (Bărbat 1938). Then, young men, forced to leave home by economic circumstances, were nonetheless able to craft some slight space for independent action in their own right. So, too, today. In fact, income earned abroad by youthful migrants and the labor contacts they provide other family members give them a voice in household affairs that is more extensive than in socialist years.

The media-driven proliferation of globalized cultural styles also erodes the authority of parents/fathers within household contexts. Such images, music, and new culture heroes such as "super models," the Spice Girls, and Michael Jackson separate the generations into distinct spheres of knowledge, experience, and imagination (Appadurai 1996) and break down continuity as well as mutual respect between generations. Economic factors also feedback on the increasing distance between the generations. People over forty have a brutal time in finding employment if they lose their current positions. Indeed, they are distrusted for their communist upbringing, and they are considered not presentable enough for careers in sales. They are viewed as expecting too much from their employers. Ceauşescu was their father. He may have disciplined them, but he also encouraged their ambitions and, until his draconian economic policies of the 1980s, gave people a sense that their labor had worth.

## Conclusions

The implications of the death of Romania's (Communist) father are as yet ambiguous. Much in the Romanian present assumes the continuation of a modified, albeit persistent, paternalism. Other forces work actively against it, however. The elimination of Ceauşescu and sere Elena, combined with the vast changes in the Romanian economy, has atomized and fragmented the field of social relations for all. This fragmentation combined with economic patronage and the continued presence of significant nationalist sentiment, whether or not supported at the ballot box, encourages retention of the paternalist model. At the same time, the disintegration of paternalism at the household level and its challenge in the political system offer a prospect for significant change in national politics, if not immediately in economic practice.

The true test for Romanian paternalism and its related psychological dependencies is just around the corner. Now that Romanian economic decline appears to be checked and growth, at least for some, is again a reality, the political system will also have greater demands placed on it by economic actors. If the political system is unresponsive, as it has too often been in the past, then it will be a simple matter for Romanians to place their affairs in the hands of those who lay claim to govern in paternalist ways. Nonetheless, changes in society have clearly shown Romanians that they are masters of their own fate and able to make decisions by themselves, for themselves.[20] Whatever the actual role of "the people" in the Romanian revolution, they themselves have become both genitor and pater to the Romanian present and future. Much more than in the communist past, Romanians view their leaders with a healthy skepticism and exhibit a willingness to engage them at all social levels. If Ceauşescu were to again return to anonymously ask people what they thought of their new leaders, their answers might surprise him: it depends on what they've done for us lately!

# Notes

1. Ceauşescu formally came to power in 1965 after the death of his mentor, Gheorghe Gheorghiu-Dej. He consolidated his power after 1971 by spearheading the so-called "mini-cultural revolution" that replaced many officials of Romanian state, Communist Party, and economic bureaucracies with Ceauşescu loyalists.
2. The exception that proves the rule here is the recently assassinated Dutch populist, Pim Fortuyn, who turned paternalism on its head by his openly gay persona and espousal of policies of social libertarianism combined with a stern antiforeigner ideology.
3. In the middle 1970s Romania became a member of the "Group of 77" developing nations which, next to the Soviet Union, were the largest outlet for Romanian exports.
4. On the strength of Ceauşescu's staking out Romania's neutrality in the Cold War, Henry Kissinger called him "my favorite Communist." To support Ceauşescu's "maverick" Communist stance, Romania was the first foreign country Richard Nixon visited after becoming U.S. president in 1969.
5. This concept was applied to officially recognized minority groups such as Magyars and Saxon and Swabian Germans. Roma (Gypsy) peoples were, however, denied such status and lumped in a category of "other nationalities."
6. Romanian statistical manuals document a ten percent increase in population, from roughly twenty-one to twenty-three million people between 1974 and 1990.
7. While walking between the two buildings in April 1990 a passerby joked that the buildings faced each other so that "the two great savants [i.e., Nicolae and Elena] could stand at their windows and telepathically bounce ideas off each other."
8. Today Romanians dub these structures "circles of hunger" *(cercuri foamei)* in reference to the disastrous nutritional conditions of Romanians in Ceauşescu's last days. In partial testimony to the extent to which Romanian society has changed, one of the largest of these structures was purchased by Arab interests and converted into the Bucharest Mall, now the most fashionable shopping center in the city.
9. Shortly after the Christmas 1989 rebellion, the interim leaders of the National Salvation Front abolished capital punishment by decree, to symbolically distance themselves from the Ceauşescu regime. Romanians, though, saw this as a way for former Communists to escape punishment and demanded reinstatement of the death penalty in a series of protests in January 1990. In one demonstration, poet Dumitru Mazilu grabbed the microphone and took up the chant of "death, death, death" along with the crowd (Binder 1990: 12).
10. Though this was a laudable goal, throughout the years of Ceauşescu's control, gaining scarce seats in university became increasingly subject to bribery and personal influence. In a campaign engineered by Elena, liberal arts and humanities preparatory schools were decimated in favor of technological education.
11. Song of Romania failed miserably and was perhaps one of the most effective vehicles for Romanian resistance to paternalistic behavioral demands. Participation in Song of Romania was so thoroughly rejected by the Romanian people that it was mainly one person—Ceauşescu, who was the spectator for an unwilling society. It was thus like Jeremy Bentham's idealized prison, the Panopticon, where a single individual kept watch on the entire penal institution (Foucault 1979).
12. One joke that particularly deflated Ceauşescu's "father of the nation" myth had him ask one of the boys from whom he received flowers, "And what is your name, little Dacian hero?" to which the boy answered "Gyula," a typical Magyar name.
13. Despite Nicu's questionable morality, he achieved some popular acclaim during socialism's last years. Put in charge of Sibiu County, he used his influence to limit its food exports, thus enabling its citizens a slightly better standard of living than elsewhere in downtrodden Romania. He reverted to form, however, during the Romanian revolt. The battle for control of the Sibiu garrison, which he commanded, was one of the fiercest in the weeklong uprising. Ceauşescu's two other children also failed to add

to his mystique. Daughter Zoie, a university mathematician, allegedly used her family connections for advancement and to support a lavish lifestyle (for which she was sentenced to a few months imprisonment after the "revolution"). Son, Valentin, said by some to have been adopted after World War II in a Communist-inspired countrywide adoption campaign, remained an anonymous academic who studiously avoided political involvement.

14. One pejorative nickname for Elena was "Adi," an acronym for "Academician, Doctor, Engineer (*inginera*)." It poked fun at her plagiarism and intellectual dishonesty by referring to titles by which she was lauded in personality cult devotions.

15. Much of this account is taken from my earlier discussion of the Romanian revolution (Kideckel 1993: 205–208), from Robert Cullen's excellent piece in the *New Yorker* (1990), and William McPherson's in *Granta* (1990).

16. The "tale of the disappearing leader" is a common genre of Romanian political rumor. For the last four decades, for example, stories have abounded of a severely incapacitated John F. Kennedy living on the Aegean island of Scorpios, once owned by Aristotle Onassis.

17. This is especially notable as Romanian television watching is characterized by extensive group sociability that goes on in its midst.

18. Cotroceni Palace was built between 1893 and 1895 as a royal residence for the families of the newly wed successor princes Ferdinand de Hohenzollern, and Maria of Saxe-Coburg Gotha, granddaughter of Queen Victoria of England. It has been the seat of the Romanian presidency since after the 1989 Revolution.

19. One bittersweet but comical vignette from fieldwork in the early 1990s illustrates the conflation of West and father. Arriving in Hîrseni, a village where I had spent much time in the 1970s, I was informed that my former host had just died and the wake at his home was ongoing. I went immediately there and, after paying my respects at his coffin, walked into the kitchen where his widow had secluded herself. She was crying profusely when I entered. "Oh, Mr. David!" she wailed when she saw me, "why did my poor husband have to die? He suffered so." She went on in this vein for another few minutes, then stopped abruptly and with red-rimmed eyes and handkerchief in hand looked up at me and asked, "And why hasn't Romania been granted Most Favored Nation status from the USA?"

20. The desire to eliminate Ceauşescu from the Romanian mind and body politic has recently been illustrated by the "yard sale" of gifts and other memorabilia received by the Ceauşescus, organized by the Museum of History in Bucharest (Perlez 1998).

# References

Appadurai, Arjun. 1996. *Modernity at Large: Cultural Dimensions of Globalization.* Minneapolis: University of Minnesota Press.

Barbat, Alexandru. 1938. *Desvoltarea şi Structura Economică a Ţării Oltului cu Un Plan de Organizare.* Cluj: Tipografia Naţională Societate Anonima.

Beck, Sam. 1990. "The Romanian Opposition's Symbolic Use of Space in June, 1990." Working Papers on Transitions from State Socialism, 90.9, Center for International Studies, Cornell University.

Benedict, Ruth. 1953. "History As It Appears to Rumanians." In *The Study of Culture at a Distance,* ed. Margaret Mead and Rhoda Metraux, pp. 405–415. Chicago: University of Chicago Press.

Binder, David. 1990. "Government in Bucharest Curbs Protests." *New York Times,* 14 January, p. 12.

Bucur, Maria. 2001. *Eugenics and Modernization in Interwar Romania.* Pittsburgh: University of Pittsburgh Press.

Ceaușescu, Nicolae. 1983. Speech to the Working Council on Organizational and Politico-Educative Problems of Labor, Mangalia, 1983. Cited in *Cîntarea României: The Journal of the Council on Culture and Socialist Education,* 12 December, pp. 8, 27.

Cole, John W., and Judy Nydon. 1990. "Class, Gender, and Fertility: Contradictions of Social Life in Contemporary Romania." *East European Quarterly* 23 (4): 469–476.

Cullen, Robert. 1990. "Report from Romania." *The New Yorker,* 2 April, pp. 94–112.

de Flers, Rene. 1984. "Socialism in One Family." *Survey* 28 (4): 165–174.

Fischer, Mary Ellen. 1989. *Nicolae Ceaușescu: A Study in Political Leadership.* Boulder: Lynne Riener.

Foucault, Michel. 1979. *Discipline and Punish: The Birth of the Prison.* New York: Vintage Books.

Gal, Susan, and Gail Kligman. 2000. *The Politics of Gender After Socialism: A Comparative-Historical Essay.* Princeton: Princeton University Press.

Gilberg, Trond. 1975. *Modernization in Romania since World War II.* New York: Praeger Publishers.

Giurescu, Dinu C. 1989. *The Razing of Romania's Past.* Washington, DC: Preservation Press.

Gluckman, Max. 1963. *Order and Rebellion in Tribal Africa.* New York: The Free Press.

Hamelet, Michel. 1971. *Nicolae Ceaușescu: Biography and Selected Texts.* Bucharest: Editura Politica.

Hann, Chris. 1996. *The Skeleton at the Feast: Contributions to East European Anthropology.* Kent, U.K.: University of Kent at Canterbury, Centre for Social Anthropology and Computing.

Helin, Ronald A. 1967. "The Volatile Administrative Map of Romania." *Annals, Association of American Geographers* 57:481–502.

Hobsbawm, Eric J., and Terence Ranger, eds. 1983. *The Invention of Tradition.* Cambridge: Cambridge University Press.

Holmes, Douglas. 2000. *Integral Europe: Fast-Capitalism, Multiculturalism, Neofascism.* Princeton: Princeton University Press.

Holton, Robert. 2000. "Globalization's Cultural Consequences." *The Annals of the American Academy of Political and Social Science* 570:140–152.

Kideckel, David A. 1988. "Economic Images in the Romanian Socialist Transformation." *Dialectical Anthropology* 12 (4): 399–411.

——. 1992. "Peasants and Authority in the New Romania." In *Romania After Tyranny,* ed. Dan Nelson, pp. 69–83. Boulder: Westview Press.

——. 1993. *The Solitude of Collectivism: Romanian Villagers to the Revolution and Beyond.* Ithaca: Cornell University Press.

——. 1994. "Us and Them: Concepts of East and West in the East European Transition." In *Cultural Dilemmas of Post-Communist Societies,* ed. Aldona Jawłowska and Marian Kempny, pp. 134–144. Warsaw: IFiS Publishers.

——. 1997. "Wealth, Poverty, and Changing Labor in a Romanian Region." Paper delivered at the American Anthropological Association annual meeting, Washington, DC, November.

Kligman, Gail. 1992. "The Politics of Reproduction in Ceaușescu's Romania: A Case Study in Political Culture." *East European Politics and Societies.* 6:364–418.

——. 1998. *The Politics of Duplicity: Controlling Repropduction in Ceaușescu's Romania.* Berkeley: University of California Press.

Lampland, Martha. 2002. "The Advantages of Being Collectivized: Cooperative Farm Managers in the Post-Socialist Economy." In *Post-Socialism: Ideals, Ideologies, and Practices in Eurasia,* ed. Chris Hann, pp. 31–56. London: Routledge.

LeBreton, Jean-Marie. 1997 [1996]. *Sfîrșitul lui Ceaușescu: Istoria unei Revoluții.* Bucharest: Cavallioti.

McPherson, William. 1990. "In Romania." *Granta* 33 (Summer): 9–58.

Pacepa, Ion. 1987. *Red Horizons: Chronicles of a Communist Spy Chief.* Washington, DC: Regnery Gateway.

Perlez, Jane. 1998. "Romania to Unload Its Ceauşescu Bric-a-Brac." *New York Times,* 1 February, p. A10.

Sampson, Steven. 1984a. *National Integration Through Socialist Planning: An Anthropological Study of Romanian New Town.* East European Monographs 148. New York: Columbia University Press.

———. 1984b. "Rumours in Socialist Romania." *Survey* 28 (4): 142–164.

———. 1987. "The Informal Sector In Eastern Europe." *TELOS* 66 (Winter): 44–66.

Shafir, Michael. 1996. "Communist Nostalgics Place Cross on Ceauşescu's Grave." *OMRI News Bulletin,* 10 May.

Tismaneanu, Vladimir. 1993. "The Quasi-Revolution and Its Discontents: Emerging Political Pluralism in Post-Ceauşescu Romania." *East European Politics and Societies* 7 (2): 309–348.

Verdery, Katherine. 1991. *National Ideology Under Socialism: Identity and Cultural Politics in Ceauşescu's Romania.* Berkeley: University of California Press.

———. 1996. *What Was Socialism, and What Comes Next?* Princeton: Princeton University Press.

Wedel, Janine R. 1998. *Collision and Collusion: The Strange Case of Western Aid to Eastern Europe, 1989–1998.* New York: St. Martin's Press.

Wolf, Eric R. 1966. "Kinship, Friendship, and Patron-Client Relations in Complex Society." In *The Social Anthropology of Complex Societies,* ed. Michael Banton, pp. 1–22; ASA Monographs, 4. London: Tavistock.

CHAPTER 5

# The Peaceful Death of Tito and the Violent End of Yugoslavia

*Tone Bringa*

This chapter places the dissolution of the Socialist Federal Republic of Yugoslavia (SFRY) and the subsequent wars in Croatia and Bosnia-Herzegovina in the context of the leadership and death of Yugoslavia's post–World War II leader, Josip Broz Tito. The violent destruction of Yugoslavia beginning in 1991 contrasted starkly with the peaceful passing of its creator eleven years earlier. Yet while the actual death of Yugoslavia and of its leader were very different, the slow weakening and disintegration preceding the death of both the leader and the state he had ruled were similar and interconnected. Furthermore, the violent death of the state structure and the destruction of the country's social fabric that paved the way for the birth of ethnonationalist independent states were more akin to the violent birth of the same state structure as a result of the Tito-led partisan struggle during World War II.

It could be argued that the war starting in 1991 was not the final destruction of Yugoslavia—it had been gradually disintegrating—but rather the instrument with which Tito's successors would implement a new social and administrative order: the ethnically homogeneous or "pure" communities and nation states. A precondition for this process to start was the absence and death of Tito. For the new social and political order to be implemented, Yugoslavia not only had to be destroyed as a state structure, but its very founding ideas had to be purged. These were ideas that had been expressed through state sponsored symbols and rituals for more than forty years and with the participation of the state's citizens from all organizational levels: the school, the workplace, and governmental bodies. The ideas, symbols, and rituals became so much part of the experience of growing up in Yugoslavia (and ultimately of identity) that they had to be purged not only from politics and public structures but from people's minds and emotions, too.

The transition in regime was dependent on a change in the transcendent, from "brotherhood and unity" among the different peoples or nationalities of Yugoslavia to ethnonationalist unity. The idea of "brotherhood and unity" was above all embodied in Tito and his image, and the purging of this idea, the antithesis of ethnonationalism, ultimately demanded the destruction of his image and Tito's final symbolic death, which was achieved through the destruction of existing multiethnic societies. This chapter discusses Tito, his life, work, and legacies, and the process whereby his successors appropriated certain aspects of his legacies and violently destroyed others. The new regimes, in other words, mark both continuity and a radical break with the Tito-past.

## Life with Tito

### Tito's Rise to Power

Tito was born as Josip Broz in 1892 in the village of Kumrovec in the Zagorje region in northern Croatia, which was then part of the Austro-Hungarian empire. His father was a Croatian peasant and Josip was one of fifteen children. The Zagorje region is near the Slovenian border, and Josip Broz's mother was from a Slovenian village nearby. Josip Broz was a metal-worker or welder by profession, and in his search for work, he traveled widely within the Austro-Hungarian Empire and in Germany. During the First World War he was drafted into the Austro-Hungarian army and fought for a short period of time on the Serbian front.[1] He was then sent to the Carpathians and the Russian front to the east where he was taken prisoner of war by the Russians. He spent a total of five years in Russia; two of these as prisoner of war and the remaining three as a migrant worker. While there he learned Russian fluently, married a Russian woman, witnessed the Bolshevik revolution and joined the Communist Party. Pelagija Belousova and Josip Broz had met in Siberia in 1917 or 1918 when she was (it is believed) sixteen years old.

When he returned to Kumrovec with his wife in 1920, he came back to a Croatia that was no longer part of an Austro-Hungarian Empire, but was instead part of the kingdom of Serbs, Croats, and Slovenes reigned over by the Serbian king Aleksandar Karadjordjević. (In 1929, King Aleksandar had imposed a dictatorship and renamed the state Yugoslavia.) In 1921, the kingdom's authorities banned the Communist Party and Josip Broz spent several periods in prison for his union and Communist Party activities. Broz rose through the party hierarchy and was appointed secretary-general of the Yugoslav Communist Party by its Moscow patrons in 1938. Meanwhile his country had been shaken by several ethnopolitically motivated assassinations: a Serbian deputy shot Croatian Peasant Party leader Stjepan Radić in the Parliament in 1928 (he died five months later), and Macedonian terrorists murdered King Aleksandar in Marseille in 1934 on contract from the Croatian Ustasha. With the establishment of the royal dictatorship, the non-Serb population in Yugoslavia became increasingly disaffected and rebellious toward a Serb-dominated Yugoslavia that favored its Serbian majority population and was carrying out a strong assimilation policy toward its minority populations. After the Yugoslav government entered a nonaggression pact with Germany, army officers staged a coup and repudiated the pact. On 6 April 1941 Germany attacked Yugoslavia, bombing Belgrade, and together with the Italian army, occupied the country. In Zagreb, Hitler and Mussolini installed the Croatian Ustasha leader Ante Pavelić who declared the "Independent State of Croatia," or NDH (Nezavisna Država Hrvatske).[2] The Yugoslav army capitulated and the rest of Yugoslavia was divided between the Axis Powers. Serbian royalist (Chetnik) forces were established, and after 1942, they joined Italian and German occupying forces in attacks against the Partisans. Both the Ustashe and the Chetnik forces committed massacres and atrocities against civilians and had fascist programs of "ethnic cleansing." The Chetniks' victims were Croats and Muslims. The Ustashas' victims were Serbs, Jews, and Gypsies.

In 1942, the Antifascist Council of the National Liberation of Yugoslavia (AVNOJ, Antifasističko Vijeće Narodnog Oslobodjenja Jugoslavije) was established, and in 1943 during the AVNOJ meeting in Jajce (Bosnia), Josip Broz became the president of the National Committee and the leader of the Partisan army, where he was known by his nickname and nom de guerre, Tito.[3] He took the title of marshal and succeeded in mobilizing all the peoples of Yugoslavia in the fight against both domestic and foreign fascist forces: the Croatian Ustasha, Serbian Chetniks, and German and Italian occupying forces. Tito won the respect of the Allies and that same year, Stalin, Churchill, and Roosevelt agreed to support him. After the liberation of Belgrade in October of 1944, Stalin and Churchill recognized Tito's provisional government. In 1945, in agreement with the Yugoslav royal government in exile, Tito formed a "unity" government. In November of that same year there was a parliamentary election and the Tito-led "People's Front" received 90 percent of the votes. Eighteen days later the monarchy was dissolved and Yugoslavia declared a federal people's republic consisting of six republics and two autonomous provinces. Tito and his new government proceeded to eliminate the leaders of the forces that had fought him during the war. The Serbian royalist (Chetnik) leader, Draža Mihailović, was executed; the Ustasha leader, Ante Pavelić, who headed the Nazi puppet regime in Zagreb, fled in May 1945 and spent the rest of his life in exile in Argentina and Spain; and the archbishop of Zagreb, Cardinal Stepinac, accused of endorsing the massacres and forced conversions of Orthodox Serbs, was given a prison sentence. In all, thousands of collaborators, anti-Communists, and opposition figures were put on trial. In 1945, as the war was coming to a close, soldiers and civilian sympathizers of the Croatian Ustashe regime fled, surrendering to the British forces in Bleiburg (Austria). The British, however, sent them back across the border and tens of thousands were executed by Partisan forces. The Partisans also committed massacres against ethnic Italians in Istrija, who were assumed to be supporters of Italy's Fascist forces under Mussolini.[4]

Although Tito was a great admirer of the Soviet Union, he soon encountered problems in his relationship with Stalin. Stalin was displeased with Tito's independent role as a major Communist player on the international scene and his ambitions to establish an association of Communist states in the Balkans. Tito seemed to be setting up his own Communist power center which Moscow saw as a threat to its own hegemony (see, e.g., Pavlowitch 1992: 54–55).[5] In 1948, Tito was excluded from the Cominform. The Soviet Union and other European Communist states introduced a political and economic blockade of Yugoslavia, and as a result, Tito broke with Stalin.[6]

## Goli Otok and the Third Way

After the exclusion from Cominform, Tito found himself invariably still in Europe, but outside of the two Cold War ideological and (later) military blocs: the capitalist West and the communist East. Tito was forced to design a third way for Yugoslavia, but first he had to deal with the pro-Stalin elements in the Yugoslav Communist Party, the "Cominformists." They (and others suspected of being "they") were sent to a prison camp on the island of Goli Otok in the Adriatic for "reeducation." The camp offered "reeducation" through physical and psychological torture; there was hard labor under harsh conditions. The prisoners were taken to work in a quarry in the summer heat—nowhere on the island are there trees for protection from the sun. The island is as indeed the name indicates: "bare." Goli Otok as a site for ideological "reeducation" was conveyed through the slogan painted on one of the main buildings of the prisoner complex on the island and still visible in 1996: "We Build Goli Otok—Goli Otok Builds Us." There were other slogans that aimed to hammer at the legitimacy of Tito's leadership and the validity of his (and, therefore, Yugoslavia's) independent, or third, path, such as "Tito—the Only True Successor to Marx and Lenin," Tito's Path—Is Our Path," "With Tito in Work and Peace." Yet a Stalinist legacy was still apparent in a slogan written above the building where the showers were: "Hygiene Is the Pride of Our Party."

According to Milovan Djilas, approximately fifteen thousand party members and sympathizers passed through the camp during the late 1940s and 1950s (1981: 87). Tito's other political opponents from within the government or higher echelons of the party (or those who were perceived as such) were purged from the government and party, including Milovan Djilas, one of Tito's close associates, who was condemned for revisionism and dismissed from the Central Committee in 1954 (see, Djilas 1981: 109). In the 1960s, 1970s, and early 1980s, it was mainly decentralizing, liberalizing, and nationalist forces which fell victim to purges and trials (see, Bennett 1995; Pavković 1997). In 1974, at age eighty-two, Tito was proclaimed president for "an unlimited term of office." He had already served seven successive terms (see, Pavlowitch 1992: 80).

## The Image and Cult of Tito

> If there is a love
> more powerful than love
> we will love You with that kind of love
>
> —Adam Puslojić (from Vidović, 1982)

As soon as Tito came to power he moved into the royal palaces and villas and established a royal lifestyle for himself.[7] This may have been an abuse of privileges to satisfy his own cravings for luxury, but it was also a clever exercise in image management. His autocratic use of power demanded in his eyes a particular kind of lifestyle to be credible. Tito knew what Djilas astutely observes: "in the eyes of people, palaces are the seats and symbols of power." And although "after the revolution, the theory of the divine origin of power was no longer plausible ... the people continued to defer to power as to something uncommon, sublime." In other words, by taking up residence in palaces and ruling from them Tito "attached himself to the monarchic tradition and to traditional concepts of power" (Djilas 1981: 95). Tito had a predilection for jewelry and pomp. He wore a diamond ring on his little finger and liked to parade in a white uniform edged with gold (as were all his official uniforms). "His belt buckle was made out of pure gold, and was so heavy that it kept slipping down. He wrote with a heavy gold pen. His chair was impressive and always placed at the center of the room. He changed his clothes four times a day, according to the occasion and the impressions he wished to create.... He used a sun lamp regularly to maintain a tan," and he had a liking for medals, both for receiving them and decorating others with them (Djilas 1981: 110–111). In his older days his vanity induced him to dye his hair and to wear a brilliantly white set of false teeth. Throughout his reign, Tito amassed or had built for himself a large collection of palaces, villas, and lodges scattered throughout Yugoslavia.[8]

After Tito's death these properties were not inherited by his relatives but remained the property of the state (or social property). After Yugoslavia disintegrated, the official residences and holiday homes were taken over by the new leadership in the new states (with the exception of Bosnia, where they were mostly looted and destroyed). For example, Croatia's President Tudjman used Tito's favorite resort on the Adriatic island of Brioni as his own summer residence. He had left Tito's private house on the small island of Vanga as it was when Tito died, using it primarily for picnics. Tito's residence in Zagreb was used as President Tudjman's palace for official purposes (offices, receptions, etc.), while the huge park surrounding it was closed to the general public. In Belgrade,

President Milošević, shortly after his inauguration as president of Yugoslavia (i.e., both Serbia and Montenegro—earlier he had been president of Serbia but since according to the constitution he could not be reelected for a third term, he organized his transfer to become president of Yugoslavia) in April 1997 moved into Tito's former royal residence and "[rode] around the capital in a vintage Mercedes custom-built for Tito."[9]

The change of regimes and transfers of power are often reflected in changes in the names of streets, squares, and cities. The Yugoslav republics have seen several such changes. Just after Tito and the Partisans came to power, new heroes were honored by having streets, squares, and bridges named after them. It was usually a question of renaming streets (which in many cases had earlier held the names of national heroes) with the names of Partisan heroes. The number of Tito streets and squares proliferated; indeed, every town throughout Yugoslavia had a major Tito street. By 1983 there were eight towns named after Tito, one in every republic and region (see, Pavlowitch 1992: 88).[10]

In the early 1990s, streets, squares, and towns were again renamed throughout Yugoslavia and given the names of national(ist) heroes (with clear Croat, Serb, or Bosniak credentials) who in many instances had been discredited during the Titoist era. The change of street names is crucial to a "politics of memory," where forgetting is part of the new mode of authority (see Borneman, this volume). In the former Yugoslavia, the politics of memory was not, however, only about forgetting a certain history and putting a new one in its place; it was about re-remembering the history that had been suppressed by Tito. Significantly, this was the history of conflict and violence among the Yugoslav peoples joined in "brotherhood and unity" during Tito's rule. An important means to remembering for Serbs, in particular, was to exhume the remains of victims of Ustasha (Croat) massacres during World War II and for the Croats to commemorate the victims of Partisan revenge killings at the close of the war.[11]

There were also numerous statues of Tito throughout Yugoslavia, and every public building (such as schools) and offices displayed a portrait of Tito in a conspicuous place on the wall. In addition, portraits of the leader were commonly found in private homes (which I believe was not the case in other European Communist states during post-Stalinist period). In Bosnia, Tito's portraits could be seen in offices and in private homes until 1990, and in some cases, even as late as 1995. The portrait had a prominent place either on the wall in the living room or else was hung on the wall in the foyer, which everyone passed through when entering the house (see Bringa 1995: 8). There were other official practices aimed at enabling people throughout Yugoslavia to identify with their common leader and thus see themselves as "Yugoslavs." The major newspapers would, for instance, print on the first page telegrams of greetings between Tito and foreign statesmen marking special events (see Djilas 1981: 111).[12]

In the beginning of his rule Tito imitated several rituals that the royals had performed before him, but most of these were later abandoned, with the exception of hunting parties, which were one of Tito's favorite pastimes, and often included his inner circle of party and government officials as well as foreign guests (see, for instance, Djilas 1981; Doder 1979). Djilas mentions in particular one ritual that Tito practiced during the first two decades of his rule. In royalist Yugoslavia, there was a custom that the monarch became a godfather to the ninth boy in any family. (The godfather, or *kum*, tradition is an old Slav custom and implies a whole set of responsibilities and duties on behalf of the godfather toward his godson. The tradition of the ninth boy in any family was, according to Djilas, a particular Serb custom that "originated in Serbia as a tribute to the fabled nine Jugović brothers, who fell in the fateful Battle of Kosova in 1389.") In Tito's socialist interpretation of the custom, there was no baptism, and the practice was often extended to the ninth child in a family independent of its sex. At the time there were quite a lot of families with nine children and some of them also claimed their right retroactively. They all asked for favors and privileges that they had a right to claim. In the end, Tito's godfathering became unmanageable and was discontinued (Djilas 1981: 113–114). This may have been an ideologically clever way of establishing identification with Tito as the substitute father representing pastoral caring and independent of the biological (genitor) and the authoritarian (pater) father roles (see Borneman, this volume). However, it was both impractical (because of the number of people and obligations involved) and had specific ethnonationalist connotations, and was therefore limited to one part of the population.

## "Brotherhood and Unity" as the New Transcendent

There were, however, other ritualized practices venerating Tito, which were specific to him and profiled him in a way that made him popular and enabled a much wider cross section of society—independent of class or ethnicity (nationality)—to identify with their leader. Like the short-lived godfather arrangement, these practices were particularly targeted at children, who were thought of as the new Yugoslavs who would embody and realize the credo of "Brotherhood and Unity." The main purpose of such practices was to cultivate "brotherhood and unity" by venerating Tito in the image of "the good father," "comrade," and cardinal role model—the Marshal of the Partisan struggle and victory. For instance, each Yugoslav republic had its Partisan or Tito pilgrimage center where schools and workers' unions organized trips, often on certain important dates on the Partisan memorial calendar such as the day of liberation for a particular republic. Such sites functioned as a ritual focus for a pan-Yugoslav identity.

In Bosnia-Herzegovina there were several significant sites: Sutjeska and Jablanica, where the Partisans fought large and decisive battles; Mrkonjić Grad, where Bosnia-Herzegovina was constituted as a republic of three equal peoples (or nations)—Muslims, Serbs, and Croats—on 25 November

1945; and Jajce, where the Socialist Federal Republic of Yugoslavia was declared on 29 November 1943. Along with Kumrovec, Tito's birthplace in Croatia, the latter site was probably visited by every schoolchild who grew up in Tito's Yugoslavia.

The official Yugoslav ideology was, in other words, revolving around the image of Tito as the heroic leader of the victorious Yugoslav partisans. This image was elaborated on in countless songs, stories, and wartime photos. It was the master image of "brotherhood and unity." (Another powerful image was that of the work brigades recruited from all the republics and nationalities to rebuild Yugoslavia after World War II.) Honoring the heroic and good death of the Partisan fighter was central to an officially sanctioned death cult, which encouraged heroic self-sacrifice for the people ("brotherhood and unity") in the name of the Father (see Borneman, this volume). Paternal love is thus tied to the image of heroic, violent, and unquestioning self-sacrifice for the group. This idea, accompanied by the emotional commitment of many "Yugoslavs" to a paternalistic leader could later be drawn on in the wars in Croatia and in Bosnia-Herzegovina, except it had by then been translated into an emotional commitment of heroic self-sacrifice for the ethnonational group and the aspiring nation-state.

The popular identification with Tito was both as a close father figure, or "dad," and as a grandfather. Such an identification between the totalitarian leader and his subjects was crucial to establishing and preserving the legitimacy of the ruler's authority (see Borneman, this volume).

Furthermore, the image of Tito as a leader above nationality was crucial to his complete identification with Yugoslavia and the Yugoslav peoples, reflected in the Communist youth movement's slogan "We Are Tito's, Tito is Ours." Tito's own ambiguous ethnic identity—of mixed Croatian Slovenian parentage—which was known but never stressed, was reinforced by an idiosyncratic accent and dialect that was difficult to pin down. According to Djilas, Tito spoke Russian and German well and could get by in English, but expressed himself worst in "Serbo-Croatian." Tito's idiosyncratic speech pattern was mainly due to his mixing of Serbian vocabulary with linguistic characteristics of the Zagorje dialect.[13] In Djilas's words, he would "confuse idioms of Croatian origin with their Serbian counterparts" and "frequently resort to Russian idioms," while his pronunciation was inclined toward the dialect of Zagorje. Hence, "his public addresses only gave credence to rumors that he was not 'our man' but a Russian" (Djilas 1981: 10). Tito's confusing language use was advantageous to an image that stressed Tito as a pan-Yugoslav with no particular ethnonational identity. But toward the end of his rule and after his death it was used to harness the new image being created of Tito in the new anti-Yugoslav and nationalist republics. Tito was then cast as a foreigner, hostile to the particular nation in question (be it Slovene, Croat or Serb).

## The Day of Youth

There was one ritual in particular that unified youth throughout Yugo-slavia in their veneration for Tito and the expression of their belief in the credo of "Brotherhood and Unity." *Dan mladosti* (or the "Day of Youth") became the core element in the state-organized symbolic representation of the new Yugoslavia. It was a national holiday and was organized annu-ally on 25 May, Tito's official birthday, by the Communist Youth Leagues (his actual birthday was not known to Tito until his official biographer Dedijer had it established).[14] As part of the celebrations, a relay was held that had started a month earlier and was timed to end up at the main sports stadium in Belgrade (the JNA, Jugoslovenska narodna armija, or Yugoslav People's Army stadium) on 25 May. At the stadium, spectacu-lar celebrations would take place in the presence of Tito himself, his wife Jovanka, and other high party officials. More than any event on the Titoist ritual calendar, the relay symbolized Tito's "brotherhood and unity." It went through all of Yugoslavia's republics and autonomous regions, and outside every town and city, students, young workers, and members of the youth organization would be ready to run the baton into town where a show would be staged at its arrival.

At the beginning of the show, greetings to Tito were read. The show consisted of a cultural-artistic (*kulturno-umjetnički*) program complete with songs devoted to Tito (cheering the youth as the future of socialist Yugoslavia, the pride of the country, and of the peoples and minorities [*naroda* and *narodnosti*] of Yugoslavia). In addition, choirs sang revolution-ary songs and there were folklore dances from all over Yugoslavia.[15] After the show, the relay continued to the next town, eventually ending up at the sports stadium in Belgrade, where the final grand rally would be held on the "Day of Youth" itself. There Tito would be presented with the cer-emonial baton, that had been carried through all the Yugoslav republics, and with school children's personal greetings written in the form of a let-ter or poem.[16] Teachers would have picked the "best" greeting written by a pupil in their school, and Tito would receive a letter of veneration from each school in each of the republics. One greeting would be read aloud at this final concluding rally. The celebratory show consisted of folklore dances and gymnastic performances from sportsmen, soldiers, and stu-dents. They would create formations, making up words such as "Tito we love you"; "Long live the Day of Youth"; or "Youth-Future." The person who had the honor of presenting the relay baton to Tito himself had been chosen among active Communist Youth League members. The show was broadcast on television throughout Yugoslavia; it was popular and widely watched. Its popularity was enhanced by the broad participation of schoolchildren at some stage in the celebrations, and not least in the preparations for the celebrations. Dan mladosti, furthermore, involved school children of all nationalities throughout Yugoslavia. This is why the claim that "The end of Dan mladosti did more real damage to the SFRY than any number of discontented nationalists of dissident pamphlets" (Thompson 1992: 233) rings true. Yet clearly the end of Dan mladosti was a symptom rather than a cause of what was to come, namely, the destruction of Yugoslavia and its multiethnic communities. Not surprisingly, the relay held particularly vivid and positive memories for the generations of Yugoslavs who had grown up with it. Persons in their late thirties, forties, and fifties whom I interviewed about their memories of Tito would all spontaneously start talking about Dan mladosti and the relay. The relay continued for another seven years after Tito's death.[17]

## Tito's Yugoslav Children

These were the generations of Yugoslavs who grew up as Tito's pioneers. A child could become a member of the pioneer organization (*pionirska organizacija*) when he or she was in the first grade of primary school (at the age of six or seven). The child was accepted as a member on 29 November, the Republic Day of the SFRY. On that day there was what could be called an initiation ceremony to include the new members in the organization and thus welcome them as active and responsible members of Yugoslav Socialist society. According to one former member, the idea was to develop feelings of patriotism, Socialist spirit, and solidarity among the young pioneers. Prior to the event, the students had rehearsed and learned by heart certain "pioneer" songs and poems. The initiation ceremony on 29 November consisted of a standard program of poems praising Tito, Yugoslavia, socialism, and "brotherhood and unity," which were read by older pioneers. The new recruits would collectively recite the pioneers' organization oath, repeating the words of an older pioneer. It was an oath to nurse and guard the heritage of the socialist homeland. That day the new pioneers became the proud bearers of a red scarf and a blue cap with a red star on the front, and would perform at school events and other public celebrations that involved schoolchildren (such as the republic's liberation day). They were otherwise dressed in a white top and a blue skirt or trousers. This would be the pioneers' uniform at all future celebrations. (The pioneer organization had a "primary cell" made up by a class in a school. These basic units were joined in a larger school organization, which again formed a larger unit with other schools from one area.) In seventh grade, a child could chose to become a member of the "Yugoslav Youth League."

There were parents who resented the competing role of the state and the party in parenting their children and instilling in them obedience to and belief in an authority other than the one taught at home—be it a religious God or parental authority. Resistance from parents, which was never public but exercised in the home, could be painful for the child who would be deprived of the pride of being a "pioneer"(see Bringa 1995: 76). The marginalizing effect of resentment and more or less subtle resistance varied greatly with the region, republic, and even the school. This was particularly true during the years following Tito's death when criticism about the cult of Tito were increasingly being voiced. But even then, however, the climate in Bosnia-Herzegovina was generally more hard-line Communist and Tito-cultivating than in Croatia or Slovenia.

The songs and poems children would learn in school, both as young pioneers and otherwise, had some recurring themes. They often contained (quasi) religious imagery that stressed Tito's pastoral, caring, and at the same, time heroic fighter roles. Numerous such poems revering Tito and promoting a certain image of him were composed during his rule and some also during the years immediately following his death. Children would learn some of these by heart and would still remember them thirty or forty years later.

Above the entrance of schools or community centers where social activities for youths such as dances took place, the slogan "Comrade Tito, mi te kunemo" (Comrade Tito, we swear [our allegiance] to you) was often inscribed. This was the first line in a so-called folk-lyric that had no identified author but was said to have originated among the Partisans during the people's liberation fight (called *pesme iz narodnooslobodilačke borbe* by one editor of a collection of such poems). The poem in the form of an oath is remembered by most Yugoslavs, and particularly by Tito's former pioneers.

| | |
|---|---|
| Druže Tito, mi ti se kunemo, | Comrade Tito, we swear to you |
| da sa tvoga puta ne skrenemo | that we will not depart from your path |
| Druže Tito, vodo komunista, | Comrade Tito, leader of the Communists |
| Partija je kao suza čista | The Party is like a clear tear |
| Kunemo se našem drugu Titi | We swear to you our comrade Tito |
| da ćemo se do kraja boriti. | that we will fight to the end |
| Kunemo se našem Titu drugu | We are swearing to our Comrade Tito |
| da gradimo omladinsku prugu. | that we will build the youth railway. |

The poems and songs of veneration would often be written by party faithfuls who were not necessarily great poets. Some were signed and others were named "folk," or *narodne*. The latter were supposed to have originated from a common worker, Partisan, or peasant, transferred through an oral tradition, and then written down (see above). These were obviously a Communist response to the rich folk song and epic traditions that had a particular ethnic or national theme and origin. The Partisan *narodne* poems and songs were for and by the Yugoslavs as a whole, sharing in the ideal of "brotherhood and unity."

In addition, there were the pictures of Tito, in every public room—in offices and above the blackboard in classrooms (and, as already mentioned, in many private homes as well). Every school grade's "reading book" had a picture of Tito on the first page and the words "Tito we swear to you." It is worth noting that Tito is addressed in the second person singular (denoting familiarity and intimacy) rather than in the second person plural (polite and formal style of address). Beside official portraits of Tito, pictures of Tito in children's school books often showed him surrounded by several children, some in their pioneer uniforms. A particularly popular one showed Tito walking with a fatherly arm around one boy's shoulders and the other hand affectionately on another boy's head. Tito is smiling and the boys look very happy. Tito's wife, Jovanka, is in the picture, too, but she is separated from Tito by children and is looking down. She has one older girl timidly holding her wrist who looks longingly over to Tito and the children surrounding him. Another popular picture in school books showed Tito with two of his grandchildren, smoking his pipe in a homely scene around a coffee table. Tito is seated on the sofa with the youngest child, holding a piece of cake, close to him and the older child sitting on a chair just opposite.[18]

In other words, children were taught to love Tito and imagine him as the "good father" to be followed loyally ("Comrade Tito we swear to you"; indicating total loyalty and commitment by the people to their leader). Aida was one of the post–world war children who had absorbed this image of Tito. She told me the story of when Tito had passed through her town in a car:

I was seven or eight years old. This is something exceptional, something truly amazing and not possible to properly convey. At the time when he passed through, everyone, absolutely everyone, came out of their houses and lined the street where he passed. People threw flowers at him along the road. These were the expressions of true feelings. I cannot describe that feeling, that atmosphere—it was fantastic, such joy. Afterwards we were given an essay to write in school about how we experienced Tito. I wrote that I wished Tito was my dad. He seemed nice. He had a car and he was smiling and waving. I thought he would be a good father.

## *Tito and His Family Relations: Separating the Roles of "Pater" and "Genitor"*

Biographies about Tito are sparse on details about the leader's private and family life. He was often pictured with his wife, Jovanka, with whom he had no children, but rarely with his two sons, grandchildren or other family, except toward the end of his life (see, for instance Pavlowitch 1992). He was reticent whenever journalists or biographers asked him about his private life. Djilas claims that Tito was trying to protect his private life and "to separate his private life from his political activity, yet he could not achieve more than partial success for absolute power subjugates private life as well as every thing else" (Djilas 1981: 136). Indeed, some of the most detailed information we have about Tito's private life is from Djilas himself.

Tito had two sons by different mothers, but it is unclear whether Tito was officially married twice or three times. According to Djilas, Tito had four wives and was "married to the first and the last, and had common-law marriages with the second and the third." They were all beautiful women committed to the Communist cause, and as Djilas pointedly puts it, "progressively younger than he" (1981: 136). His first wife was the Russian Pelagija Belousova. She and Tito had four children but only one, a son, Žarko, survived. Tito never spoke of her, and Djilas was warned by another close associate never to mention her (see Djilas 1981: 137–138). When Josip Broz was arrested in 1928 for his workers' union activities, Pelagija went back to Russia with their son. There she remarried, became involved in Communist Party activities, and was imprisoned during the Stalinist purges. The son was placed in a children's home. It is unclear where Žarko spent his childhood, or who looked after him, but at one point his father must have brought him back to Croatia. Tito's second wife, Herta Hass, was a Slovenian student. They had met in 1937. They had a son in 1941 named Aleksandar (Miša), but while she was taking care of their son, Tito was commanding an army and having an affair with another young student from Belgrade. Davorjenka Paunović was known under her code name, Zdenka—a typical Croatian name. Zdenka and Tito stayed together throughout the war—she working as his personal secretary. Meanwhile, Herta had been arrested and sent to an Ustasha camp. In 1943, Tito managed to secure her release through a prison exchange. After the war, Herta married another man and had two daughters. Zdenka died in 1946 of tuberculosis and was buried in the garden of the White Palace. Djilas remarks that Tito had kept her death secret and that "no party official or comrade attended her funeral" (1981: 142).

Tito married his last wife, Jovanka Budisavljević, an ethnic Serb from Croatia, in 1952. Jovanka was a dutiful Communist from a peasant background. She had been hired to be in charge of Tito's household, and thus became part of Tito's security guard and entourage. The best information we have on Jovanka and her life with Tito is to be found in Djilas's biography of Tito, thanks to Djilas's wife's friendship with Jovanka. According to Djilas, Jovanka was often treated with disrespect by Tito and the relationship was unhappy and destructive. She wanted children but Tito did not. She was a dutiful and somewhat subdued wife who after some time as the president's wife was "carried away by the glitter of power." Djilas continues: "Jovanka soon appeared overpowering—too much laughter, too much adornment, too much smugness, excess, excess. But it was Jovanka who lived up to Tito's concept of his own prestige" (1981: 148). In 1977, three years before his death, Tito suddenly separated from Jovanka and she continued her life in seclusion. They never formally divorced (see Pavlowitch 1992: 80). After Tito's death, Jovanka became the main target of popular misgivings about the lavish excesses of the Tito regime and the press depicted her as an unattractive, greedy, and manipulative woman. The image of her as an intriguer had been established when Tito separated from her. It is believed that Tito's chosen successors had schemed to remove Jovanka to prevent her from influencing Tito to have them removed from power before his death (see Pavković 1997: 76; Pavlowitch 1992: 80).

The image of Tito as a father to his own sons—or rather the absence of such an image—was in stark contrast to his official image as the "father" to all Yugoslav children. Furthermore, Tito would have no children with Jovanka, the woman who accompanied him throughout most of his life as the president of Yugoslavia. During the last years of his life, Tito seemed more keen to appear as a family man, and did appear on official photographs with his family.[19] The most widely publicized was perhaps the one of Tito with two of his grandsons, described above. The role as grandfather did not interfere with his official role as Yugoslav pater, in the way his role and image as a father to his children would have done. By being careful not to appear as a social father (or pater) to his two sons, but still acknowledging his role as genitor, his two father roles did not interfere with each other. Indeed, his father role was split up between the genitor (biological father) to his children and pater (social father) to Yugoslavia and its children (for a discussion of the conceptual relationship between "pater" and "genitor," see di Bella and Borneman, this volume). As an extension of this pattern, Tito never resorted to nepotism. So neither his two sons nor any of his relatives were given any high official posts (see Djilas 1981; Pavković 1997). So while "fathering" all Yugoslav children, his own children remained separate from office. Tito, alone personified the office of the people—his people: the Yugoslavs. He consumed himself and his power while leaving no dynasty or successor, thus enabling "illegitimate sons" to claim succession.

The presence of a strong paternal authority in the public domain (Tito as the leader of all Yugoslavs), was mirrored in the domestic domain by a gradual weakening of paternal authority throughout Tito's rule. The changes in socioeconomic structure and in ideological outlook after World War II as a result of increased availability of wage labor through migration abroad and modern education, affected both the role and status of younger men in relation to their fathers and of women in relation to men. Young men's positions as junior and dependent members of a patriarchally ruled and patrilineally structured household had traditionally been weak. This was particularly true for agricultural communities throughout Yugoslavia, although in some regions changes were more apparent than in others. Sons became economically independent of their fathers' agricultural land, and as a result, authority in the family and household often shifted from father to son. Socialist policies, that encouraged education and wage labor for women, together with new values favoring the consumer society and the nuclear family, gave women both an independent economic platform and an ideological legitimation for pursuing more autonomy (see Bringa 1995: 41–50). With the deaths of Tito, and later of Communist Yugoslavia and its egalitarian ideals, the appearance of state-sponsored ethnonationalism and male-dominated violence and war also implied a return to patriarchal structures, the introduction of pronatality politics, and the official cultivation of the image of the woman as mother and nurturer. As Bracewell observes, the "calls for the national rebirth [placing the mother at the center] have taken on a literal meaning" as women were made responsible for increasing the birthrate and winning the nation's demographic race (1995: 27).

## Tito's Yugoslav Model

> In this country lives the man and comrade and leader
> Josip Broz Tito.
> And all those who love freedom,
> love him.
> And all those who fight for justice,
> know his name.
>
> —Jure Kaštelan, 1957

Tito's victorious command of the Partisan forces that liberated and unified Yugoslavia established his rule with a popular legitimacy which none of the Soviet-installed Communist leaders in Europe had. His legitimacy was further bolstered by his leading Yugoslavia onto a path that was independent of its former Communist masters in Moscow. The hallmark of this independent path became the "self-managing system," implemented by law in 1950 in a direct response to the exclusion from Cominform. Self-management was the distinguishing feature of Tito's own brand of socialism, permeating all levels of official institutions and workplaces. The self-managing system "meant the installation of a multiple hierarchy of assemblies, from the communities to the republic and the federation," and by 1986, 649,525 delegates were elected to self-managing bodies (Thompson 1992: 32). There was self-management in the workplace, which resulted in "a hierarchy of workers' councils" in relation to property, which in turn introduced "social property" as a new category of ownership, and in the field of the military and defense produced "a network of civilian defense militias" in every workplace and local community (Thompson 1992: 32). The system could never, however, become a truly democratic one. First, Communist Party members constituted the vast majority of representatives in official committees and assemblies. Second, the system was "subsumed within a political system characterized by a monolithic party and an autocratic leader"(Djilas 1981: 74–75). Indeed, the conflict of interests inherent in the relationship between "self-management" on the one hand, and an autocratic leader and a monolithic party on the other, reflected the ambivalence in a system of autocratic rule that relied on populist ideologies for its legitimacy but by its very nature had to prevent any real power to the people (which could challenge the leader). Its value was therefore primarily ideological, and as Djilas points out, "self-management provided the basis for a new kind of ideological mobilization" and "assumed utopian inspiration" (1981: 75). Not only did self-management provide an image of Yugoslavia as the most independent, open, democratic, and benign of the European Communist states—so popular with many Western European liberals and socialists; it also took on transcendent values in the sense that nobody really knew what it meant—it was beyond practical experience—but it was nevertheless central to the society's social structure and permeated all aspects of it and imbued Yugoslavia both with its very separate identity and an apparently populist legitimacy.

All children who received their primary education in the SFRY learned that Yugoslavia was built on three pillars: Self-Management, Nonalignment, and "Brotherhood and Unity."[20] All three were part of defining Yugoslavia's third path with its identity rooted both in the communist East and the capitalist West and outside it. To most people, nonalignment was the most abstract principle, a principle that bore little relevance to their experiences as "Yugoslav" citizens. (It was brought to people's attention mainly through news coverage of foreign non-Western diplomats visiting Tito or of Tito's numerous trips to developing countries).[21] Self-management, however, affected the daily work routines of everybody who worked in so-called socially managed enterprises or public services, as well as those who were the beneficiaries of such services. (Every sector had its own so-called Samoupravna Interesna Zajednica, or SIZ, so there was a SIZ for housing, health, education, and so forth. Each SIZ was responsible for collecting and allocating resources within each sector and was made up of representatives from a wide range of institutions and work organizations.) The self-management system became particularly elaborate and encompassing after the 1974 decentralizing constitution.

In the 1970s and 1980s, the often burlesque character of the self-management or "enterprise culture" was a favorite theme in literature, film, and popular television comedies. They portrayed frustratingly long meetings producing no results, conflicts between workers and self-management boards (and corrupt directors), so-called social self-defense exercises, and mismanagement of resources.

At the core of Tito's Yugoslav creation was the idea of "brotherhood and unity" of the South Slav peoples, which was achieved in the struggle against fascism (see Shoup 1995: 56). It was the founding element in a multinational federation, ultimately embodied by Tito himself. The SFRY was built on two main institutions: the League of Communists of Yugoslavia (LCY, or SKJ—Savez komunista Jugoslavije)[22] and the armed forces—the Yugoslav People's Army (or JNA, Jugoslovenska narodna armija). Tito formed and headed both institutions. Six republics constituted the federation, five of which had an officially designated *narod* (people, or nation) that lent its name to that republic (Serbs in Serbia, Croats in Croatia, Slovenes in Slovenia, Macedonians in Macedonia, and Montenegrins in Montenegro). They were what we could call titular nations. Bosnia-Herzegovina consisted of three peoples (or narod) Muslims, Serbs, and Croats, and was the significant exception; it had no titular nation.

Rivalry and conflicting interests among the different peoples in the South Slav lands had previously caused violent infighting. Tito had experienced the discontent of the non-Serbian population in a strongly Serbian-dominated royal Yugoslavia. In contrast to the previous government, however, Tito's Communist government "sought to create a multinational federation of equal and putative sovereign republics, linked through the one-party system" (Shoup 1995: 56). He believed that the key to success for the second Yugoslavia was an institutionalized balance of power system that secured the influence of the weaker nationalities (or minorities), and even attempted to diminish the influence of the most numerous groups. Serbian influence was reduced by establishing two autonomous provinces within Serbia (Vojvodina and Kosovo). Top jobs in state institutions went to active Communist Party members, and immediately after the war, to prominent Partisans. In other words, appointments were not so much on the basis of merit as on the basis of political loyalty. This created an impression among some of the Yugoslav peoples that Serbs (who were also the most numerous) dominated the more powerful and prestigious positions in society.

## The Politics of Many Heads: The Beginning of the End

The Yugoslav constitution was comprehensive and complex, and became even more intricate with every new amendment. With every new amendment there was a trend toward the devolution of power from federal institutions to republican ones. The most radical in this respect, and the one that had the most repercussions for the future of the Yugoslav state after Tito's death, was the 1974 constitution enacted when Tito was eighty-two years old. This was Yugoslavia's sixth and last constitution, designed to secure a smooth transfer of power after Tito's death. First, it outlined a collective state presidency to replace the office of president after Tito's death. The position as president of the presidency would rotate annually between the eight presidency members from each of the republics and autonomous provinces. It was intended to prevent any individual from acquiring as much power as Tito himself had. At the time, Tito's health was deteriorating and during the last years of his life, Yugoslavia was ruled by his close circle of trusted associates, while Tito himself had become a leader beyond politics. He did not any more carry the authority and strength to keep Yugoslavia on an even keel and make sure federal politics were Yugoslav-oriented and transcended local, ethnonational and republican interests. At the same time he had "made himself more indispensable to Yugoslavia than he had ever been before" (Bennett 1995: 74).

Second, the 1974 constitution set out a series of checks and balances to prevent any of Yugoslavia's peoples from dominating the federation (see, e.g., Bennett 1995: 70; Pavković 1997: 74). The 1974 constitution was a reaction to the upsurge in reform movements, both among the Albanian population in Kosovo and particularly among Croats in Croatia, which had started in the late 1960s and reached a more militant and nationalist expression in the early 1970s. In 1971, Tito decided to purge the Croatian

Communist leadership and clamp down on nationalist and reform leaders. Acting on the principle of "equal treatment" of Croatia and Serbia, Tito likewise purged the top Communist leadership in Serbia of its so-called liberals. The 1974 constitution was partly a response to this movement and was Tito's attempt at defusing "the nationalists' appeal by devolving yet more authority from the federal to the republican level" (Bennett 1995: 74). However, as Denitch points out, "the Yugoslav constitution of 1974 practically gave each republic and each province a veto over any legislation that might affect it negatively. The result was an almost complete paralysis of the federal system when economic and political crises arose during the 1980s." In other words, devolution was leading to disintegration (1994: 105).

The disintegration process took place on two interconnected levels: the economic and the political-administrative. Throughout the 1970s, huge foreign debts had been amassed, borrowing that had mainly been used for consumption and investment in failed projects. Indeed, the economic and political crisis came to a head about the time of Tito's death. Loans had dried up and Yugoslavia had to begin repaying a national debt at a time of high interest rates. The Yugoslav crisis was further aggravated by the fact that it coincided with the oil crisis of 1979 and recession in Western Europe (see, e.g., Bennett 1995; Pavković, 1997). After Tito's death the economic and political crisis continued to deepen. Living standards were dropping dramatically (by 40 percent from 1982 to 1989) and inflation rose to more than 2,000 percent in December of 1989 (see Bennett 1995: 69). There was no strong unifying federal government to take action, and the republics shied away from individual responsibility, squabbling among themselves over increasingly scarce resources.

While Tito was still alive he used "the party" to preserve the country and keep a check on the expression of exclusive national interests. After his death the political fragmentation of the LCY became obvious. The republican divisions of the LCY largely pursued their own political agendas, which were often at odds with federal all-Yugoslav interests. Indeed, "the republics rather than the federation had become the real loci of power and thus the indispensable power base for the new generations of politicians" (Denitch 1994: 59).

The movement from a monarchical type of rule to a multiple, rotating leadership principle could not result in a democratic government. The system outlined in the 1974 constitution was that of a liberal government model, that was federalist and limited in power. It encouraged wider participation but without allowing for the opposition necessary for a functioning democracy. The significant change that resulted from the new constitution was that the "people-as-one" principle characteristic of totalitarian rule was moved from the Yugoslav to the ethnonational level (see Borneman, this volume). The scene had been set for the appearance of the new parochial, nationalist leaders trained in a one-party and authoritarian tradition.

# The Death of Tito

> TITO's death does not exist
> In every language
> He is light
> Not a shadow
> But a teacher for
> All homelands
> TITO the grief of all of us
> TITO—HERE WE ARE ALL OF US
> TITO—THAT IS LIFE
> ONE AND THE SAME BLOOD AS US ALL

—Veseljko Vidović, 1982

## Death of the Father

In the beginning of January 1980 at the age of eighty-eight, Tito took ill with circulatory problems in his left leg and was admitted to hospital in Ljubljana on 16 January. After several unsuccessful operations, his left leg eventually had to be amputated on 20 January to save his life. Tito lay dying in the Ljubljana hospital for four months. During this time medical bulletins concerning the state of the president's health were published daily, as were the comings and goings of his closest associates and the members of the collective presidency. At his deathbed were both his sons—the sons whom, as Djilas (1981: 150) points out, Tito rarely saw and who had never been involved in his work or his life—and official photographs were issued showing his sons visiting him. It is unclear whether Tito's estranged wife, Jovanka, was allowed to visit (biographers disagree, and if she was, it was not made public). Tito died 4 May 1980 at 3:05 P.M. His death was not publicly announced until about 6:00 P.M. that day. Indeed, at 4.30 P.M. the daily medical bulletin declared only that Tito's health had reached a critical stage (see Pavlowitch 1992: 85–86). In the meantime, solemn music was played by all radio stations, and many "Yugoslavs" suspected that Tito was already dead.

They knew that Tito was seriously ill, and considering his great age, his death should have come as no surprise. Yet knowing these facts would not prevent the deep shock and sorrow most people felt when his death was announced. Sarajevans have told me that just after Tito's death was announced, the streets were filled with people even though it was Sunday. Gordana said: "I remember this day very well. It was very strange. People were running in all directions, hurrying to work. Some were crying. People were crossing the streets without paying attention to the cars. It seemed to me that it was as if they had to go and look after their firm or office because the father was dead."

In the soccer stadium in Split that day, the Belgrade (Serbia) soccer team, "Red Star," and the Split (Croatia) team, "Hajduk," were playing a match as the news of Tito's death was announced over the loudspeakers. The players immediately stopped playing and many broke down in tears while a full soccer stadium spontaneously started to sing the hymn that the World War II generations of Yugoslavs had learned in school: "Comrade Tito We Swear to You, from Your Path We Will not Depart."[23]

## The Burial

Tito's coffin was taken from Ljubljana in Slovenia through Zagreb in Croatia to Belgrade in Serbia in the president's private "Blue Train." This was an opportunity for people who lived outside Belgrade to say farewell to Tito, but also an opportunity for the numerous party organizations to stage a farewell. People lined up along the railway track to watch when the slowly running train passed by. Some people, most of them young, lined up with placards carrying slogans such as "Count on Us"; "Tito, Here We Are All of Us"; "We Are Tito's, Tito Is Ours." The procession was transmitted on television and cameras often focused on the crowds along the tracks and the slogans some of them were carrying. According to several people I asked in Zagreb, the writing of placards was no spontaneous act but staged by members of the Communist Youth League who had received the order from their superiors. In some cases, school classes were ordered out to watch the train, but this depended on the ideological outlook of the teacher. This is in line with Djilas's argument that demonstrations of public tribute to Tito were rarely spontaneous and that "what started out as spontaneous celebrations such as the May Day celebrations were soon taken over by organization" (1981: 112). But even though the organizational aspects of the public mourning may have been staged, the emotional outpouring was, for many people, spontaneous. Thousands, and perhaps millions, of people throughout Yugoslavia were truly mourning Tito's death, as is evident from pictures of people's faces as they learned about Tito's death or watched his coffin passing by on its way to Belgrade, or from interviews with people who are old enough to remember the event.[24]

This is the account of one young woman who was present at the main railway station in Zagreb that day:

> I was in the crowd in front of the Main Station that spring afternoon when the Blue Train with Tito's coffin stopped in Zagreb. Tomislav Square was so packed with people that you could literally feel the breath of the people behind you on your neck. Yet there was also such an incredible, thick silence that you could also hear a fly's buzz. I don't remember seeing any slogans or inscriptions. Accompanied by the tunes of a funerary march, members of Tito's Guard brought the coffin out onto a small stage in front of the building. There was a speech—a relatively short one for the political standards of the time—and then a choir sang a single song that had a deep impact. As the choir sang, some people near me sobbed. There could not be any doubt in my mind that the event was a genuine and spontaneous expression of deeply felt emotions.

Shock, sadness and weariness about the unknown future were on people's faces. I had had a critical perspective on many aspects of Tito's rule, but that cathartic event nevertheless left a lasting impression on me. In retrospective, I see it as the precise moment when an era ended.

The song that was sung was "Fala" (Thank you) a traditional, well-known eulogy, a so-called *starogradska pjesma,* or old-town ballad, written in the Zagorje dialect by a Zagorje native poet.[25] The original poem expresses love and praise for a mother, but for that occasion, verb endings were changed from feminine to masculine forms, sacrificing the rhymes, but in this way personalizing the poem for Tito, turning the song into an expression of love for the father. In other words, the farewell to Tito in Zagreb was expressed by a poem of a private kind, mourning a parent, that is; the father. It was even sung in the dialect of Tito's childhood, taking the cycle of his life back to its beginning. The song was reserved for intimate social gatherings and considered unsuitable for political purposes. Choosing that particular song, which was known to have been loved by Tito, the crowd in front of the main railway station in Zagreb said their good-byes by showing gratitude, but also by acknowledging and taking pride in his local Zagorje identity.[26] While the farewell in Zagreb was directed toward a dear son of the Croatian region of Zagorje, the burial ceremony in Belgrade was the official farewell to an international, Partisan, and Communist leader, and Yugoslav president.

The burial took place in Belgrade on the 11 May, a week after Tito's death. His funeral was staged with great pomp in the presence of 209 delegations from 128 countries, including 31 presidents, 4 kings, 8 vice-presidents, 11 prime ministers, 12 deputy prime ministers, and 47 ministers of foreign affairs, according to the official report (see also Thompson 1992: 234).[27] No wonder that fifteen years after Tito's death and at least eight years of more or less intensive debunking of Tito's image, the independent Croatian newspaper *Arkzin* commented on the fifteenth anniversary of Tito's death that "turbulent times still do not allow for a truly historical assessment of his stature and achievements, but the appraisal which the world showed those days in May 1980, confirms that small nations and small states may produce world giants" (*Arkzin*, 4 May 1995).

Tito had wanted to be buried in the garden of his Belgrade residence. A tomb had been built and the house within which the tomb lay was called the "House of Flowers." The whole complex, including the house and a museum is called the Josip Broz Tito Memorial Centre. As late as 1990, Thompson noted that "the guard of four, framing his white sarcophagus in the House of Flowers, still changes every fifteen minutes, as it has done since his funeral" (1992: 233).

When Tito died on 4 May, the 36th Josip Broz Tito relay had already started. It was decided it would ride with the train that took Tito's coffin to Belgrade. In retrospect, it was perhaps telling that the relay never made it through Bosnia-Herzegovina that year. The president of the youth organization for Bosnia-Herzegovina had the honor of bringing the baton into the city hall in Belgrade.

During the next ten years fourteen million people filed by Tito's tomb, and every year on 4 May at 3:05 P.M. sirens wailed and the country was supposed to observe a one minute silence (see Pavkowitch 1992: 88).

## Mourning Tito

The public speeches and newspaper commentaries in the aftermath of Tito's death were full of assurances that they (i.e., the Yugoslav people) would continue Tito's legacy and deeds. The declaration by the Central Committee of the Yugoslav Communist Party and the Presidency of the Federal Republic of Yugoslavia, ended with the following words: "It was an honor to fight and live with Tito. Present and future generations who are deeply grateful to Tito will continue his immortal life work."[28]

An editorial in the Zagreb newspaper *Vjesnik* (1 June 1980) comments on the fears cited abroad that Tito's death would lead to chaos, but at the same time, it stressed that the only way forward for Yugoslavia was to continue on Tito's path. The article pointed out how it must have been difficult for foreigners to understand the closeness the Yugoslav people felt toward Tito, explaining: "He is so much more to us than just a dear man. Tito, that is us, too, and the symbol of the existence of this country. After us will come generations of people who will continue our legacy, Tito's and our deeds, for they will have no other choice. For such a country with so many nationalities, different languages, historical conditions, and such richness in variations, there is no other path if its people want a free and peaceful life, worthy of man, there is no other chance than to develop socialist self-management. Tito and his achievements we cannot betray, for we would then also betray ourselves." These comments highlight how completely Tito was being identified with Yugoslavia, and in turn, with "us," the people, not only through rhetoric but in the minds of many "Yugoslavs." In other words, Tito is Yugoslavia and Yugoslavia is "us," so that the three entities—Tito, Yugoslavia (the state), and "us" (the "Yugoslav" people)—form a kind of trinity. The loss and death of one of the entities (Tito) caused a disequilibrium in and rethinking of the relationship between the two remaining entities, which eventually resulted in a complete restructuring of the relationship. In combination with other later developments (i.e., the end of communism and the Cold War, which deprived Yugoslavia of its status as a nonaligned state balancing between the "East" and "West," and a deep economic crisis as well as the rise of new leaders with an aggressive, nationalist agenda, which stifled the democratic, pluralist alternative), this disequilibrium caused a serious and, as later became evident, unsolvable crisis for Yugoslavia and the Yugoslav identity.

The Belgrade-based newspaper *Borba* wrote on 7 May 1980: "Yes, this country is mourning—from the heart, but proudly dignified. We're being separated from Tito, but know that we continue with Tito. And that, too, he taught us: to believe in life. So also when in tears we are together in friendship, we know that life does not end with death."[29] The newspaper interviews a worker from Belgrade outside the city hall. He says that he was waiting in a mourning procession until midnight to get into the city hall where Tito was lying on a *lit de parade*. "It was not hard to wait, to walk. But that thought [that Tito was dead] is heavy like a stone—I was myself Tito's fighter. He was like a father to me, and not only to me. And people are saying, 'when the head of the household dies, that must necessarily be felt, that it hurts.'"[30]

According to Pavlowitch, "the unease felt by most Yugoslavs stemmed from fear that their way of life might be disturbed" (1992: 86). A year before Tito died, Doder quotes "an elderly lady of bourgeois background in Sarajevo" who told him: "Honestly, the people have never had it so good. He [Tito] lets them live and enjoy life" (1979: 118). But the fear of what was to happen after Tito's death was not only founded on a liking for consumerism and good living standards (i.e., the fear of loss of "the good life") as Pavlowitch claims. There were other more specific and still less pronounced fears that had very much been fed by the official rhetoric. Friends in Bosnia have told me that on 4 May they had to report to their local military unit (see earlier on the self-management system in defense) and people holding managerial jobs were told over the radio that they had to go to work (although this was a Sunday). The military was put on alert and the fear was of an attack from the Soviet Union.

However unrealistic this may have been at the time, it is consistent with how Tito and the ruling Communist Party built their legitimacy after 1948—and even more so after the Soviet invasions of Hungary in 1956, Czechoslovakia in 1968, and Afghanistan in 1979—as the patron and guarantor of an independent Socialist Yugoslavia. This conditioning is reflected in the assessments made by "ordinary people" in different parts of Yugoslavia quoted in Doder's book, for instance: "I am for Tito. As long as he is alive I know the Russians will not come here" (1979: 118).

Gordana, a journalist from Sarajevo who was thirty years old when Tito died, was reflecting on these fears fifteen years later when she expressed her belief that the fear of an outside Soviet attack following Tito's death was manufactured by the authorities to create internal cohesion, but also to divert attention from internal strife and discord. "At the time I was working at the newspaper. Prior to his death there had been a four-month state of alert. The media had been informed that his death might come soon. Editors had to make sure they had his obituary written. There was fear about what was called *diverzija* (sabotage). Someone, and I suspect it was the army, was inventing dangers that might occur in the event of Tito's death. A feeling was created that as soon as Tito died, the country would immediately be exposed to an external threat. There was, in fact, a kind of internal state of war. All firms and institutions were on state alert, and newspapers had prepared a special edition in the event of Tito's death."

Nenad from Zagreb was nineteen when Tito died and remembers: "We thought there would be a war. But a war against Yugoslavia and not from within Yugoslavia." Aida, a teacher in Sarajevo was twenty-three years old when Tito died. She says: "When my friends and I thought about the future after Tito, we were worried about the economic situation, about Yugoslavia's future (not about nationalism, or that Yugoslavia would disintegrate). I cried terribly at the news of his death—we all did. It was the 1 May holidays. I was returning from the seaside with my husband and some friends. We stopped to drink coffee at Jablanica—and there we heard the news on television. They declared a "state of alert." The program announcer said Tito was in critical condition and everyone who had any critical state function should immediately call in at their workplace. Later we learned that Tito at that point was already dead." Yet Aida from Bosnia recognized in her mother a different kind of fear: "With my mother it was different, she wondered: 'What will happen now when there is no more Tito?'" Aida then proceeded to tell me the stories her mother had told about how she survived massacres and rapes committed by Serbian nationalists in her village in 1943. Indeed, the threat many people who had experienced World War II were recalling was not external but internal. Tito's absence from the scene brought back memories of animosities and feelings of injustice whose existence the era of "brotherhood and unity" had denied.

After Tito's death there was uncertainty about the future. A fear of looming chaos and an outside attack were present among younger citizens, while for many older citizens, Tito's death brought back silent fears of the return of the World War II era oppressors and their ethnically targeted violence. This made for a fragile society where emotions could easily be stirred up in the interest of ruthless ethnonationalist leaders.

## Life without Tito

### *"After Tito—Tito": The Posthumous Cult*

When Tito died there was an apprehension that Yugoslavia would enter a precarious and even dangerous situation. The country entered a liminal period where the collective presidency ruled, but federal government was fraught with inertia while important political decisions were taken at each republican level. After Tito's death, the process that had started with the 1974 constitution which decentralized power to the republics had gained momentum, and almost all domestic political issues were decided by the party leadership of each republic. Tito himself had made sure there was no one successor to step in and lead a crisis-ridden Yugoslavia after his death. But arguably he was not a head of state whose office could be filled by someone else. He was Yugoslavia, Yugoslavia was Tito(ism), and Tito and Yugoslavia embodied the credo of "Brotherhood and Unity."

Indeed, in private conversations with foreign visitors, Tito himself expressed the belief that Yugoslavia would not survive his death.[31] However, his party, army, and federal government successors wanted to keep Yugoslavia (and their own power base and privileges) intact. They realized that Tito, his image, and ideology, and Yugoslavia were so intimately connected in the minds of citizens that keeping the memory of Tito alive was a way of keeping Yugoslavia together.

During the first few years immediately following Tito's death there was a desperate need to uphold the reverence for and the presence of the great leader. In order to preserve the Tito myth and maintain his authoritarian hold on the Yugoslav people, the Yugoslav authorities passed a law in 1984 that made any disrespectful public comments on or abuses of Tito's name and likeness a criminal offence. The law laid down "precise guidelines to preserve the dignity of his memory, with the term of imprisonment for flouting these ranging from three months to three years" (Pavlowitch 1992: 88). The law was enforced and arrests were made. (For one particular case involving a popular Sarajevo band, which did not, however, lead to an arrest, see Ramet 1992: 92).

It is telling that in the 1980s, while the Yugoslav state structure was crumbling and the unifying institutions (built on the Communist partisans' victory in World War II) were starting to lose their legitimacy, new monuments commemorating Partisan battles during World War II were erected in many places in Yugoslavia. In Bosnia—as late as seven years after Tito's death—the Partisan memorial park in Sutjeska had been extended with a new monument at the alleged spot where Tito, according to a well-publicized myth, had been saved by his dog when a grenade exploded nearby.[32]

In addition, writing Tito's name in red paint (or slogans in conjunction with his name) on conspicuous mountainsides or on slopes by cutting the trees or the grass or forming his name with the help of boulders, continued after Tito's death. Slogans such as "Tito, We Swear to You," "Tito—Peace," or just "Tito," cut into the natural terrain, were visible from long distances both in Bosnia-Herzegovina and along the Croatian Adriatic coast even as late as 1995. These images must have been repainted or reshaped several times after Tito's death, which is consistent with the continued building of statues and other memorials related to Tito and his Partisan battles after his death.

But the reverence and positive memory of Tito was perhaps strongest among the peoples who thought they owed him most: the Macedonians, Bosnians (and particularly "ethnic" Muslims), and Albanians. All three peoples had been exposed to strong assimilation pressure in pre-Tito Yugoslavia. Tito gave the Macedonians their own republic and nationality status (as one of six Yugoslav narods). Kosovo was given the status of an autonomous province and the Albanians obtained a high degree of cultural autonomy. The Bosnians had seen a particularly ferocious civil war (feeding off a larger war) ended by Tito's Partisans and were now taking part in the reconstruction of their communities in the spirit of "brotherhood and unity." In 1971 the Bosnian Muslims were granted status as a separate Muslim *narod* and thereby obtained the same political and cultural rights as their Croat and Serb neighbors in Bosnia-Herzegovina. (In 1994, the narod designation Muslim was officially changed to Bosniak.)

## Tito's Orphans

Symbolically, Tito was the Father of the Yugoslavs, and not of those with a specific ethnic identity. (Indeed, his own children were of mixed ethnic/national parentage.) Significantly, during Tito's rule the number of children from so-called mixed marriages increased. Although there had always been a certain number of cross-ethnic marriages, during Tito's rule, exclusive ethnic identification was de-emphasized and a common Yugoslav identity stressed, and it became socially more acceptable to marry and have children with a person of a different ethnic origin than your own. It happened all over Yugoslavia, but became particularly common in Bosnia-Herzegovina, which already had a history of intermarriage as well as close and often tolerant coexistence between Bosniaks (Bosnian Muslims), Serbs, and Croats. It is difficult to establish an accurate number for Bosnians of a mixed ethnic parentage (statistics are usually based on the number of people who declared themselves as Yugoslavs on the population census), but the highest numbers were found in the major cities such as Sarajevo and Mostar (see Bringa 1995: 151). After Tito's death, when nationalism and the credo of ethnic purity gradually replaced Yugoslavism and the credo of "Brotherhood and Unity," those of mixed ethnic background were viewed as an anomaly and became distrusted and despised. This development hit particularly many people in Bosnia-Herzegovina and also had the most extreme consequences there. In the new divided Bosnia of "ethnically pure" regions there was no place for those Bosnians of ambiguous ethnic identity. Nor was there any place for those people who identified themselves as Yugoslavs. Yugoslav identity was declared (through the national census) by only a minority of the population in the SFRY, but typically by a much higher number in Bosnia-Herzegovina than any of the other Yugoslav republics.

Immediately after World War II, Tito and his Communist Party may have hoped that over time the different Yugoslav peoples would merge into one Yugoslav narod. The official policy on nationalities, however, did not encourage this, as "Yugoslav" never referred to a person's nationality—only to her citizenship (and in some population censuses to either an ethnic minority or an "undeclared" category); (Bringa 1995: 25).[33] Some Yugoslav officials and intellectuals hoped that the "nationally undefined" Bosnian Muslims would spearhead such a Yugoslav nationality. Indeed, on the census the Muslims made up the largest number of "declared Yugoslavs." However, the number of Muslims who declared themselves

"Yugoslavs" dropped dramatically in 1971 when they got the right to declare themselves as "Muslim."

Yugoslav identity was inextricably linked to Tito's multiethnic Yugoslav state. When Yugoslavia dissolved and Bosnia-Herzegovina was torn apart by ethnonationalism, "Yugoslavs" and Bosnians of ethnically mixed heritage became persons without a nation and eventually without a state. The nationalist successor regimes portrayed them as the product of an invention, of Communist propaganda geared toward weakening the ethnically defined nation—be it Bosniak, Croat, or Serb. They had become Tito's orphans.

## Destructive Forces: War on Identity

Tito's serious illness and eventual death coincided with an economic crisis and demonstrations in the autonomous province of Kosovo, the poorest region in the former Yugoslavia.[34] There the majority Albanian population (who constitute 90 percent of the total population of Kosovo) demanded more independence from Serbia while the minority Serbian population felt their politically dominant situation threatened. Albanian nationalism had grown strong during the 1970s when Kosovo Albanians obtained increased cultural autonomy. In the 1980s, part of the Serbian leadership and intelligentsia in Belgrade used the plight of the Serbian minority and Albanian nationalism in Kosovo to whip up Serbian nationalist feelings. After Tito's death, Serbian intellectuals increasingly voiced misgivings about the treatment of Serbia during Tito's rule. They claimed Tito ruled by the doctrine of "a weak Serbia means a strong Yugoslavia." The Serbian-Orthodox church became an outspoken champion for the Serbian cause and gained in popular appeal. The novelist and nationalist dissident Dobrica Ćosić, a former Partisan and Communist Party official, introduced a slogan that would later be adopted by Serbia's President Slobodan Milošević: "Serbia won all wars, but lost the peace."[35] In 1986, Ćosić drafted a memorandum on behalf of the Serbian Academy of Arts and Science, of which he was a prominent member. The "memorandum" is a fifty-page document "elaborating on two nationalist themes, the victimization of Serbia and Serbs and the conspiracy of non-Serb Communist leaders against Serbia" (Pavković 1997: 89). It refers to the "present state of depression of the Serbian people, against a background of chauvinism and Serbophobia" and calls for a stop to the alleged assimilation of Serbs in Croatia and genocide of Serbs at the hands of the Albanian population in Kosovo.[36] It proclaimed that the only way to ensure the very "existence and development" of the Serbs was the "territorial unity of the Serbian people," that is, uniting all Serbs in a single Serbian national state (see Cigar, 1995: 23).The "memorandum" was condemned by the Serbian party leadership as nationalistic, but it struck a chord among many disillusioned Serbs and caused a stir in the other republics where Serbian dominance and nationalism were feared.

In 1986, Slobodan Milošević became the leader of the Serbian Communist Party and was then elected president of Serbia in 1987. He was a shrewd and cynical political operator who was seeking to build his legitimacy as a strong leader filling the vacuum left by Tito. He realized the popular appeal of Serbian nationalism, especially after a visit to Kosovo in 1987 when, after a meeting with local Serb officials, he faced a group of Serb demonstrators. One of them was telling Milošević that he had been hit and Milošević uttered the words that are seen as marking his new populist approach: "No one should dare to beat you." Although the man apparently had been hit with a baton by a policeman who was there to constrain the demonstrators, the exchange was shown repeatedly on Serbian and Yugoslav television stations. Milošević's words became a rallying cry for Serbs to unite against (ethnic) enemies; whether Albanians, Croats, or Bosnian Muslims. Slobodan Milošević had found his cause as the new tough protector of all Serbs and their interests (Silber and Little, 1996: 37).

Initially, Serbia wanted a more centralized rule of Yugoslavia from Belgrade. The other republics (except Montenegro) were against it, fearing Serbian dominance and preferring a decentralized confederation of the six republics. Slovenia was particularly critical of Belgrade's and Milošević's treatment of Kosovo, but both Croatia and Bosnia-Herzegovina found developments toward an authoritarian and aggressive Serbia ominous. (In 1989, Milošević stripped Kosovo of its autonomous status and effectively disenfranchised the Albanians.) In Croatia, the leadership did not, at the outset, seek to secede from the Yugoslav federation; instead it was arguing for a loose confederation (which was also favored by Bosnia-Herzegovina). But it became clear that if Slovenia left Yugoslavia, Croatia would follow suit, and with the majority of its population being non-Serb, Bosnia-Herzegovina would not want to stay in a Yugoslavia that would be no more than Greater Serbia.[37]

Ten years after Tito's death, and a year after the fall of the Berlin Wall, all the Yugoslav republics decided to hold democratic multiparty elections. They were poorly prepared to do so as little time and resources were invested in educating people and institutions. In Tito's single-party state the only opportunity to express political diversity was through ethnicity. Indeed, in many instances, political representation was based on ethnicity, that is, every governmental body had to be represented by a member from each of the ethnic groups in that republic. Thus, the foundation for a political system based on ethnicity was already in place. Furthermore, during the Tito era, political dissidents were often branded as nationalists and persecuted on that basis. Not surprisingly, then, the 1990 multiparty elections in the Yugoslav republics swept to power nationalist parties and their leaders.

While Croatia was consumed by Croatian nationalism from within and Serbian nationalism from outside, Bosnia-Herzegovina developed three nationalisms: Serb, Croat, and Bosniak. Each of these was associated with a political party, the SDS (Srpska Demokratska Stranka), HDZ (Hrvatska Demokratska Zajednica), and the SDA (Stranke Demokratske Akcije). But while the SDS and the HDZ had strong ties to nationalist parties in Serbia and Croatia respectively, the SDA had no patrons in neighboring countries. Although the SDA was the only party without an ethnic/religious identifier in its name, it was founded as the party for Bosniak, "members of the Muslim cultural-historical sphere" (SDA statutes, article 1). The different armies that developed and operated in Bosnia during the war were (and in the case of the Bosnian government army, became) the military arm of the nationalist parties.

Yet the SDA's nationalism was ambiguous. The electorate considered it the party of and for the Bosnian Muslims, but its platform called for a multiethnic and unified Bosnia-Herzegovina. However, as polarization increased and international support for an undivided Bosnia dwindled, the ruling SDA members started identifying themselves publicly with the plight and fight of their Bosniak compatriots. Their policies increasingly favored the Muslim population, while official rhetoric and symbolism were dominated by Bosniak and Islamic imagery.

In 1991 (after a week long war in Slovenia in June 1991, after which the JNA withdrew) war broke out in Croatia, starting in those areas with a large Serbian population, which Serbs hoped would become part of their new Serbian Yugoslavia. Within five months, the Yugoslav army, working with local Serb paramilitary, had occupied more than one third of Croatia. Fifteen thousand people were killed and more than two hundred and fifty thousand, mainly Croats, were driven from their homes. In early 1992, UN troops were deployed to the Serb-held areas of Croatia, which remained under the effective control of Serb warlords until reconquered by the Croatian army in May and August of 1995. After the Croatian recapture, thousands of Serbs fled their homes and those who remained were harassed and intimidated. Although it was not the official policy of the Tudjman regime to "cleanse" or "purify" Croatian territory of Serbs, it fully expected the Serbian population would flee military action and took every possible step, including tolerating widespread burning and looting of Serbian property as well as killing of individuals who refused to leave, to ensure that the Serbian population would never return. Serbs did not feel safe in Croatia and left for Serbia or Serbian-controlled areas of Bosnia.

While war raged in Croatia, the Bosnian leadership of Bosnia-Herzegovina and many of its citizens hoped that war there could be averted. From 29 February to 1 March 1992, Bosnia-Herzegovina held a referendum on independence, although Serb-controlled areas did not participate. More than two months earlier, warlike martial law conditions were reigning in numerous cities and townships in Northern and Eastern Bosnia, areas bordering on Serbia and with large Serbian settlements. Here the Serb nationalist party, the SDS, which had not gained a majority in the elections, had organized a parallel Serb administration called the

"Crisis Committee." These "committees" were secretly arming local Serbs with weaponry coming from Belgrade and the JNA (Yugoslav People's Army).[38] In November 1991 the SDS organized a referendum in those areas they considered Serbian on whether the Serbs wanted to remain in Yugoslavia (with Montenegro, the Krajina, and Eastern Slavonija—the latter two areas in Croatia). This was, in effect, a vote for Greater Serbia and an overwhelming majority voted yes (there are no reliable figures for how many Bosnian Serbs actually voted). On 9 January 1992, the SDS declared the foundation of the Serbian Republic of Bosnia-Herzegovina, later renamed Republika Srpska (see Judah 1997).

On 5 April 1992, Serb snipers from across the river of Bosnia's Parliament building fired at a large Sarajevo peace demonstration, killing two young women as the crowd crossed the Vrbanja bridge in defiance of those who were shooting.[39] The Sarajevans had been chanting "we want to live together" and "peace." Overnight Sarajevo turned into a divided city under siege when barricades were put up by armed men at various sites in the city. The 6th of April has become the official date for the start of the war in Bosnia-Herzegovina; it was the day war came to the capital, Sarajevo. From that date on, the siege of cities, shelling of civilians, massacres, death camps, the burning of homes, mosques, and churches, and the forced expulsion of hundreds of thousands of people, became daily news in the Western media. By the summer, Serbian forces had taken control over and ethnically cleansed 70 percent of Bosnia-Herzegovina. An alliance of ill-prepared Croat and Bosnian (Muslims and others) army units held out against the militarily superior Serb forces, until January 1993 when it just became too obvious that the Croatian forces were working hand in hand with the political forces that wanted an independent Croatian Republic of Bosnia-Herzegovina. Now the Bosnian, and by now mainly Muslim, government forces were fighting a two-front war against the Serbs and against the Croats. There was more "ethnic cleansing," destruction, camps, refugees, death. The fighting between Croatian forces (Hrvatsko Vijeće Odbrane, or HVO) and Bosnian government forces (Armija Bosne i Hercegovine, or ABiH) ended with the signing of the U.S. sponsored Washington agreement in March 1994, and is echoed in the Dayton peace agreement signed in the United States on 21 November 1995. The agreement and final settlement divides the country in two entities: a Serbian republic (Republika Srpska), and a joint Croat-Bosniak-run federation.

The war in Bosnia probably cost the lives of about 250,000 people (this number includes thousands who remain unaccounted for). Of a prewar population of 4 million people, 1.8 million people were displaced or became refugees (1,259,000 were exiled outside Bosnia-Herzegovina), and about 30 percent of all residential buildings were damaged or destroyed (with a much higher percentage in some regions than in others).[40] In addition, many public buildings such as mosques, churches, schools, libraries, and hospitals were destroyed.

## The Destruction of the Myths

> Tito ... built himself up into something above and beyond the people and the movement. That "grandeur" will be taken from him because it is not his. But he will survive as a historical figure, politically gifted and in many ways creative.
>
> —Milovan Djilas, 1981

In the village of Kumrovec on the Slovenian border in the region of Zagorje, approximately fifty kilometers northeast of Zagreb, lies Josip Broz Tito's birthplace. The house where he was born and the nearby museum have seen radical changes since the breakup of Tito's Yugoslavia in 1991. First, it no longer lies in Yugoslavia, but in the Republic of Croatia, and between Croatia and nearby Slovenia now runs an international border. The exhibitions with maps and photos from Partisan commander Tito's military maneuvers and battles during World War II have been removed, and so has other Tito paraphernalia, such as his uniforms. On a table in the entrance to this modest house is a visitors' guest book, which contains critical, often disrespectful and even rude, comments about Tito. These are in sharp contrast to the grateful and admiring comments contained in guest books from before 1991.[41]

Comments from 1995 reflect the reevaluation of Tito and his edifice— a Yugoslavia of "brotherhood and unity"—which had taken place among Croats since the breakup of Yugoslavia and the establishment of a nation-state for Croats. They are often written in the style of a personal communication with Tito, who is addressed in the second person singular, the pronoun of familiarity and equality. He is, in other words, not addressed in the third person plural, the pronoun used to express social distance, although some people would write the pronoun *ti* (second person singular) with a capital *t* to express both intimacy and reverence. The rudest comments seem to have been written by young people (judging from the handwriting), and several pages have been pulled out or scribbled over. The young generations to whom Tito was not a living memory (they were either too young or not born when Tito died) appear to have been most susceptible to the recasting of Tito as the stepfather who favored the other son: "Dad you were a Communist" (by 1995, "Communist" was more or less a swearword and being accused of being a Communist was analogous to being accused of not being a "good Croat"). "Tito—you do not deserve that your name is written in capital letters, for you were a Chetnik [a Serbian nationalist]." "Thanks for all you did not give us, because you gave the Serbs everything"; "Tito, a traitor to his people." At the same time, in Serbia Tito was being accused of being a Croat who wanted a weak Serbia. So Tito himself is finally turned into a nationalist, but since his ethnic identification was ambiguous, nationalists on all sides see him as a traitor.

The few respectful and grateful entrances are written by older people (with careful handwriting), or foreign guests. Among these there were one Croatian woman, two Muslims from Bosnia, and a Macedonian. A few people had written short, thank-you messages, which were as much directed to the present as to the past. They are as interesting for what is understated as for what is stated. The following are examples from the 1996 guest book: "Comrade Tito! May you rest in peace. Thank you for everything"; "Comrade Tito, it was after all beautiful to live with You"; "Thank you, Tito, for fifty years of a beautiful and happy life"; "In loving memory of Him, the man who loved us, Tito"; "Truly, in this book vulgar expression does not belong, for we lived beautifully in Tito's Yugoslavia." All messages stress the beauty of life under Tito or Titoism (i.e., before separatist wars in the 1990s); they are implicit critiques of the present regime as the authors allude to a contrast with present life, which is full of war and suffering. These messages were written at the height of Croatian President Tudjman's repressive nationalist regime, a regime that was scornful of the Yugoslav (Communist) past, a time when using the word for "comrade"—*drug* or *drugarica*, which was also a commonly used word in everyday speech for "friend"—was seen as unpatriotic and was risky.

Expressing such views in the guest book at Kumrovec could be read as a public declaration of opposition to the new nationalist regimes. There were few platforms for expressing such defiance at the time, and it was not without personal risk in a regime where people who voiced opposition to the regime were routinely kept under surveillance (which also explains why most of these entries are anonymous).[42] A personal address from a Bosnian refugee reads as follows: "Beloved Comrade Tito, With your departure I lost a lot. All that remains are the memories of a beautiful past living under the system that You built. After your departure, I feel lost, and only now do I understand how beautiful, and what an honor it was to live with You. I am proud that I, as a Bosnian refugee forced to leave for Germany, I succeeded once more in coming to Your birthplace and reminisce about Your—Tito's time. You were a beloved man and forever you will remain in my heart." The words of this young Bosnian (Muslim) woman (who signed her full name) convey how intimately Tito, Yugoslavia, and the "good life" are connected in her mind, particularly when compared to the horrors that followed the war of succession after Tito's death. Retrospectively, then, for this young woman the death of Tito merges conceptually and emotionally, not only with the death of a state, but with the loss of an inalienable part of herself. Through mourning the loss of Tito, she is mourning the loss of home.

In Belgrade in 1994, people expressed views similar to those discussed above directly to a resurrected Tito. The independent media sponsored the film *Tito: For the Second Time among the Serbs*, conceived by the filmmaker Želimir Žilnik. For the purpose of the film, an actor was dressed up as Marshal Tito and wandered the streets of Belgrade, while people's reaction to his presence was filmed. People reacted as if the actor were the real Tito and let him know what they thought of him and his lack of presence (see Judah 1997: 135–136). Judah provides some examples: "As he toured

Belgrade, women crowded around the dead leader to give him flowers."
"Scores engaged their former leader in conversation. 'I am a Serb and you
are a Croat, said one man, 'but I used to admire you.' Another said that
after his death he had been part of his honor guard. 'Yes, I remember
you,' said Tito encouragingly. The man said, 'You were everything for us,
you used to warm us like the sun.' Another disagreed, telling the former
communist leader that he was 'guilty,' a 'bandit,' and accused him of hat-
ing Serbs. 'I used to be one of your soldiers,' said another, 'but now there
is no bread in the shops.' Another said that during his time there was only
one Tito: 'Now there are fifty-five.' In the most pathetic scene of all, Tito
finds an old man sitting alone by the tombs of the Marshal's old comrade-
in-arms. Their busts have been removed. 'Who was bothered by them?'
asks Tito. 'Those who don't like order, those who don't respect the past
… those who are irresponsible,' says the old man. He does not look up.
Tito asks him where he is from and he replies that he is a refugee from the
war in Bosnia. 'When will it end?' asks Tito. 'There is no end, my friend,'
says the old man" (1997: 135–136).

In spite of the nostalgia many people whose lives were ravaged by war
in the 1990s may have felt for the Tito era, the change in official discourse
and public mood during the years following Tito's death were dramatic.
So what had happened in the time period between the official insistence
on upholding Tito's memory and following his ideological path, to the
popular expression of disrespect in the Kumrovec guest books after 1991?

As the years passed, it was becoming increasingly difficult to keep
Tito's memory alive. While the public discourse and political leadership
during the first years following his death strove to continue with business
as usual, the late 1980s was the time for demythologizing Tito and breaking old taboos. In Croatia the story that Tito was not the original Tito, and
that not even his old mother had acknowledged the present Tito, was circulating. The real Tito, it was claimed, had died at the end of World War
II. Thus, the heroic Tito of the songs and poems, the emotionally close
Tito is preserved, while the Tito that founded and governed Yugoslavia
for thirty-five years, only to leave the country to dissolution and war, can
be comfortably disavowed. The period of mourning was drawing to an
end and the process of restructuring values and paving the way for new
truths had begun. The process of demythologizing Tito, was at the same
time, a process of delegitimizing his creation, Yugoslavia, and its ideals.
It had to take place to make way for a new kind of leader—the parochial
leader of only one people, or narod.

*Replacing the Lost Father: The Rise to Power of the "Illegitimate Sons."*

In the late 1980s there were popular rumors circulating in the press about
Tito's many allegedly illegitimate children. These rumors were part and
parcel of the stories about Tito's numerous extramarital affairs. They culminated in allegations that developed separately in Serbia and Croatia

that Tito's main successors, the ethnonationalist leaders of the two most populous republics, Slobodan Milošević and Franjo Tudjman, were in fact, illegitimate sons of Tito's. It is significant that it is the kinship idiom of son that is used and not, for example, that of cousin or nephew (brother would not be possible because time and generational distance is required). The kinship term "son" conveys the idea of direct succession and of legitimate inheritance (i.e., political office and the right to rule Yugoslavia, or parts of it). It furthermore implies ideas of filial duty, and it implicates the role and legacies of the father. However, the new leaders are said to be "illegitimate sons," that is, sons that Tito fathered but did not acknowledge. These claims leave an interesting ambiguity as to whether they are concerned with biological fatherhood or social (i.e., political) fatherhood. (Interestingly, the allegations were voiced mainly by the critics of the two leaders.) Both leaders adopted some of the symbols and images used by Tito, they both admired Tito, and most important they both bastardized central parts of the Tito legacy.

Both Milošević in Serbia and Tudjman in Croatia had a previous history in the Communist Party hierarchy. However, while Milošević never really broke with his Communist past and was too young to have made any real connection with Tito (he was a war child), Franjo Tudjman had been an officer in the Partisan army, and it is said that he was Tito's youngest general. In 1967 he was thrown out of the party and stripped of his two official positions, and in 1972 he was sentenced to two years in prison, charged with espionage in the purges of nationalists after the Croatian spring. (After Tito intervened, however, he spent only ten months in prison.) Tudjman was again sentenced to three years in prison in 1981 for his continued nationalist and dissident activities (see Pavković 1997; Thompson 1992).

As a historian, Tudjman was known for his revisionist history writing, of which the most contentious points were his views on the NDH regime as a benign expression of Croats' dream for independence (treating its fascist policies and Nazi collaboration as irrelevant, or even as misunderstood) and his contesting the official figure of the number of people (Serbs, Jews, and Partisans) killed at the Ustasha-run concentration camp at Jasenovac, claiming it was much lower. In 1990 he rose to power on a ticket of nationalism, preaching the rebirth of the Croatian nation and the realization of the nation's "thousand-year-old-dream" for a separate Croatian state. Although Franjo Tudjman was of an age that made the idea of him being Tito's illegitimate son feasible, it was merely symbolically compelling. Tudjman was from the same region as Tito (Zagorje) and had a similar accent. He spent many years in Belgrade as an officer in the Yugoslav People's Army, and like Tito, he sometimes used *ekavski* (or Serbian variant words) when he spoke.[43]

Like Tito, Tudjman had children who grew up in Belgrade, and at least one of his grandchildren still lives there (his daughter was once married to a Serb). Although this is a fact that has been downplayed and even denied by Tudjman's supporters, it is something his adversaries like to point out. These are merely coincidental similarities with Tito's biography, but Tudjman seems to have copied other aspects relating to Tito's image as a leader more consciously. In addition to Tudjman's autocratic leadership, many Croats as well as Serbs, Slovenians, and Bosnians have commented on the way Tudjman liked to dress, his love for handing out distinctions and medals, and for military parades as being reminiscent of Tito's style. This is particularly evident in the white military uniform he sometimes wore. He kept Tito's holiday, and official guest home on the Adriatic island of Brioni. Tito's house on the tiny island of Vanga with all his belongings remained untouched. He even kept up Tito's ritual of honoring his special guests with a bottle of wine from the wine cellar bottled in the same year as the guest was born.[44]

The analogy the successor and his supporters were attempting to establish with Tito, his powerful predecessor and mentor, was crowned by plans to establish a "Kumrovec-like" museum at Tudjman's birthplace in the Zagorje region. This plan was taking form as Tito's birthplace was being stripped of many of its Tito-era memorabilia and turned into an ethnographic park where Tito's birthplace merely happens to find itself.

The rumor that Milošević is Tito's illegitimate son is again a metaphor used by his opponents to express what they see as his illegitimate claim to and bastardization of Tito's legacies. Yet in Milošević's own biography there are elements that make this claim less fantastic than meets the eye. The interesting twist to this theory, however, is that it is also rumored that Milošević's wife, Mirjana Marković, who herself is a skilled political operator and manipulator, is Tito's daughter. (It is not clear whether one rumor excludes the other, or whether the married couple would be considered half siblings, and therefore their relationship incestuous.)

Slobodan Milošević was born in Pozarevac (a small town in Serbia) in 1941. His parents, who were both teachers, had moved there from Montenegro. His mother was a Communist activist and Mirjana Marković, whom he met in school and later married, came from a prominent family of Partisans and Communist politicians. Her mother had been secretary of the Belgrade party but was shot as a traitor to the party in 1942, apparently for having given names of Communists to the enemy under interrogation and torture. Davorjanka (Zdenka) Paunović, who had been Tito's wartime secretary and lover, was a relation of Mirjana's mother. There are even rumors that she was Mirjana's mother's sister, and indeed, that Mirjana is really the daughter of Zdenka and Tito. Mirjana herself grew up with her grandparents and spent summers with her father (who had become the party boss of Serbia) on Brioni together with other Communist elite members and their families (see Judah 1997; Silber and Little 1996: 42).

Slobodan Milošević, the bureaucratic, Communist Party boss, did not imitate Tito's image to the obvious extent that Tudjman did, and although his leadership was autocratic, he did not appear as a successful new father. However, he did carry the Communist and Yugoslav part of the

Tito legacy, but it is a bastardized version of the legacy. The communism is in the leadership and government style, and in the rhetoric against foreign enemies (see Bringa 2002). But the rhetoric of class struggle and solidarity among all Yugoslav peoples was replaced with that of the Serb nation's superiority and need for unity. The claim to the Yugoslav part of the legacy became a way of seeking international legitimacy for a "Greater Serbia" as Yugoslavia's legal successor state.

## Getting Rid of Tito Posthumously

During the transition from the Tito-era, to the nationalist era when establishing legitimacy had been critical to establishing a solid hold on power, the new nationalist governments engaged, as already mentioned, in demolishing the image and memory of Tito, Titoism, and the Yugoslav past.

In October 1991, Serbia's minister of urbanization announced at a press conference that they wanted to dig Tito's body up. According to a report by *The Guardian* journalist David Hearst, "he had just discovered that the memorial park, built twelve years ago never had the requisite planning permission. 'There are no judicial and moral reasons not to move the body to another Belgrade cemetery,'" he told a press conference. His proposal was echoing one put forward by the right-wing Serbian nationalist and paramilitary leader Vojislav Šešelj, appointed as Serbia's deputy prime minister in 1996. He demanded that Tito's remains should be disinterred and returned to Croatia. Tito, he claimed, had been anti-Serbian and an Ustasha.[45] Or, he argued, if Croatia did not want him, each republic could receive parts of his remains. The issue of where Tito should be buried then became a theme in the press and in popular discussions. As it turned out, the Croats did not want him either; they claimed Tito had been pro-Serbian and had only done damage to the Croatian cause (cf. the claim of a Croat in one of the Kumrovec guest books that Tito was anti-Croatian and a Chetnik). Slovenia had declared independence in May 1991, and was de facto independent by October; for the Slovenes, Tito had become irrelevant, in spite of the fact that Tito was half Slovenian.[46]

Tito's body was the most potent symbol of a multiethnic, united, and federal Yugoslavia. Tellingly, in Bosnia, a prominent politician suggested he be buried in the city of Tuzla, and in Sarajevo people listened to the various suggestions with a mixture of disbelief, disgust, and a good portion of black humor and the punch line: "If you don't want him, give him to us!" The director of the Tito memorial center in Belgrade (which includes Tito's mausoleum) told David Hearst: It will not happen. Rationality will prevail. Since the urbanization minister's press conference, I have been flooded with letters of support. Many of them say we used to live in peace and that they preferred Tito's peace to the so-called peace we have today." "In Tito's time, you were not free to say what you wanted, but at least you could sleep where you wanted. Now you can say what you want, but you can't lie where you want." "Least of all when you are dead," the journalist added (*The Guardian*, 1 October 1991).

In 1996, the new Yugoslavia's president, Slobodan Milošević, declared that Tito was an important part of Serbian history and should remain buried in Belgrade. As of 2002, Tito is still buried in the House of Flowers in Belgrade.

## The Death Cults: Recovering Memory and Establishing Political Authority

The most striking similarity between the two "illegitimate sons of Tito," apart from their manipulation of nationalist sentiments, xenophobia, and fear, is their cultivation of a relation to the death cults.[47] Toward the end of the 1980s, war crimes committed during World War II, which had been omitted from Yugoslavia's official history or not properly acknowledged, became widely publicized and welcome tools in the hands of the new nationalist leaders. Both would celebrate and help ritualize certain deaths as significant markers on the nationalist calendar and thereby turn them into ritual expressions of national mourning and unity while at the same time reviving fears of repetition while holding themselves up as the sole protectors should their people again be attacked. The death cults obviously revolved around different events for the Serbian and the Croatian leaders. For Franjo Tudjman, the defining death cult of his regime was the commemoration of the Ustashe soldiers and supporters killed by Tito's Partisans after being returned by British forces in Bleiburg (Austria).[48] His suggestion that the Bleiburg dead should be reburied at Jasenovac next to the victims of the regime they fought for met with so much resistance (particularly from the West) that the president's suggestion was never realized. In October 1996, however, Croatian radio reported that in the small town of Omis on the Adriatic coast, 104 "homeland defender" soldiers (the official word for a soldier who fought in the 1991–1995 war) and 6 Ustasha soldiers were dug up from a mass grave near Omis and reburied with two Partisans from the city' s cemetery. A representative from Tudjman's ruling nationalist party, the HDZ, said that the reburial represented "the historic reconciliation of the Croatian people."[49] Hence the forced homogenization of Croatian citizens through war and the manipulation of history were even extended to the dead. In April 1996, President Tudjman called for "a balanced historical view of all major personalities and movements in modern Croatian history." He praised Tito "as the most successful modern Croatian politician and traced the roots of the current Republic of Croatia back to Tito rather than Pavelić." He said, "it is time to bring back to Croatia from abroad the remains of Tito, Pavelić (the wartime Ustasha leader of Croatia) and Vladko Maček (who led the powerful Croatian Peasant Party in the 1930s)."[50] Tudjman's idea of joining the victims and their perpetrators in death in a common memorial at Jasenovac and of bringing back "Croat-born historic personalities" to Croatian soil to bury them by the wall of the "famous" at Mirogoj is reminiscent of Franco's "valley of the fallen," where the fascist dead and the republican dead from the Spanish civil war were buried in a mood of national reconciliation needed to build a strong nation-state. For the Croatian president, the ultimate celebration of death cults would be steering his country into war, first with the Serbian attackers in Croatia and then with the Muslims (Bosniaks) over territory and control in western and central Bosnia.

In Serbia, we have seen how Milošević used the emotionally charged Kosovo issue as the defining issue of his new nationalist path. However, an even more critical defining moment of his leadership was another episode also related to Kosovo, which took place already in 1989, before the breakup of Yugoslavia. This was the celebration of the six hundred years anniversary for the battle of Kosovo when Serb forces were defeated by the Ottoman Turks on 28 June 1389 (also known as St. Vitus Day), a defeat that marked five hundred years of Ottoman rule over "Serbian lands." On this day six hundred years later, a million Serbs flocked to Kosovo to worship at Milošević's feet. The Serbian Prince Lazar was killed in the battle, and according to a revered and popular Serbian epic, on being given the choice between capitulating or killed by the Turks, Prince Lazar chose the heavenly kingdom rather than to capitulate to the foreign enemy.[51] In their book, *The Death of Yugoslavia* (1996: 72), Silber and Little have captured the mood of the anniversary celebrations very well:

> Pilgrims stood in line at the Orthodox monastery, Gračanica, to view Lazar's bones. The remains would be passed round monasteries in Yugoslavia, places which would be claimed as Serb lands when the war broke out in 1991. This journey, the first time that Lazar's bones had been seen in public there, was celebrated as a holy national rite. In an aggressive defiant mood Serbs flocked from around the world to take part in the ceremonial union of all Serbs under one leader. In this fevered atmosphere, Milošević descended from the heavens by helicopter to deliver his grandest snub to the federation. Yugoslavia's top politicians stood on the stage, looking decidedly uncomfortable. Milošević was out in front totally in command.

The journey of Prince Lazar's bones was reminiscent both of the last journey of the dead Tito traveling by train from Ljubljana via Zagreb to Belgrade and of the baton for the Youth relay traveling through all of Yugoslavia's six republics—except this time, the journey was conspicuously defining Serbian territory and was, as such, a marker of Serbian unity as against non-Serbs within Yugoslavia. In his speech at Kosovo Polje, Milošević showed his readiness to go to war on behalf of the Serbs in order to gain control of what was defined as Serbian land, and was preparing his fellow Serbs for the possibility of such a war. The enemy were those fellow Yugoslavs whom Tito had joined in "brotherhood and unity," and Milošević's cultivation of the death cults (among others, through the very public celebration of the battle of Kosovo and the rehearsing of World

War II deaths) created a psychological atmosphere of war, and violent deaths that were eventually confirmed by personal experience.

War and death had been central elements in both Tudjman's and Milošević's life experiences. While Tudjman fought in World War II himself, Milošević was a war child; both men's parents died a violent death. In Milošević's case, his parents both committed suicide. The circumstances of Tudjman's parents' deaths just after World War II are more difficult to ascertain. His father had fought with the Partisans, and after the war he was appointed chairman to a Communist Party committee in Zagreb. In 1946, both his parents were found shot dead in their house. According to one Tudjman biography, the police said they had committed suicide, but Franjo Tudjman contended forty years later that they had been killed by the Communist secret police (*Bruns International* 1999: 2).

Indeed, the cultivation of death cults was not innovative; rather, it was very much continuing the ritual and symbolic repertoire of the Tito era, with the only difference being the cause the celebrated dead heroes represented. During Tito's reign it was the Partisans who had fought for a multinational Yugoslavia, whereas in the immediate years after Tito's death and before the appearance of the successors, the object for the death cults was the dead Tito. With the appearance of the "illegitimate sons," the death cults centered on exclusively Serbian or Croat heroes, and often those who had fought against people defined as belonging to the groups against which the new regimes were now waging war. Historical terms that had denoted the supporters of a particular political system and regime were now adopted by opposite sides and used to brand all members of an ethnic group or nationality. Croats became Ustashe, Serbs became Chetniks, and Bosnian Muslims became Turks (or *balija*, a derogative term originally meaning "primitive peasant"), or depending on the context, Ustashe. This renaming worked because the Ustasha was established and run by Croats (and there had been a Bosnian Muslim Ustasha unit), the Chetnik forces were established and run by Serbs, and the Ottoman administration in Bosnia-Herzegovina and Serbia had been dominated by the Muslim landowning class. This categorization blurred the fact that thousands of Bosnian Muslims, Croats, and Serbs fought with the Partisans against the Ustashe and the Chetniks, and there were Bosnian Muslims who fought against the Ottoman regime. It did help the internal process among the three groups for national (or ethnic) unity, however. Yet it seems that President Tudjman was the most successful in creating national unity, first, by acknowledging that Croats had fought on opposite sides during World War II, and second, by attempting to reconcile the two through the idea of Croatian national unity based on political and ethnic homogeneity. Serbia's Milošević never seemed to have properly addressed the split among Serbs during World War II, when Partisans and Chetniks were engulfed in a civil war in Serbia, Montenegro, and Bosnia; therefore, he had to go much further back in history to be able to create a sense of unity (albeit a mythical one).

As they were seeking popular legitimacy as the new rulers, Milošević's and Tudjman's positions as Tito's illegitimate sons in popular imagery enabled them to take over for the father, without actually following him. In other words, they established for themselves a legitimate successor status by establishing continuation with the past through an identification with Tito, and at the same time, they were breaking with the past through a rejection of multiethnicity and replacing it with the credo of ethnic superiority and purity.

## The End of "Brotherhood and Unity" and the Sacrifice of Bosnia-Herzegovina.

Tellingly, Bosnians wanted to be the keepers of Tito's true legacy, as reflected, for example, in their welcoming Tito's remains when other republics wanted to discard them, but Bosnia was also the place where legacies of Tito were most brutally dismembered, while the Bosnians were forced into the role of executioner. Alija Izetbegović, leader of the Bosniaks and the president (or, chairman) of the Bosnian presidency during the war of the 1990s was the only leader without a Communist past (i.e., he was a genuine dissident). Of Bosnia's three leaders, he least fashioned his image after that of Tito, and, significantly, there were never any rumors that he was Tito's illegitimate son; indeed, there were never even humorous attempts at establishing any sort of relationship, symbolic or otherwise, between Tito and Izetbegović.

Yet Izetbegović was the only one who, at least during the first years of the 1990s, represented Tito's ideal of a multiethnic society. In addition, he tolerated opposition. Indeed, Izetbegović was the only successor in the republics of Serbia, Croatia, and Bosnia-Herzegovina who acted as a caretaker of the core element of Tito's Yugoslavism—"brotherhood and unity." Alija Izetbegović, and many other Bosnians, however, saw their multiethnic society not primarily as a legacy of Titoism but as a Bosnian tradition preceding Tito and Yugoslavia, which Tito had merely confirmed. In this respect, Alija Izetbegović could be said to be Tito's only true successor, whose successor status was eventually totally undermined by his ethnonationalist counterparts, first by disclaiming his right to represent a non-ethnically defined population, and then by destroying (or not recognizing) the geopolitical unit he had been elected to head. However, as the war progressed and international and domestic support for a multiethnic, and unitary state dwindled, Izetbegović increasingly gained status as an ethnic father-leader. His picture was held up by soldiers in military convoys and in some public buildings controlled by his ruling SDA party, his portrait replaced that of Tito's. The personality cult of Izetbegović, if there ever was one, however, was never comparable to that of Tudjman, Milošević or Karadžić (the Bosnian Serb separatist leader). This may have been partly due to Izetbegović's personality and his lack of populist appeal (for instance, in not using populist rhetoric)

and partly the dire situation his country and people were in, which gave
no incentive to celebrate political leadership.

In Croatia and Serbia, Tito's residences had been taken over by the new
leaders, whereas in Bosnia Tito's official residence and his hunting lodges
were destroyed in the war. In Bosnia, too, there were the forgotten dead
from massacres in World War II, but while Serbs dug up the bones of their
ethnic brethren, the Muslim leadership did not parade the bones of their
dead. The massacres of thousands of Muslim civilians by Serbian Royalist
(or Chetnik) forces in Eastern Bosnia during World War II, which had been
silenced by official history ("the history we never learned in school," as
one Bosnian Muslim told me in 1991), could have provided a source for
emotional appeals to Bosnian Muslims to spread fear and mobilize people
in settling scores against the Chetniks (i.e., the present Serbs). Izetbegović,
however, did not cultivate a relation to death cults, which were so central
to establishing authority for Tito's two main successors. The reason for
this again may have been Izetbegović's reluctance to use divisive and
inflammatory rhetoric, but more important disinterment and displaying
of the bones of the dead would have been contrary to both Bosnian Muslim tradition and Islamic belief. Contrary to what is the case in Catholic,
and particularly Orthodox Christian, traditions (which in some regions
include a second burial), death cults are much less pronounced in Bosnian
(Sunni) Islam. This is among others reflected in the lack of attention most
Muslims pay to the graves of their relatives (see Bringa, 1995: 176).[52] However, there is a tradition in Bosnian Islam for celebrating the heroic dead,
that is, Muslims killed in battle, the so-called *šehits*. This created a problem
in Sarajevo where many of those who fought and were killed in the
defense of Sarajevo were not of the Muslim faith. While some Muslim
fighters were posthumously honored by being buried at a special burial
ground for šehits, their non-Muslim colleagues were buried alongside
other "ordinary" citizens.[53] This means that the contribution and sacrifice
of non-Muslims in the defense of Sarajevo, and indeed a multiethnic
Bosnia, was not publicly acknowledged. This served to undermine the
Sarajevo government's own allegiance to multiethnicity and to alienate its
non-Muslim defenders. When the fight against nationalist separatists and
the siege of Sarajevo were publicly monopolized by the members of one
ethnically defined community, and the contribution of others were not
publicly acknowledged, the conflict was further ethnicized.

The bone-digging on the eve of the recent war was about reclaiming a
particular part of history, which Tito had ignored or suppressed; it was
about the collapsing of time and of identifying present neighbors with the
enemy of yesterday. These emotionally very powerful rituals of disinterring
the dead and victims of atrocities were both about creating internal cohesion and unity within the relevant ethnic community and external divisions
and hostility. The disinterment could have served to acknowledge the suffering of people who were not included in Socialist Yugoslavia's official history, and thus serve to start a process of reconciliation between people

who found themselves on different sides during Yugoslavia's civil wars and World War II (sides that actually cut across ethnic communities). Instead, it was used to inspire fear in people and ferment antagonisms between ethnic communities.

The exhumation of what Verdery (1999) has called the "nameless dead" would serve to collapse or "reconfigure" time as well as identifications, so that people, battles, and power structures of the present and the World War II era (and in the case of King Lazar, the Ottoman era) would become indistinguishable, and the intermittent period of Titoism would be erased. Furthermore, as Verdery has argued so well, exhumation of "the nameless dead," who during the Tito regime had been officially known as either Partisans or Fascists, were now finally being publicly identified as Serbs or Croats. This helped the living establish exclusive ethnic ownership to the land through their dead ancestors (see Verdery 1999). Bosnia-Herzegovina would be the major grounds for the Serbian and Croatian leadership and their proxies in Bosnia-Herzegovina, headed by Radovan Karadžić and Mate Boban, respectively, to play out their fascination with death cults.[54]

In 1990, Bosnia was preparing for democratic multiparty elections scheduled for November that year. A Zagreb-based news journal commented on its front page: "The Bosnian elections—exam for Yugoslavia." An article asked the question whether members of the electorate body in Bosnia would turn toward national parties, or whether, to the benefit of the multinational parties, they would turn their backs against them? "In any case, it continues, the multiparty elections in this republic makes for one of the key points in the unraveling of Bosnia-Herzegovina and Yugoslavia" (*Danas*, 27 January 1990). The point was made quite clear: the fate of Bosnia-Herzegovina was construed as closely connected to that of Yugoslavia. There was an obvious political advantage, in for instance, the Croatian President Tudjman's insisting that the disintegration of Yugoslavia would imply the dissolution of Bosnia-Herzegovina. By the same token, he would oppose any political settlement for Bosnia-Herzegovina that could be construed as the Yugoslav model. Likewise, the Bosnian Serb and Serbian political leadership and media would, throughout the war, insistently refer to Bosnia-Herzegovina as "the former Bosnia-Herzegovina." Under the leadership of presidents Tudjman and Milošević respectively, official Croatia and official Serbia legitimated the destruction of Bosnia-Herzegovina in the dissolution of Tito's Yugoslavia.

## Conclusion

The upsurge in nationalism and the ensuing war was both a revolt against (and purging of) Titoism and its central idea of a multiethnic Yugoslavia built on "brotherhood and unity," and a result of conditions created during Tito's rule. The Titoist system was built from the "top down," and any nascent reforms were quashed by a combination of a frozen self-management ideology and the fear of nationalism. After Tito's death, "the republics were dead-locked over the issues of constitutional reform, economic policy, and democratization of the political system" (Shoup 1995: 60). Tito himself had made sure that democratic reform movements were weak and that there were not any democratic leaders who could lead Yugoslavia through a peaceful democratic transition. He had furthermore prevented a constructive and open discussion about the nationalities question. Any disagreements or conflicts of interests be- tween the different republics or peoples were glossed over with the doc- trine of "brotherhood and unity." Political dissenters were branded nationalists and persecuted. As Shoup points out, "the Communist ide- ology ... never addressed underlying attitudes while it did encourage people to think in terms of 'the enemy' and 'domination' by one group over another—"a way of thinking easily transferred from questions of class to those of race and ethnicity" (1995: 61). Furthermore, the state administrative and political structure already had a system in place that implied that people were recruited not on the basis of membership of diverse political parties, but on the basis of allegiance to one and the same political party and membership of different ethnic communities. Hence, during the 1990 elections, people voted according to the principles of a one-party system with ethnicity as the basis for representation.

In a similar vein, Zwick (1983) argues that there are numerous impor- tant similarities between nationalism and Communism; for instance, both Communism and nationalism emerged in transitional societies and are, as such, "expressions of social collective grievances," and their "revolutions are both essentially rites of social exorcism." Furthermore, they have both "quasi-religious characteristics" and are "millenarian world views in that they promise secular deliverance and salvation in the form of a perfect world order. Therefore, the followers of these 'faiths' tend to be messianic, and they are willing to justify virtually anything in the name of their millenarian goals" (1983: 11–12). Both movements arise as a reaction to an (imagined) enemy or enemies. While in the case of Communism, another class and the capitalist "foreign" West- ern world are depicted as the enemy, in the case of nationalism, the pri- mary enemy is the other nation (see Zwick 1983: 11). In Yugoslavia the switch from Communist to nationalist ideology thus implied a redefin- ition of the enemy as no longer the outside foreign capitalist or Soviet powers as defined by Tito, but the other competing "Yugoslav" nations within. This redefinition of the enemy was necessary because the two dominant former Yugoslav republics, Serbia and Croatia, did not be- come more democratic. Indeed, their mode of authority remained the same. Presidents Milošević and Tudjman both pursued an autocratic leadership reminiscent of Tito. The mode of authority in the newly inde- pendent Serbia and Croatia remained the same as under Tito's Yugoslavia. The transcendent, however, changed from the ethos of "brotherhood and unity" among all the peoples of Yugoslavia to a bigoted, exclusionist ethnonationalism.

Bosnia-Herzegovina has often been called a Yugoslavia in miniature. Its primary similarity with Yugoslavia, however, was that it was the main ground for playing out contesting claims between Serbs and Croats. Presidents Tudjman and Milošević saw Bosnia-Herzegovina as the living legacy of "Titoism," and therefore as an obstacle and direct challenge to their perceived power base—the ethnically pure nation state.

To create a basis for their authority and build a new social order, these leaders would not only have to destroy Titoism but also what was seen as its legacy: a multiethnic state based on power-sharing between the different South Slavic peoples. In Bosnia-Herzegovina, where no one nationality formed a majority, the consequence was that the nationalist leaders pursued a political strategy of ensuring that their "nation" or people would form a majority, either by redrawing state boundaries, and/or by the expulsion, terrorizing, and murder of other Bosnian "nationalities." For Tito's main successors it was therefore not enough to discredit Titoism; the very social fabric of Bosnia with its tradition of pluralistic social life (expressed in its ethnically mixed villages and urban neighborhoods) had to be destroyed, too. The fact that the Bosnian Muslims refused to be nationalized as either Serbs or Croats and were blocking a straightforward two-way partition of Bosnia-Herzegovina made them into enemies of the Serbian and Croatian nationalists and a target of their intolerance and "ethnic-cleansing" campaigns. Tito's successors purged his legacy and simply denied that there had ever been substantial periods of voluntary, peaceful coexistence. In Bosnia, the nationalists set out to destroy a sense of community based on a shared history and social practices. They replaced it with ideas of centuries-old hatreds among now sharply delineated national groups. The Croat leader, Franjo Tudjman, even invoked the idea of a deep civilization clash between the primitive oriental East (represented by Eastern Orthodoxy—Serbs and Islam—Bosniaks) and the civilized West (represented by the Catholic Croats) (see also, Lindstrom and Razsa 1998).

In Bosnia-Herzegovina, where Tito had been most popular, attempts were made to keep "brotherhood and unity" alive as much in Tito's spirit as in its pre-Titoist form of Bosnian multiethnicity and neighborliness. But while Croatia and Serbia found their new fathers, in Bosnia no political leader, even by symbolic analogies, established himself as Tito's successor. This is perhaps the reason why in Bosnia Tito's image was never successfully erased.

In Bosnia, the post-communist government of Alija Izetbegović initially broke with Tito's authoritarian model where the ruling party controlled the state apparatus, the military, and the media. Faced with violent attacks from Serbian and Croatian nationalist, authoritarian regimes, Izetbegović's SDA eventually adopted a similar leadership model to that in Serbia and Croatia, maintaining a commitment to diversity in name only. The outcome could have been different had there been a viable opposition to each successor-leader and a mourning process after Tito's death that was not preempted by the state but allowed to follow a course of open discussion and retribution. Since this did not happen, no other mode of authority was allowed to develop, and the only one available was the "Tito, we swear to you" model of paternal authority. This was also true for Bosnia-Herzegovina, where opposition and multivocality instead were translated into paternal loyalty for not just one, but for three ethnically defined leaders.

## Postscript: The Absence of the Father

In Sarajevo, 4 May, the anniversary for Tito's death, has been remembered every year since Tito's death. In 1992, a month after war had broken out, flowers were put at the foot of the Tito statue outside the military barracks. In 1993, I was told that there was too much shelling to put down flowers, but the national broadcasting still remembered the day. On 5 May 1995 the news reader for Sarajevo BiH television reminded his viewers that it had been fifteen years since Tito's death and asked the rhetorical question of whether anyone would have remembered if there was not a war going on. In Sarajevo you could still come across Tito's portrait on the wall in offices and shops.

In April 1995 I was walking through the bombed-out city of Mostar in Herzegovina. From a former front line, I was looking at the once-proud old city, now piles of rubble, thanks first to shelling by Serbian forces, then by Croatian forces. High up on the mountain face my eyes caught sight of two words painted in red letters, faded but still readable. The first word was "TITO" and beneath the word was "MIR" (peace). I have been told that the second word was added in 1991. In Bosnia people continued to honor the man who they believed had brought them peace and prosperity. Indeed, throughout the war on 4 May, individual citizens or groups of friends would enter an obituary or a *sjećanje* (remembrance) for Tito in the main Sarajevo newspaper, *Oslobodjenje*.[55] This was still the case in 1999. During the 1992–1995 war, however, a new generation grew up in the shadow of war and intercommunal fighting. In Sarajevo the young men whose education, lives, and dreams for the future were shattered by a war waged by former fellow Yugoslavs adopted a new, favorite curse. You could hear it during the war in the queue of people waiting in line for water or bread, exposed to shells and sniper fire. I am told you could hear it too among the young Sarajevo fighters in the trenches up in the hills. These young men are the sons of a generation that claims that had only Tito been alive, this war would never have happened. So when something goes wrong they curse; " F— Tito." The reprimand from older people who remember better times and still honor the memory of Tito is met with silence. Perhaps they think of the graffiti on a downtown Sarajevo wall in

1992. Someone had written "Tito come back!" (*Tito vrati se!*), and someone else had added "Don't want to!" (*Neću!*) and signed it "Tito," copying his characteristic signature.

As of 2002, the three main successors to Tito—Franjo Tudjman in Zagreb, Slobodan Milošević in Belgrade, and Alija Izetbegović in Sarajevo—are no longer in power. Tudjman died in 1999, Izetbegović retired in October 2000, and Slobodan Milošević lost popular elections and was finally forced to step down by mass demonstrations against his refusal to accept the outcome. In the summer of 2001, Slobodan Milošević was arrested and transferred to the International Criminal Tribunal in the Hague to face charges of war crimes, crimes against humanity, and genocide. While pluralist governments have won the elections in both Zagreb and Belgrade, the ethnonationalists are still strong in parts of Bosnia-Herzegovina (i.e., the Serb separatists in Republika Srpska and Croat separatists in Herzegovina and western Bosnia where the Croat nationalist party are pushing for a third and Croat-ruled state entity that would imitate Republika Srpska). In areas with a Bosniak majority, particularly in the cities, the nationalists are losing ground and the non-ethnically defined political forces are gaining power. Bosnia-Herzegovina has not yet emerged from the breakup of Yugoslavia and the ensuing wars as a functioning state. The reasons for this are complex, but one major factor is the state-governing structure laid down in the Dayton peace accords. In many respects it prevents Bosnia-Herzegovina from moving beyond the ethnically based citizen rights system that favors those who identify with either the Bosniak, Croat, or Serb nationalities. It defines political representation and office, as well as allocation of resources, on this basis. Ethnonationalist political forces will stand to lose if an attempt is made to change the system, and will fight it with all means available. As long as politicians do not need to appeal to an electorate beyond their own ethnic community to be elected, the ethnonationalist rhetoric of homogeneity and separation will continue to stifle people's imagination and offer their only hope for security, prosperity, and influence, while the Sarajevo government based on the principle of a rotating presidency among a Bosniak, Croat, and Serb candidate will remain. In principle, this is the system that Tito designed for the Socialist Federal Republic of Yugoslavia to replace his office after his death. It leaves Bosnia-Herzegovina in a time warp, with its regime transition yet incomplete.

The living quarters at Goli Otok

"Tito! We are here. Don't shoot!" Inscripton on a bombed-out house on the frontline of the Dobrinja neighborhood in Sarajevo. The "We are here" echoes posters held up by youths along the railroad track from Ljubljana to Belgrade where Tito's coffin traveled in May 1980.

Statue of Tito by the Croatian sculptor Antun Augustincic in front of the Kumrovec Museum

A page from one of the guest books at the Kumrovec Tito museum. It reads: "Tito, you are not worthy that we write your name in capital letters for you were a Chetnik, you are a Chetnik, and you will always remain a Chetnik."

All photos by Tone Bringa, 1996 and 1999

# Notes

An earlier and shorter version of this essay was presented at the American Anthropological Association meeting panel "The Death of the Father: An Anthropology of Changes in Political Authority" in Washington, DC, 1995. I thank the panel participants for constructive comments at our working seminar in Bellagio in Italy, August 1996. I am indebted to John Borneman for his inspiring ideas and comments. I have benefited from the insights and comments of Keith Brown, Kemal Kurspahić, Ivana Maček, and Olga Supek, all of whom read a later version of the essay. Interviews and research for this essay, including visits to major Tito sites were undertaken in Croatia and Bosnia in 1995–1997. I thank friends who contributed, and particular thanks go to Peter Galbraith, Maja Povrzanović, Zeljka Jelavić, Gordana Knezević, Aida and Džemal Sokolović, and Margaret Soltan, who proofread the essay. The discussion of the Tito cult and the effects of his death on people and the region is particularly informed by ethnography from Bosnia-Herzegovina. Abbreviated sections of this essay pertaining to the political developments in Yugoslavia and Bosnia in the late 1980s and early 1990s are also published in Bringa 2002. Unless otherwise noted, all translations for quotations are my own.

1. This fact was left out of Tito's official biography, most likely because of Serbian sensitivities, but also because of the damage it might do to Tito's image as a leader above nationality and (ethnic) partisan loyalties.
2. The "Independent State of Croatia" was declared on 10 April 1941 under the Ustasha leader Ante Pavelić and encompassed inner Croatia, Slavonija, Srem, those parts of Dalmatia that had not been ceded to Italy, and all of Bosnia-Herzegovina (see West 1994: 72).
3. The popular explanation of Tito's nickname is that it is a pun on the fact that Josip Broz as the commander of the Partisans was always giving orders, saying *ti to!* meaning "you that!" However, Tito himself explained to one of his biographers that Tito was a common nickname in the Zagorje region where he grew up.
4. After the Partisan victory in 1945, many thousands of Ustasha sympathizers in particular, but also Chetniks, emigrated overseas to South America, the United States, Canada, and Australia (although many Chetnik soldiers and sympathizers joined the Partisan forces toward the end of the war). These émigré Croats and Serbs established strong networks abroad and continued to fight Tito's Yugoslavia from afar. When Yugoslavia dissolved, Croat émigrés helped finance the new Croatian government in various ways; including through arms purchases. In many instances, their political influence was considerable and they returned to high positions in Croatian society. When the Croatian president Franjo Tudjman (1991–1999) referred to the size of the Croatian nation, he cited a number that included an assumed number of diaspora Croats (irrespective of whether these people were citizens of another state or not).
5. Archives at the Woodrow Wilson International Research Center in Washington, DC, which were made available in 2000, show that Josef Stalin, through the Soviet secret services, was making plans to kill Josip Broz Tito. The plan was scrapped in 1953 when Stalin died.
6. The relationship between Yugoslavia and the USSR was normalized in 1955 when Khrushchev visited Yugoslavia and acknowledged its right to an independent path to socialism.
7. Djilas claims that only "a few days after the liberation of Belgrade, on 20 October, 1944, by Yugoslav and Soviet forces, Tito made a tour of inspection of the royal palaces at Dedinje and ordered their restoration. Before the war was over, the White Palace was repaired and Tito moved in. Tito also retained the Royal Palace [for official guests and functions] and the villa on Romanian Street [renamed Užička Street after 1948]" (1981: 93).
8. According to Pavlowitch, "by 1974, the number of official residences had grown to thirty-two, and more would be added " (1992: 81). But there were also villas built or

dedicated to Tito by local party bosses and used by them, which Tito never visited (personal communication, Kemal Kurspahić).

9. Philip Smucker, "Holbrooke to Find Milošević in Grandiose Tito-Style Mode," *Washington Times*, 8 May 1997.

10. Djilas states that: "In 1953, it was decided to allow towns, streets, factories, and co-operatives to revert to their old names—names that had been replaced by names of party leaders. Tito went along, but it was agreed that he was exempt from that rule" (1981: 22).

11. In 1990, a group of Serbs lead by Christian Orthodox clergy went to the Surmanci ravine in Herzegovina where about five hundred Serb women, young girls, and children under the age of fifteen from the village of Prebilovici were hurled to their deaths down a four-hundred-foot pit by local Ustasha men in 1941. They wanted to excavate the bones and give them a Christian Orthodox burial in Serbian soil. "The bones lay in the depths until 1961, when the government ... raised a memorial to the dead and sealed the pit with concrete" (Hall, 1994: 207). This pit was excavated along with twelve others in Herzegovina. "Afterwards, the hole was resealed, and in the new cover was embedded a black marble Orthodox cross. Accompanied by Serbian television teams, a procession of pickup trucks transported the bones, in hundreds of small caskets draped with the Serbian coat of arms ... to the old site of Prebilovici" (Hall 1994: 208).

12. Interestingly, this practice did not disappear with Tito but was continued by Tito's two main successors, President Tudjman of Croatia and President Milošević of Serbia.

13. Anthropologist Olga Supek offered a popular pun from "Yugoslav" times to illustrate this point: Tito, influenced by his Zagorje dialect, would only have one sound for the pronunciation of *l*'s and *lj*'s, which in a phrase such as *spoljnji poslovi* (external affairs) would sound like *spolni poslovi* (sexual affairs). In Tito's native dialect, and in most Croatian dialects, the word for "external" would be *vanjski* rather than *spoljni*, which is common in Serbian dialects.

14. Djilas claims that as a response to the denunciation of Stalin's cult of the personality at the Twentieth Congress of the Communist Party of the Soviet Union in 1956, Tito suggested that the day be designated the "Day of the Youth" and no longer be associated with his birthday. However, it continued officially to be associated with his birthday and "the celebration itself became even more gigantic, more popular" (1981: 30). Furthermore, it seems that after Tito's break with Cominform and Stalin, the cult of Tito "served to strengthen Yugoslavia's capacity for independent resistance" (Djilas 1981: 22).

15. In the new independent Croatia, "cultural programs" continue to be part of major political events, except the dances, folk costumes, and so forth, shown are from different regions within Croatia.

16. My colleague Željka Jelavić in Zagreb has given me the following example of such a greeting: "Dear comrade Tito, at the occasion of Your birthday, we pioneers, youth and citizens of Zagreb, wish to assure You that we will continue to guard and nurse the achievements of the socialist revolution and nurse brotherhood and unity of all of Yugoslavia's peoples and minorities [*naroda and narodnosti*]."

17. By 1987, the Slovene League of Communists was publicly criticizing the grandiose celebrations venerating a dead man and the relay was held for the last time, indicating, as Thompson points out, how tenuous Yugoslavism had become (1992: 233).

18. In school textbooks issued in Zagreb in the latter part of the 1980s, Tito's picture and poems are absent from the sixth grade upwards, but still present in fourth grade books, although there is no longer the official picture of Tito on the first page.

19. In 1990, the Belgrade daily newspaper published a family photograph from 1977 with Tito surrounded by twenty-eight family members, over four generations (see Pavlowitch 1992: 80).

20. I owe this point to Olga Supek.

21. One tangible aspect of nonalignment for people living in larger cities was the presence of African and Arab students at Yugoslav universities, which included dating, marriage, and children with native "Yugoslavs" (personal communication, Olga Supek).

22. The Yugoslav Communist Party changed its name in 1952 to the League of Communists of Yugoslavia to further mark its independence from Moscow (see, e.g., Thompson 1992).
23. The coffee-table sized book *Bilo je časno živjeti s Titom* (It was an honor to live with Tito), edited by photographers Valent Grobenski, Ivo Eterović, and Mladen Tudor, and published in Zagreb in 1980, contains several pictures of the reactions of the soccer players on hearing the announcement of Tito's death over the loudspeakers.
24. The contrast with the reaction of Croatians to the death of their post-1990 leader and president Franjo Tudjman, in December 1999 is striking. The crowds were solemn and emotions subdued. After his death, aspects of his authoritarian rule disappeared almost overnight (such as limitation on the freedom of speech). Two months later (February 2000), the Croatians elected a new president who was the most vocal of the presidential candidates in his criticisms of Franjo Tudjman's leadership style.
25. The song is often included in music collections of "Yugoslav songs" from various regions of the former Yugoslavia.
26. Olga Supek shared with me her insights and thoughts on the role of this song.
27. The funeral of Croatia's President Franjo Tudjman was, by contrast, attended by only two heads of state, the Turkish and Macedonian presidents. This reflected Croatia's low international regard and isolation as a result of the policies pursued by Franjo Tudjman. This was ironic, as Tudjman was the one successor to Tito who had conspicuously emulated him.
28. Quoted in *Bilo je časno živjeti s Titom*. This book contains copies of the day-by-day medical bulletins, official pictures from his burial, and printed texts of speeches, poems, and quotes relating to the president's death.
29. This kind of religious imagery was prevalent in many of the poems written in veneration of Tito, and particularly in the eulogies written after his death, which used the imagery of sacrifice, suffering, and eternal life associated with Christ.
30. All newspaper quotes are from *Bilo je časno živjeti s Titom*.
31. Personal communication, Peter W. Galbraith (U.S. ambassador to Croatia, 1993–1998).
32. Sutjeska is a river canyon in a rough mountain area in south-eastern Bosnia. In 1943, several thousand Partisans under Tito's command were killed as they were trapped in the valley surrounded by German, Italian, and Croatian troops.
33. For a fuller discussion of the peculiarities of the nationalities system in Tito's Yugoslavia, see Bringa 1995.
34. An abbreviated version of this section appears in Bringa 2002.
35. Milošević, appointed Dobrica Ćosić as president of the new and unrecognized Yugoslavia (consisting of Serbia and Montenegro) in January of 1992.
36. The "memorandum" is published in English in *Former Yugoslavia through Documents: From Its Dissolution to Peace Settlements* (1999), edited by Snezana Trifunskova
37. Slovenia, with its distinct language and strong (Austrian) and Central European orientation, was the richest and most reform-friendly republic in Yugoslavia. It was moved by strong nationalist sentiments and a desire for independence. With Serbia, Slovenia held the key to the dissolution (or preservation) of Yugoslavia (see Shoup 1992: 63).
38. For more details on the transference of political and military control to Serb-controlled parallel structures in Bosnia and Herzegovina, see Final Report of the United Nations Commission of Experts, S/1994/674/Add.2/ (Vol. 1), 28 December 1994.
39. The women, Suada Dilberović, a student of medicine from Dubrovnik of Bosnian Muslim descent, and Olga Sučić, a mother of two young children and of Bosnian Serb descent, were killed on the Vrbanja Bridge as the peace demonstrators were crossing the bridge to Grbavica (a neighborhood taken over by Serb snipers). A commemorative plaque with the names of the two women has been erected on the bridge.
40. This number is from "Bosnia and Herzegovina: War-Damaged Residential Buildings and Status on Repair/Reconstruction and Funding Requirements," report by International Management Group, Housing Sector Task Force, Sarajevo, January 1999.
41. I am grateful to the curator at the Kumrovec museum for letting me study earlier guest books.

42. I am indebted to Olga Supek for her analysis of the overall Croatian political context of these guest book comments. Also, she tells me that in June 1998 when she visited Kumrovec, criticisms of Tudjman's regime had become more open, and she observed a group of seventh graders from eastern Croatia giggling in an act of bravado, eagerly squeezing around the "guest book table" to (again) write positive and loving messages.

43. The most publicized example is during President Clinton's stopover at Zagreb airport in January 1996 when the Croatian president used the word for "happy" now considered Serbian, *srećan*, rather than the word *sretan*, which is considered Croatian. (At the time, President Tudjman's words were replayed time and again by the Zagreb opposition radio station 101.)

44. Personal communication, Peter W. Galbraith.

45. In the much referred to "Memorandum" of the Serbian Academy of Science and Arts, the author(s) claim(s) that Slovenia and Croatia plotted against Serbia to realize political and economic domination over Serbia, and that the coalition between the two republics was solidified through the cooperation between Tito, a Croat, and his ideologist, Edvard Kardelj, a Slovene (see Rogel 1998: 122–123). In other words, Tito was recast as an anti-Serb Croat.

46. It is interesting to note that Slovenia, which was the first republic to drive public criticism and debate about the legacy of Tito, and indeed, as already noted, the first to pull out of the Dan Mladosti relay, is also the region where a new "post-Yugoslavia" public nostalgia for Tito—a kind of "Tito revival" was first expressed through a web site where people were invited to talk to Tito. The web site, www.titoville.com, called "Tito's home page," was posted on the Internet in 1994. It provides a collection of photographs of Tito, his speeches, and songs and movies revering him, but also jokes about Tito and a list of his alleged lovers. It is, perhaps, appropriate that the former Yugoslav republic that was the site of both Tito's physical death, and the beginning of his symbolic death was also the first to symbolically resurrect him.

47. John Borneman drew my attention to the importance of cultivating a relation with the death cults in order for the new leaders to establish political authority.

48. On the fiftieth anniversary of Bleiburg, the Croatian Parliament held a special session to commemorate those who died in the forced march back to Yugoslavia. The march was officially referred to as the "way of the cross." Clearly, the Croatian government was seeking to establish an analogy between the suffering of Christ and what they saw as the suffering of the Croatian people, symbolized through the fate of the fleeing Ustashe supporters.

49. Maple Razsa generously provided this information from his fieldwork notes.

50. Patrick Moore, BosNet, 28 April 1996, summarizing a report in the Croatian newspaper *Večernji List* on 23 April 1996.

51. In a speech that Milošević held that day, he appears to ask for the same choice from his followers. He said, for example: "The Kosovo heroism does not allow us to forget that at one time, we were brave and dignified and one of the few who went into battle undefeated. Six centuries later, again we are in battles and quarrels. They are not armed battles, though such things should not be excluded yet" (Silber and Little 1996: 77).

52. According to Goldziher, "Desecration of a saint's grave is considered a crime which will be avenged by terrible divine punishment, and exhumation—which is also disapproved of for ordinary human beings—is considered as such a desecration" (1971: 286).

53. Personal communication, Ivana Maček.

54. Radovan Karadžić has been charged with war crimes, crimes against humanity, and genocide by the International Criminal Tribunal for the former Yugoslavia (ICTY) and is hiding in the Serbian-controlled part of Bosnia-Herzegovina. Mate Boban was removed from political office in January 1995 and died of natural causes in 1997.

55. This information was provided by Kemal Kurspahić, the chief editor of *Oslobodjenje* at the time.

# References

Bennett, Christopher. 1995. *Yugoslavia's Bloody Collapse: Causes, Course and Consequences.* New York: New York University Press.
Bracewell, Wendy. 1995. "Mothers of the Nation." *WarReport: Bulletin of the Institute for War and Peace Reporting* 36:27–29.
Bringa, Tone. 1995. *Being Muslim the Bosnian Way: Identity and Community in a Central Bosnian Village.* Princeton: Princeton University Press.
———. 2002. "Averted Gaze: Genocide in Bosnia-Herzegovina, 1992–1995." In *Annihilating Difference: The Anthropology of Genocide,* ed. Alex Hinton. Berkeley: University of California Press.
Bruns International. 1999. "Obituary: Tudjman Dead, Opening Door for Political Change in Croatia." 11 December [accessed 6 July 2002].
Cigar, Norman. 1995. *Genocide in Bosnia: The Policy of "Ethnic Cleansing."* College Station: Texas A&M University Press.
Denitch, Bette. 1994. "Dismembering Yugoslavia: Nationalist Ideologies and the Symbolic Revival of Genocide." *American Ethnologist* 21:367–390.
Djilas, Milovan. 1981. *Tito: The Story from Inside.* London: Weidenfeld and Nicolson.
Doder, Dusko. 1979. *The Yugoslavs.* New York: Vintage.
Eterović, Ivo, Valent Grobenski, and Mladen Tudor, eds. 1980. *Bilo je Časno Živjeti s Titom: Kako su Jugoslavenski Novinari i Foto-Reporteri Zabilježili Dramu Posljednje Titove Bitke i Sedam Najtužnijih Dana Jugoslavije.* Zagreb: SOUR Vjesnik.
Godhziher, Ignaz. 1971. *Muslim Studies.* Vol. 2. London: George Allen & Unwin.
Hall, Brian. 1994. *The Impossible Country: A Journey through the Last Days of Yugoslavia.* Boston: David R. Godine.
Judah, Tim. 1997. *The Serbs: History, Myth and the Destruction of Yugoslavia.* New Haven: Yale University Press.
Kaštelan, Jure. 1957. "Pjesam o Titu." In *Stihovi Borbe i Slobode.* Belgrade: Narodna armija.
Lindstrom, Nicole, and Maple Rasza. 1998. *Reimagining the Balkans.* www.ksg.harvard.edu/kokklis/GSW1/03%20Lindstrom%20Rasza [accessed 6 July 2002].
Pavković, Aleksandar. 1997. *The Fragmentation of Yugoslavia: Nationalism in a Multinational State.* Basingstoke: Macmillan.
Pavlowitch, Stevan K. 1992. *Tito: Yugoslavia's Great Dictator: A Reassessment.* London: Hurst.
Ramet, Sabrina P. 1992. *Balkan Babel: Politics, Culture, and Religion in Yugoslavia.* Boulder: Westview Press.
Rogel, Carole. 1998. *The Breakup of Yugoslavia and the War in Bosnia.* Westport, CT: Greenwood.
Shoup, Paul. 1995. "The Bosnian Crisis in 1992." In *Beyond Yugoslavia: Politics, Economics, and Culture in a Shattered Community,* ed. Sabrina Petra Ramet and Ljubisa S. Adamovich. Boulder. Westview Press.
Silber, Laura, and Allan Little. 1996. *The Death of Yugoslavia.* London: Penguin and BBC.
Thompson, Mark. 1992. *A Paper House: The Ending of Yugoslavia.* London: Vintage.
Trifunovska, Snezana. 1999. *Former Yugoslavia through Documents: From Its Dissolution to Peace Settlements.* The Hague: Martinus Nijhoff.
Verdery, Katherine. 1999. *The Political Lives of Dead Bodies: Reburial and Postsocialist Change.* New York: Columbia University Press.
Vidović, Veseljko. 1982. *Tito Svjetionik Mira.* Šibenik: Širo štampa.
West, Richard. 1994. *Tito and the Rise and Fall of Yugoslavia.* London: Sinclair-Stevenson.
Zwick, Peter. 1983. *National Communism.* Boulder: Westview Press.

# CHAPTER 6

# Doubtful Dead Fathers and Musical Corpses: What to Do with the Dead Stalin, Lenin, and Tsar Nicholas?

*John S. Schoeberlein*

The Soviet experience is replete with authoritarian bodysnatching. Either the body must be rendered eternal, like Lenin's waxy remains lying forever in state on Red Square, or the body must be spirited away, like Stalin's corpse taken to commune with the Kremlin wall after a short joint residence in Lenin's tomb. Actually, a sly combination of posterity and oblivion is the ideal: simultaneous extermination and resuscitation. Eliminating the god-king while seeking to retain the symbolic structure of his authority. Political patricide and visitation of the shrine to the dead father.

That Stalin has been difficult to kill off is a well-known fact of Soviet life. The year of Stalin's death, 1953, was neither the end nor the beginning of adulatory ambivalence about his mortality. During the Gorbachev glasnost era, a film was made in Stalin's homeland of Georgia, called Penitence (Abuladze 1986). In it, the unfortunate children of a perished father—a man whose identity is unmistakably Stalin writ small—are plagued with his reappearing corpse. Since the end of glasnost, Stalin has reappeared ever more frequently on the exalting lips of former-Soviet citizens wishing to resuscitate him. Khrushchev meant to do away with him already in 1956 with his "secret speech" to the Twentieth Party Congress. But a few years later, Stalin revived to silence Khrushchev instead, and many hoped the unpredictable if benign Khrushchev would be succeeded by someone more similar to Stalin.

In many modern authoritarian states, the authoritarian leader has a dual identity as "father of the nation." The father image situates the leader as simultaneously "of us" and "above us." To help sustain such imagery, the connotations of military order serve well. The soldiers are the nation's sons. The general is their caring father. Stalin was buried in the outfit of the generalissimo, and his crowning achievement in the minds of most former Soviet citizens today was delivering the blood-soaked Soviet people from Hitler's assault upon them. The uniforms of modern generals are tailored to look very much like those of other soldiers. Medals were pinned on dead Stalin's chest, just as many a Russian veteran pins them on his chest on every public holiday. The army is a model for the family just as the nation is. The Soviet nation, marching against a hostile world, would have perished without their father's caring leadership. The turning point in the history of the world was when Stalin won the Battle of Stalingrad. And when he marched from Stalingrad to Berlin, what greater pride could there be for his redeemed family? For many who heard the news, losing Stalin was more devastating than losing the war might have been. Even in Stalin's prison labor camps there were tears of confusion and also undoubtedly genuine grief. The crush of mourners pressing to assuage the pain and confusion of their loss through a glimpse of his dead remains lying in state resulted in the trampling to death, it is said, of over a thousand people.

Meanwhile, there is a paradox of succession in such modern authoritarian states. The father is beloved. The nation is beholden to him. But there can only be one father. And fathers are not selected; they are there by nature and destiny. The image of a nation bereft of its father is a shattered one. The Soviet state, if it was to survive in a hostile world, could not sustain this shattered condition. The family must be kept whole. Nothing must be allowed to change. The same radio announcement that broke the news of Stalin's cerebral hemorrhage and paralysis declared that Stalin would be withdrawing temporarily from the leadership. His eulogies declared that he would live forever in the quadriumvirate of Marx-Engels-Lenin-Stalin.

The paradox of succession follows from the fact that to succeed the father is to usurp his position. Usurpation was fine when the body of the tsar was cast aside, for the Bolsheviks were brothers casting off an unworthy father, a delegitimized father. But they didn't want to lose the legitimacy of Stalin's rule with the loss of him. Later Soviet leaders could be shuffled in one after another—Andropov, Chernenko, and Gorbachev in rapid succession. By then, the authority of the state, for better or worse, was no longer as tightly attached to an image of the nation's father. Indeed, changes in the leader's authority after Stalin had turned the Communist Party first secretaries from heroes to government functionaries. By Gorbachev's time, rejecting the previous leader had become habitual in the Soviet regime. When Stalin died, authority was severely challenged.

Like each of the chapters in this volume, this contribution examines the end of a form of political authority in which those who control the state, aspiring to maintain total control over the society, seek to legitimize their rule by promoting a form of identification with a leader as the father of the nation. The Soviet case is the earliest and most enduring case of a regime figured on this model. As such, it may be considered the most successful, serving as a model for other regimes. Further, it created the conditions for its own destruction and that of the other regimes built on the same conceptual frame.

This chapter explores the manner in which the leader's authority was established in the Soviet Union under Stalin. After the revolution, everything was supposed to be different, and having slaughtered the imperial family, the Bolsheviks had to construct a new concept of the leaders' authority that would sustain legitimacy of the new state in a world where ideas of national and popular self-determination were not only prevalent among many political leaders and intellectuals, but were embraced by the Bolsheviks themselves. At the same time, they had no intention of dismantling the "Prison House of Peoples," as they had dubbed the tsar's realm. Furthermore, they felt the need to establish unprecedented levels of control over their population, which far exceeded the authoritarianism of the tsar which they had railed against. It is impossible to assess, ultimately, whether the forms of authority that were constructed to sustain this political system were conceived of self-consciously as tools of authoritarian control, or instead were the only way that Stalin and his cohort could conceptualize the relationship between the ruler and the ruled. The thrust of the Western Cold War ideology was to figure the Soviet Union as uniquely evil, but in many states that aspire to their own forms of "democracy"—and the USSR also called itself the most democratic country in the world—the paternal relationship and aspiration to control that we see played out under Stalin are also reflected in, for example, J. Edgar Hoover's FBI and the policy of removing Native American or Aboriginal children from their families in the United States, Canada, Australia and elsewhere.

The creation of Stalinist authority may be characterized as a product of prevailing revolutionary ideologies such as anti-imperialism and democratic populism. At the same time, the connections are obvious between Stalinist authoritarianism and the tsarist model of autocratic rule—both in the model of the paternal leader and in their totalitarian aspirations. Yet in important ways, the project of building Stalin's authority was radically new, and it is astonishing to see the prolific use of the father image in constructing the figure of the leader—though there is nothing in the concepts of communism or revolution that would sustain this. The conceptual frame that generated Stalin as state father clearly has other sources, in the conceptualization of the modern state and the logic of paternal authority itself. In creating the ideology surrounding Stalin, certain materials were drawn from Stalin's own existence as an actual family man, and his own deeds as a public figure, though the growing power of the new media in the course of Stalin's rule created new possibilities for the construction of images. The image became all-pervasive in Stalin's public persona. For example, as aviation caught hold of the public imagination in the late 1930s, Stalin was on hand to greet the pilots arriving home after a new feat, and accounts not only have him referred to as "father to the aviators," but even have the pilots addressing him as "father" (Fitzpatrick 1999: 72). This chapter explores the various dimensions of the construction of this image.

In the context of this volume, and in the world generally, the case of Stalin's model of authority is peculiar in that his demise as authoritarian leader did not correspond with the end of a regime. The Soviet Union persisted without any systematic public disavowal of Stalin's form of authority. On the contrary, Stalin himself disappeared without extensive public discourse surrounding the event, and most of the statues and portraits of Stalin that peppered the Soviet landscape vanished in the night and without official comment. Khrushchev's "secret speech" to the Twentieth Party Congress, which initiated de-Stalinization, was not presented to the Soviet public. The "Cult of Personality," which became the timid official explanation for what went wrong under Stalin, has loomed as one of the logical options to be emulated by his successors, however unconvincingly. Brezhnev and Andropov had cities named after themselves. Brezhnev had the Lenin Prize for literature awarded to himself. Brezhnev was an extraordinarily noncompelling figure as a national father figure, yet this did not discourage him from trying. He was rewarded by being made the subject of a large corpus of derisive jokes. Though no successor was able to embody the nation-father as effectively as Stalin, no strong alternative model emerged to replace it.

Conditions are most conducive to this form of authority when the regime is new. Successors cannot readily occupy the role of nation-father, though this did not prevent Stalin's successors from trying to assume the position he seemingly left vacant. Still, the form of authority that people associate with Stalin (and not with his successors) is the most compelling one today for many former-Soviet citizens, even among those who never knew Stalin's rule firsthand. This chapter also considers the emergence of new national fathers on the Stalin model in many of the Soviet successor states. The authoritarian father model lost its efficacy in the USSR after Stalin's death, and the regime was sustained subsequently by an array of other institutional mechanisms less contingent on the figure of the leader. Correspondingly, we are now faced with the question of whether these new regimes can effectively be built on the model of the nation-father in the manner of Stalin, or whether the paternal model will lose its compellingness before the current leaders meet their political or mortal ends. It is clear that such figures as President Saparmurat Niyazov of Turkmenistan, universally mocked outside of his country as an egomaniac and unabashed Stalinist, believe they can re-create the relationship between leader and population that existed under Stalin. To what extent was the model of the national father compelling because of the time of transition into a new regime under the Bolsheviks, and because of the possibilities to control the production of images that existed then? Can these conditions be re-created in the twenty-first century?

In many respects, Stalin was imminently plausible to his population as a national father. He strove for this image more deliberately and comprehensively than perhaps any of the other leaders addressed in this volume. And by many, he was held with that characteristic mixture of feeling with which fathers are often held, blending awe, esteem, fear, and submission. And yet Stalin's figure as a national father and the regime centered around him embodied crucial contradictions: the creation of a strict hierarchy of authority on the background of an ideology of revolutionary egalitarianism, the positing of a unified nation superimposed on a multinational empire, and the necessity of perpetual revolution to validate an eventually entrenched status quo.

## The Good of a State Father

In the modern age of nation-states, the tsar could no longer embody the realm. The egalitarian premise of nation-states—that each member of the nation had an equal stake in its destiny—left no room for kings except as symbolic faces of the nation. The premise of equal stakes had a powerful mobilizing force, for the realization of the nation promised to realize every individual. With communism, this egalitarian premise was intensified. The collectivization of land and addressing everyone as "comrade" promised that nobody's chances would be infringed by somebody else's status.

The father is a convenient model for strong political authority in such situations. In certain respects, the father is no different from others. The image pictures him as sharing the blood tie that unifies all members of the nation. He shares their experience and their aspirations. At the same time, the father stands above the nation—loving it, looking after its needs, and arbitrating its destiny. Stalin's image was predicated on his humble origins. He made a point of wearing worker's attire in public. The propaganda apparatus publicized pictures of him with happy industrial and collective farm workers throughout the land. The image that Soviet citizens were to envision of their leader was expressed in a poem sent by an amateur poet to the Eighteenth Party Congress in 1939:

> Heroes grow all over our land.
> And if you suddenly ask each one:
> "Tell me, who inspired your exploits?"
> With a happy smile, he will joyfully reply:
> "He who is the creator of all that is wonderful,
> The masterful architect, our friend and father
> Comrade Stalin. We are Stalin's children."
>
> —Siegelbaum and Sokolov (2000)

Meanwhile, Stalin's own status as a son was essentially without the image of a father—an opportune condition for a revolutionary. In Bolshevik ideology, lineages of authority were initially taboo. The authority of the leadership was predicated on their worthy personal qualities. Tsar Nicholas II had been conceptualized as an unfortunate happenstance—an individual who by virtue of his heredity and in spite of his own personal weakness came to head an empire and brought it to the brink of disaster with spectacular losses to the Germans in World War I. The claim to authority of Bolshevik leaders had to rest on their personal strength. Stalin himself, far from the product of a dynasty, was of shaky paternity. His father, a poor shoemaker, came from a lineage distinguished by participants in peasant rebellions in rural Georgia, but contributed to Stalin's nurturing mainly by his beatings, and Stalin's mother soon excluded him from participation in her son's life. Stalin's father, then, did not become a part of the official myth of Stalin's creation once he rose to power. Perhaps because of this, and because of a residual desire for authority based on lineage, there was much popular speculation about Stalin's actual paternity, with rumors attributing him as the offspring of various members of the Russian nobility who might have passed through his mother's village.

It is noteworthy that both Lenin and Stalin were mythologized as having "international" parentage—that is, parentage that reflected some of the diversity of the empire. With a Georgian mother, Stalin, as mentioned, might have been a Russian by his father. Lenin was thought to have Tatar, Kalmuk-Mongol, German, and Jewish heritage, though officially he was a Russian and nothing else. This unofficial mythology might have been useful in sustaining these figures' position as the leadership of the Russians, who were the leaders of the international revolution. Internationalism in the Soviet Union was an expression of loyalty to the regime, and the Soviet citizen—especially the citizen who aspired to advancement within the party—was encouraged to mix blood in his or her children to assure that there was no loyalty to a group other than that defined by Soviet communism.

Lenin and Stalin were both raised in fatherless families. Lenin's father died when Lenin was fifteen, and Stalin's was a drunkard who died when Stalin was eleven. Both Lenin and Stalin had doting mothers who sacrificed for the education of their sons. Stalin and his mother initially planned that he should be a priest—a "father" in the more modest of senses. She had to reconcile herself with him becoming first a fervent atheist, and later, a "god."

Lenin was the first father of the revolution and the Soviet state. He lived in a time when the main agenda was the destruction of traditional authority. The revolution unleashed attacks on everything traditional, from dynastic authority, to the position of the paternal figure in the traditional village community, and to the concept of family itself. The Bolsheviks often eschewed marriage, with an ideal of "free love" applied to both women and men. Part of both the appeal and the danger of the Bolshevik movement was a notion, which was broadly associated with them and which many in the leadership sustained in their own behavior, that sex would be dissociated from marriage. Tradition—most particularly, parental domination—would no longer interfere with the individual's sexual freedom (Clements 1989). This concept, which was part of the Bolshevik movement's initial program of social destabilization and revolution, was dispensed with as state ideology once the Bolsheviks moved from being a leadership of brother-comrades to state fathers.

## Dubious Succession

Lenin produced no heir, and thus no possibility for institutionalized familial authority. The only way his authority could endure beyond his death was to make him immortal. However, Lenin's authority was most useful to his successor, Stalin, if he could render his predecessor into a father-myth and then assume his position as the national father. Stalin, too, was ineffective as the genitor of a dynasty, for although he had two legitimate sons, both were beset by alcoholism and personal problems, and both died early deaths—one in a suicide after Stalin repudiated him and before Stalin's own death, and the other after a period of alcoholic degeneration that began before Stalin's demise (Richardson 1993: 167–182).

Lenin's death at the beginning of 1924—just six years after the revolution he led and only very shortly after the Bolsheviks' definitive victory in the traumatic civil war—cut short the development of Lenin's leadership as a mundane routine. Instead, he occupied the readily mythologizable position of a revolutionary leader whose shortcomings could all readily be attributed to his difficult circumstances rather than his personal failings. It was also possible to posit that he was somehow distanced from the day-to-day implementation of the revolution, especially since his last years were spent in isolated convalescence in Gorky, with his comrades filtering the realities of the political situation from him to protect his fragile health. His convalescence itself was portrayed as a heroic act, since he had suffered an assassination attempt and was generally thought of as having lived a hard life in revolutionary exile.

Lenin's final decline and death were events that could only be carefully revealed to the public. Lenin himself thought it odd how his grave illness, even after suffering a stroke, was represented to the public as a bad stomach ailment. Reports of his iron disposition appeared almost until his final demise, but his disappearance from public life and official obfuscation helped to establish the Soviet tradition of disbelief and rumor, which in his case, had him dying of syphilis. In the absence of having his own offspring, the thing imagined to bring the great man down was a presumed by-product of sexual prowess.

Lenin's early death was inopportune for the revolution, but well-timed for Stalin's rise to power. In his aspirations for death, Lenin was in line with his Bolshevik comrades, among whom there was a strong ethic of subordinating the personal to the common cause. According to this principle, the common practice was to cremate remains because there was no need for an enduring embodiment of the individual. Stalin developed a different scheme—in opposition to some of his colleagues and Lenin's own wishes—to render the person of Lenin immortal (Conquest 1991: 110). He mobilized cutting-edge mortuary technology to make Lenin into something that would last forever (Zbarsky and Hutchinson 1999). In addition, he promoted a cult of Lenin that would replace the Orthodox tradition of small household shrines decorated with icons in the homes of the population, and substitute these with shrines to Lenin, called "Lenin corners" (Tumarkin 1983: 126–127). For Lenin's eternal remains, Stalin commissioned a mausoleum, which would become the locus of public ritual for the Soviet state. For the rest of Soviet history, the public symbolization of a political figure's position in the power hierarchy was atop Lenin's monumental display case on Red Square.

At the time when Stalin was taking these initial steps to deify Lenin, he was by no means the most prominent amongst Bolshevik leadership in the public eye, and it was not clear who would succeed Lenin, nor even if there would be a single figure to succeed him. Stalin assumed the reins of power, not through public charisma and prominence, but through his clever manipulation of alliances, which entailed a different kind of charisma. When it came time to present to the Soviet people their new leader—after several years during which Stalin systematically eliminated his rivals behind the scenes—the next problem was to sculpt an image that would capture their imagination. The transformation of Lenin into a near-deity was one of the crucial tropes for the establishment of Stalin's authority. Lenin was to become the background for Stalin, as is plain in a children's verse that appeared in 1938:

> Lenin! Who does not know him?
> From the Kremlin, where he soundly sleeps,
> To the mountain tops of the blue Altai
> The glory of Lenin brightly shines.
> Higher than the mountains, wider than every sea,
> Heavier than the very earth
> Was our people's grief
> When he died, our dear one.
> Lenin died. But stronger than steel,
> Firmer than the flinty mountain races
> Came his pupil—splendid Stalin.
> He is leading us to victories and happiness.
>
> —Lane (1981: 217)

In a comprehensive study of the Lenin cult, Nina Tumarkin writes, "A regime that derives its legitimacy from a single ruler risks instability upon his death. But if after death that ruler becomes the object of a cult predicated on his continuing living power, then that cult can serve as a stabilizing force" (1983: 165). The creation of a cult of Lenin was a way of pushing him into the background and making Stalin the operative figure.

In effect, this created a new concept of a trinity modeled on the familiar one: Marx was the inspirational spirit, Lenin was the creator, and Stalin was the embodiment on earth. Nothing that Stalin did would be a contradiction of Marxism-Leninism, yet it would all be done by the person of Stalin. Tumarkin points out that even the Lenin Mausoleum, when it was completed six years after his death, was ultimately "presented to Soviet Russia as nothing more than yet another accomplishment of the Five-Year Plan.... Under Stalin's rule the cult of Lenin grew as cold and lifeless as the stone mausoleum" (206). Lenin's figure had become a platform upon which Stalin stood.

However, Tumarkin's assessment underestimates the importance of Lenin's image for Stalin's authority. Lenin remained eminently important in an attempt at creation of a new kind of dynasty. Stalin's credentials as leader were clearly conceptualized in his status as heir to Lenin. The two men together became one of the crucial images representing the formation of the regime. While Lenin was made remote, he was also put forth as eternal and omnipresent. Stalin and his successors made no attempt to displace Lenin, or to diminish him in their own favor. Rather, as "grandfather" of the nation, he became the most stable element in regime legitimacy. Even as the Soviet icons began to be torn down with glasnost in the late 1980s, many still defended Lenin as a benevolent genius whose cause was betrayed by his successors.

## Soviet Subjects

With the advent of Stalin's rule, the tasks of the revolution had changed somewhat. The dynastic realm was gone, but most of the task of a radical transformation of society was still ahead. Lenin left the Soviet Union in the midst of the New Economic Policy (1921–1928), which in many ways was merely a reconfiguration of capitalism. The creation of a communist society—the end of private property, the collectivization of agriculture, the rapid industrialization, the eradication of feudal cultural carryovers, including the paternalistic family and the opiate of religion—still remained to be executed. The radical transformation of the family included a prescription that families should be nuclear, and this was accompanied by concepts of communal living, reduction of parental authority, and autonomy of the children. Loyalty to the state should exceed loyalty to parents, as exemplified by the figure of Pavlik Morozov, whom all children were to revere for his famous betrayal of his counter-revolutionary parents (see Fitzpatrick 1999: 73).

The state took over important roles of child nurturing, with proliferation of preschools for small children and the obligatory participation in the Pioneer organization, where state values were inculcated. In an extreme form that would be replicated in other Soviet bloc countries, orphans—many of them created by a system that uprooted and destroyed whole segments of society—became the children of the state. The communist ideal was lived out in large orphanages that could accomplish the otherwise unachievable task of eliminating all intermediaries between the individual and the authority of the state.

The problems of social transformation were intensified a decade into Stalin's rule with Germany's invasion. To make himself a compelling figure for the population, new tactics were employed drawing in part on the tsarist Russian tradition and in part on modern egalitarian images to create a father-leader that was at once distant and severely controlling and at the same time benevolent and penetratingly intimate. Photographs of Stalin receiving flowers from children, and especially kissing his own daughter, were among the rather monotonous images of the leader that the population was constantly shown.

Stalin's image as father was also built on the notion of the military family: the father with his boys undertaking a task of sacrifice for the family and posterity. So much of Stalin's leadership was framed as a warrior struggle: first the revolution growing into cultural revolution, the building of socialism, the campaigns for electrification, collectivization, industrialization, and against Trotskyite and other heresies, and later, the war against German aggression, Japanese spies, and so forth. In his authority as father, he could call upon the nation's sons to sacrifice their lives if necessary. Many perished in Stalin's repressions, thinking that of course certain people must perish for the cause, but they personally had been chosen for this fate by mistake.

The impact of this image was intensified by some particularities of the Soviet system. The creation of Soviet society was thoroughly predicated on the destruction of what went before it. Instead of church, community—even family—citizens were called upon to place themselves in Soviet comradeship. The state penetrated downward toward ordinary people through the establishment of collective and state farms and the incorporation of all enterprise into the state. People's lives were stripped bare of other connections by civil war, rapid industrialization, repression, and other disruptions, and they were drawn out of disjointed desperation toward the image of Stalin as father and the collective family offered by the state under him. Stalin personified the state, which assumed ever increasing importance in people's lives.

The war greatly increased other trends that were developing in the structure of the family as well. First, the emancipation of women, already a part of the Soviet program of social transformation, was greatly pushed forward by the necessity of women's involvement in the war economy, making women less dependent on men in the household economy and more dependent on the state. The role of men was further diminished by their physical absence and ultimate elimination. Between the civil war, collectivization, the great repressions of 1928–1937, and World War II, an entire generation of men was effectively decimated. Since then, the Soviet family—especially in the European parts of the USSR—has never been the same. Later it was alcoholism and male irresponsibility which helped to sustain the norm that the family would have at its core a woman who could not rely on men but instead was dependent on the state to guarantee the family's well-being.

## A Peculiar Sort of Nation

In contrast to the founders of many modern states, the Bolsheviks were not nationalists, and what they took over was not some nation-fragment of an empire, but rather an empire nearly in its entirety. Thus, the collectivity to which Stalin sought to appeal was not a nation in the usual sense. This was potentially destructive of his image as father to a unified family. This problem would seem to have been compounded by the fact that soon after the establishment of the Soviet government, it diminished the state's unity by dividing off parts of the empire as national republics.

Yet the Soviet government sought to establish a notion of Soviet citizenry as a common collectivity, and it achieved this goal to a remarkable degree. It promoted a concept called the *Sovetskii narod*—the Soviet people—which was understood to be a new kind of collectivity. This, with the help of socialism, would overcome national distinctions. It is often asserted that the Soviet nationalities policy failed to produce the "New Soviet Man" since people retained cultural differences and distinct identities. However, there is a very real sense in which the consciousness of a common Soviet collectivity was achieved. The image of Stalin as father of the nation was key to the formation of this collectivity.

For example, the sacrifices that virtually everyone made during the war—ranging from combat to starvation—were made in the name of Stalin and the Soviet people, and not some smaller national entity. It is a measure of the strength of this image that, in some ways, it endures intact to this day. It may be that the Baltic states have abandoned the exercise of celebrating the Soviet victory because they don't see the Soviet victory as their victory. But, for example, when Tajikistan continues to celebrate the anniversary of the war's end, there was little talk asserting that this war was Russia's war, not Tajikistan's. Tajiks fought to defend the Soviet people as a whole. In Tajikistan, the worth of having defended the Soviet Union has not diminished ten years after independence, and the combatants in that war are considered more worthy of commemoration than those who fought in the post-Soviet civil war.

That Stalin was a Georgian did not disrupt this image of a "national father," in fact, it may have enhanced it. The interchangeability of a non-Russian leader for a Russian meant that blood was not the decisive criterion. Meanwhile, Stalin did very little to indicate that he was not a Russian. During World War II, Stalin took on the qualities of a Russian nationalist, evidently supposing that this might enhance the Russians' willingness to sacrifice for the Fatherland. The "Great Russian people" was celebrated as the "leading" people of the USSR, and Russian culture was praised as lavishly as Stalin himself (Martin 2001). The Russian Orthodox Church came to occupy an extraordinary position in spite of the militant atheism of the Bolshevik state. At the same time, national symbols of other Soviet peoples were also given public emphasis in a way that earlier would have drawn criticism as "bourgeois nationalism." Western observers have called this an obvious, cynical bid to mobilize popularity, but it seems it had precisely the desired effect: to encourage loyalty, not to narrow concepts of nation, but to the Soviet people and its great historic struggle against fascism.

The image of Stalin as father thus sustained a tremendous amount of paradox. He was leader in a land that promised national self-realization to all of those formerly captured in the so-called "Prison House of Peoples" under the tsars. New national languages and cultures were codified and promoted, yet Russian culture was clearly dominant. Stalin's image was as an internationalist father, in spite of his being a Russified Georgian.

Furthermore, the Bolshevik regime continually defined itself as a radical break from the tsarist government, yet Stalin's leadership was increasingly defined with the same attributes as the tsars' leadership had been. He became increasingly aloof and regal. He played up images of military leadership reminiscent of the tsars. And in the same way that much of the Bolshevik government's imagery placed Stalin in the same symbolic frames once occupied by the tsars, much of the new Soviet government's administrative practice was drawn directly and obviously from tsarist models—the structure of administrative departments, the role of the secret police, and so on (Ulam 1973: 523). During World War II, the Red Army abandoned many of the qualities that had distinguished it from the tsar's army: the lack of officers' privileges, the rank of general, and so forth. Frequent reference was made to great tsars as glorious figures of Russian history, emphasized as the patrimony of the contemporary Soviet state. The tsars, too, had been conceived of as fathers to their people, and Stalin increasingly drew on this more distant, more exalted paternal model.

The war played a crucial role in creating the image of Stalin in a number of ways. Victory was personified in Stalin, and soldiers were asked to fight for him as much as for national survival. But the war also served a key role in achieving the disruption of traditional social order that the construction of the Soviet state sought to achieve, particularly in the realm of the family, with the increasing displacement of the functions of the family by the state. That this was congenial to Stalin's strategy for building the new Soviet society is apparent in that instead of attempting to rebuild society by welcoming the return of soldiers who had been in German captivity, Stalin intensified the disruption by sending many thousands of returning soldiers off to Siberia on the pretext that their capture by the Germans indicated treason.

With the millions of Soviet citizens that suffered various forms of repression under Stalin, there is a problem of how the image of a benevolent father could be sustained. Many people refused to believe that Stalin had a role in the repressions, accepting instead that they were the deeds of underlings, of which the leader was unaware. Of course, many of those who suffered purges were precisely those who had been functionaries implementing the previous round of repressions, so people might imagine that gradually the culprits were being caught. The belief was almost universal that indeed the West was determined to destroy the "First Socialist State," and all sorts of sabotage could readily be imagined. Even those who attributed the horrors of Stalinism to Stalin himself commonly fell under the spell of adulation of the leader who so dominated their lives. In the traditional family of the Russians and other Soviet peoples, the figure of the father was a severe one. Russian folklore is riddled with aphorisms to the effect that you don't really know if a man loves you unless he beats you.

## Stalin's Death

When Stalin died, there was only one previous model for the death of a Soviet head-of-state. Lenin had had a much more transient presence as a Soviet leader, and at the time of his death the Soviet state was still quite new. Lenin's living image had been quite unlike Stalin's, whose rule had penetrated concretely into everyone's lives. Thus, the dead Lenin was ripe for a particular kind of mythologizing. He would be rendered into a symbol of Bolshevik enthusiasm, sagacity, and purity. His corpse, on display in its tomb, was an object of purity, seemingly unaffected by the corruption of death. A shrine was built to him on Red Square, and the populace would visit his enduring physical presence, and see with their own eyes the image that was now portrayed everywhere, alongside of Marx and Engels, as well as Stalin, who embodied these deities in life.

Lenin, on death, was quickly turned into a distant, yet warm figure. He was assigned the status of grandfather—all Soviet children would eventually learn to call him "Grandfather Lenin" with the proper affection. He became a dead ancestor. He was kept alive in the hearts of the people, by visits to shrines constructed everywhere to honor him. The place that had formerly been occupied by icons and candles in people's homes—now in schools and club as well—was occupied by the so-called Lenin Corners composed of icons of him as well as mass-produced artifacts of his life. Lenin museums were built in all of the capitals of union republics. His name was on everyone's lips and written everywhere. His bald head and goatee were rendered into an iconic stamp that appeared on every newspaper and currency note. His various determined poses proliferated in statues before public buildings and in portraits and busts in every public space.

In life, Stalin had been placed in some of the same symbolic frames that Lenin already occupied in death. Marxism-Leninism had become a triumvirate with Stalinism. Lenin and Stalin stood together as young geniuses and revolutionaries. But next to Lenin, Stalin was swarthy, dark, and hairy. The plan had been to keep Stalin next to Lenin in death, but this was actually impossible. Lenin's persistent presence in death was to accompany the continuing revolution. He was the one who conceived it, and his image provided ongoing inspiration. Stalin, by contrast, was chiefly the one who executed the revolution. His actions were pervasive in Soviet life, and this same role could not be sustained in his death—or so thought his successors.

The original plan had been to build a huge new shrine to Lenin and Stalin on Red Square. Within days of Stalin's death, however, plans were changing on how to deal with his remains. Within a couple of weeks, newspapers, which had been full of him for years, began to mention his name much less frequently. A new edition of a standard Russian dictionary appeared scarcely a week after his death with the entry "Stalinist" having been removed. The newsreel footage shot of his funeral was not to be shown anywhere (Bortoli 1975: 175). Stalin's death, in spite of his advanced age and the obvious deterioration of his health, has been the object of conspiracy theories—something only broached by Soviet authors after the end of the Soviet Union (Radzinsky 1996: 566–578). Though after a lengthy embalming, he was placed alongside of Lenin in the tomb in November 1953, eight years later in 1961 his body was removed and placed in the Kremlin wall with other Bolshevik heroes, but only with a simple stone marker, later modestly complemented with a bust.

The public grieving at Stalin's death is famous. In the Western formulaic myth-narrative of his death, the motif is always mentioned that people whom Stalin had put in Siberian prison labor camps wept at the news of his loss. There must have been colossal doubt and confusion as to what would happen next.

It was time for Stalin's close circle to attempt to usurp him—to eat his body and attempt thereby to re-embody him. This proved to be rather indigestible fare, however. It was a relatively simple matter to remove the physical signs of Stalin, and this began soon after his death and proceeded with great vigor in 1956 following Khrushchev's "secret speech." Khrushchev sought a domestic profile with his campaign to grow maize wherever it would sprout, and he cut a bold international figure as he threatened the United States with missiles in Cuba, and as he beat his shoe on the table at the UN. Efforts to displace Stalin as the nation's father were unsuccessful, and Stalin's authoritative presence in Soviet politics endured long after Khrushchev's had vanished (Volkogonov 1991).

In any case, there could not have been an immediate successor to Stalin who assumed his aura as the nation's father, unless he had first been assigned the aura as Stalin's son—which Stalin had been careful never to do. Even usurpation by a son is problematic for he must aspire to the beloved and respected position which the nation-family had held for the father, and which they may be reluctant to accord to the son. There was no precedence for a happy transfer of this role in Soviet experience. Tsar Nicholas's slaughtered body was deliberately lost, lest it come back to interfere. Lenin had abandoned his country in crisis by his early death from disease, and Stalin usurped his role as leader in the mayhem without having to explain the act to a broader public.

Brezhnev was in an easier position than Khrushchev had been, because he did not have to be responsible for an act of patricide in the usurpation of Stalin. On the contrary, the image of Stalin was free to transform Brezhnev. Although he never assumed the figure of father in the way that Stalin had, Brezhnev was assigned some such attributes by his political milieu. Like Stalin, he sought to seem a man of ordinary roots, and yet attempted to maintain an image of wisdom and aloofness. Lenin and Stalin were configured as the purveyors of wisdom, with their collected works published in massive and frequent editions, and Brezhnev similarly was put forward as a man of literary gifts and theoretical wisdom, and his collected works were available in every bookstore alongside those of Lenin and Marx. Some of the same adulation was accorded to Brezhnev as to his predecessors, though it was devoid of sincerity. Instead, he became famous for his simplicity, his slurred speech, and a public appearance of stupor, which increased with age. The image of the father was draped over him, but he was unable to give it life.

## Newer Stalins and Musical Corpses

Stalin's paternal model, meanwhile, has occasionally been more inspirational. First secretaries of republican communist parties occasionally enjoyed personality cults reminiscent of Stalin's. For example, Sharaf Rashidov, the Brezhnev-era leader of Uzbekistan (1959–1983), acquired a form of authority similar to Stalin's, as did Dinmuhammed Kunaev, Kazakhstan's First Party Secretary (1959–1962, 1964–1986). Under Brezhnev, republican leaders were given considerable autonomy, and thus, the opportunity to promote their authority locally. However, this was always tempered by their subordinate and dependent status in relation to rule from Moscow. Both of these leaders were discredited by the Gorbachev regime under perestroika, but both have been rehabilitated by the post-independence regimes, and given net status as the worthy predecessors of the independent leaders. In the case of Rashidov, his burial place also became a point of contention, much like that of Stalin and the last tsar. Rashidov died in 1983, bringing his twenty-four-year rule to an end, and was buried in a prominent public location in Uzbekistan's capital, later to be removed when he was accused of corruption. The current regime in Uzbekistan has revised Rashidov's status again, however, and although the former grave remains empty, a statue has been erected, a major avenue has been given his name, and his birthday has become a public celebration. Similarly, Kunayev has had a street named after him in Almaty, and those who were killed in demonstrations opposing his ouster have been officially honored as martyrs.

The post-independence years, meanwhile, have seen a much more dramatic burgeoning of regimes modeled on Stalinist paternal authority. The most impressive case is that of President Saparmurat Niyazov of Turkmenistan, who has styled himself as *Turkmenbashi*—i.e., father or leader of the Turkmens. This title caries echoes of Mustafa Kemal's chosen epithet of Atatürk—Father of the Turks. Niyazov has imitated Stalin in a great many ways, including not only his penchant for eliminating all opposition and his aspiration to bring the country's citizens under nearly total control. The echoes of the Stalin personality cult are apparent in the proliferation of images and statues of the leader, the multitude of entities that have been given his name, vanity engineering projects such as the creation of the "Turkmen Sea" to be established in the middle of the Qara Qum desert. Like Stalin, Niyazov has issued works that are meant to be read by every citizen for guidance. He declared his book, entitled *Ruhname*, to be comparable to the Bible or the Qur'an, with the purpose to "determine the main criteria for the development of the Turkmen people and their moral qualities in the 21st century" (AFP 2001). Under Niyazov, applicants to university are required to declare their allegiance to "the Great Saparmurat, Father of the Turkmen" (Ashirova 2002). In his own variation on the Soviet Era interventions into the sphere of the family, Niyazov declared that foreigners seeking to marry a Turkmen woman would have to pay the state $50,000 in *kalim*, or bride wealth. In his own version of calendrical reform reminiscent of moves made by French and Russian revolutionaries, Niyazov has moved to have all the months and days of the week renamed, giving his own adopted name of Turkmenbashi to the month of January.

Other post-Soviet leaders have been more restrained, but the model upon which they seek to build their authority is much the same. President Emamali Rahmanov of Tajikistan has sought to draw parallels between himself and the founder of the Samanid dynasty, which is figured as the "first Tajik state" in history, whereas Rahmanov's own regime is portrayed as the second Tajik state. Many of the post-Soviet leaders have followed Stalin and Brezhnev in producing books containing their wisdom. Even President Askar Akaev of Kyrgyzstan, who otherwise aspires to a relatively democratic model, has published works that are distributed by the country's embassies as the essential wisdom of the president. Akaev has aspired to a mythical legitimacy, much like other post-Soviet leaders, by drawing links between himself and the medieval "progenitor" of the Kyrgyz people, in the legendary figure of Manas, subject of the most famous epic of the Kyrgyz people. In the ceremony connected with his second presidential inauguration, President Nursultan Nazarbayev of Kazakhstan had himself elevated on a white carpet, in a reference to the ritual by which past Kazakh khans were raised to the position of leadership of their people. Similar to Turkmenbashi in Turkmenistan, Nazarbayev has designated himself as "El Bashi," or leader/father of the homeland. President Karimov of Uzbekistan, like his colleagues, seeks to present a public image of the father of the nation, looking after his people, at times in a firm authoritarian manner, but always as an engaged paternal figure.

In very important senses, the dominant conceptions of legitimate authority thus have not changed. Though Stalin was replaced politically, and ferreted away physically, his model of authority remains one of the most compelling, particularly for those who were born during his rule. The weak leaders who have followed have failed to generate new, compelling models. Amongst those who lament the passing of the Soviet Union, it is Stalin, even above Lenin, who is seen as the model of redemption. It is not certain that Stalin cannot again be resuscitated.

After the retreat of Stalin's corpse from Lenin's tomb, the Soviet leadership was more careful about where it placed its deceased. No one was mummified, or even given a prominent grave. Still, the old graves and cadavers have presented some persistent dilemmas for Russia's leadership. With de-Stalinization, even the more modest placement of Stalin's grave has presented the leadership with some embarrassment, as Stalin's grave is more often visited with spontaneous devotion than that of any other Soviet leader aside from Lenin. With the withdrawal of communist ideology already more than a decade ago, Lenin still cannot be denied his position of prominence amidst the symbols of Russian statehood. No longer is there the massive stream of people passing through the tomb to get a glimpse of the chemically preserved state icon. But it is still impossible to displace this image. Former President Yeltsin, in his bid to distance himself from his own communist past and that of his society, suggested on several occasions that the time had come for Lenin to go, but these suggestions have not been taken up. The debate about relocating Lenin's remains has been a focus of tremendous political symbolism, much as other corpses have been in contention in the wake of communist political legitimacy (Verdery 1999). In April 1997, the Russian Duma (Parliament) passed a resolution denouncing the government's intentions to displace Lenin from Red Square. In the previous month, an underground leftist group blew up the only standing Russian monument to Tsar Nicholas II in protest of the government's plans, as they put it, to "profane a national shrine" by removing Lenin's remains (RFE/RL Newsline 1997). The issue has subsequently been on hold; the power of Lenin's body as a symbol of continuity and legitimacy is yet too strong.

Meanwhile, another corpse has reappeared on the Russian political scene. An excavation, drawing on the authority of foreign forensic experts, has reproduced the bodies of the last tsar and his murdered family from the nongrave that the Bolsheviks had left them in. But what is to be done? Many symbols of the continuity of Russian statehood from pre-Soviet times have been given new prominence, but there is an ongoing debate about what kind of prominence the tsar's body can be given. The Orthodox Church itself has latched onto this issue to promote its own image of sanctity, for although Nicholas II was canonized as a saint in 2000, the Church opposed any reburial, raising doubts about the authenticity of the remains. Ultimately, the political authorities prevailed, and the remains of the members of the imperial family, murdered by the Bolsheviks on 17 July 1918, were reburied in the Romanov dynasty's family vault on the eightieth anniversary of their deaths.

## How to Finally Kill Stalin?

The experience of the post-Stalin years has only served to enhance the legitimacy of Stalin's model of authority in the eyes of many of the inhabitants of the former Soviet Union. It has often been supposed by Westerners and the indigenous intelligentsia that if people simply knew all of the terrible things that Stalin did to attain power, then he would be rejected as a valid model. The cause of the Soviet population's acceptance of authoritarian rule is thus assumed to be their ignorance and their inability to understand proper legitimate political authority. But underlying this assessment is the assumption that as leaders and citizens make their judgment of what constitutes compellingly legitimate political order, they are counterposing the love of freedom and the affinity for order—and many are assumed to be favoring the order, however authoritarian it might be. However, in the Soviet case, as indeed in others, the choice is not being made between true, enlightened leadership and a mythical paternal alternative. Rather, the model of political authority is created and given credence because the image of the nation-father is compelling. Leaders and populations alike find that they have no other way to think about how political authority can be constituted.

The conditions of the new regime in the twentieth century conjured the image of the nation-father. Lenin could be supplanted by Stalin as leader through a transformation of the former into a new kind of image, more removed and eternal, like the image of a god. Stalin, as the crafter of state and society, could not be made so ethereal so as to get him out of the way, and thus, the options for new authority under his successors were greatly limited. They could not assume his position as nation-father, nor could they devise an alternative form of authority with which to replace it. In effect, though Stalinism was not meaningfully repudiated by the subsequent Soviet regime, the effective paternal regime ended, though aspirations to this form of paternal authority persisted. As a result, post-Stalin authority in the Soviet leadership was inherently unstable, and the end of Stalin contained the seeds of the end of the Soviet regime.

The persistent compellingness of the paternal model echoes now across the former-Soviet space. Various political systems, following their own newly independent trajectories, gravitate in one way or another toward this paternal model. Because the regimes are in some sense new—despite the continuity of personnel from the communist system to the current one—the model works to some extent. Yet the disintegration of this form of authority appears inevitable with the advent of successors, or even with the aging of the current regimes. While the model itself may remain compelling, it may be impossible for anyone to render the model into life.

Is it the case, then, that current conditions make such a model of leadership impossible in the former Soviet space? A crucial element of Stalin's rule was his ability to implement in large measure the goal of state control over all aspects of society. This is probably impossible in a political domain where it has become difficult to silence all dissenting voices, and where power grows out of a complex array of social institutions. Another crucial element was that Stalin had the opportunity to create a new regime unencumbered by explicit continuity with its predecessor. Meanwhile, it is another question whether credible alternative models of political authority will be found that can decisively destroy the legitimacy of Stalin's model. The death of Stalin's model has been very halting and slow. His portrait is being lifted now by a generation who may never get a chance to enjoy his rule.

# References

Abuladze, Tenghiz. 1986. *Monanieba* [Repentance; in Russian, *Pokaianie*]. Feature film, 151 minutes, in Georgian. Tbilisi: Gruziia fil'm.

AFP (Agence France Presse). 2001. "Turkmenistan: Citizens Given 'Great Book' to Improve Spiritual Lives." *Agence France Presse*, 20 February.

Ashirova, Chemen. 2002. "Personality Cult in Turkmenistan's Universities." *Primanews*, 17 July. Available online at: http://www.prima-news.ru/eng/news/articles/2002/7/17/16274.html [accessed on 17/7/2002].

Bortoli, Georges. 1975. *The Death of Stalin*. [Originally published as *Mort de Staline*, 1974]. New York: Praeger.

Clements, Barbara Evens. 1989. "The Birth of the New Soviet Woman." In *Bolshevik Culture: Experiment and Order in the Russian Revolution*, ed. Abbot Gleason et al., pp. 220–237. Bloomington: Indiana University Press.

Conquest, Robert. 1991. *Stalin: Breaker of Nations*. London: Weidenfeld and Nicolson.

Fitzpatrick, Sheila. 1999. *Everyday Stalinism*. New York and Oxford: Oxford University Press.

Lane, Christel. 1981. *The Rites of Rulers: Ritual in Industrial Society—the Soviet Case*. Cambridge: Cambridge University Press.

Martin, Terry. 2001. *The Affirmative Action Empire: Nations and Nationalism in the Soviet Union, 1923–1939*. Ithaca: Cornell University Press.

Radzinsky, Edvard. 1996. *Stalin: The First In-depth Biography Based on Explosive New Documents from Russia's Secret Archives*. New York: Doubleday.

RFE/RL Newsline. 1997. "Duma Opposes Lenin Reburial." RFE/RL *Newsline* (Prague), 3 April.

Richardson, Rosamond. 1993. *Stalin's Shadow: Inside the Family of One of the World's Greatest Tyrants*. New York: St. Martin's Press.

Sigelbaum, Lewis, and Andrei Sokolov. 2000. *Stalinism as a Way of Life: A Narrative in Documents*. New Haven and London: Yale University Press.

Tumarkin, Nina. 1983. *Lenin Lives! The Lenin Cult in Soviet Russia*. Cambridge: Harvard University Press.

Ulam, Adam B. 1973. *Stalin: The Man and His Era*. London: Allen Lane.

Verdery, Katherine. 1999. *The Political Lives of Dead Bodies: Reburial and Postsocialist Change*. New York: Columbia University Press.

Volkogonov, Dmitri. 1991. *Stalin: Triumph and Tragedy*. New York: Grove Weidenfeld.

Zbarsky, Ilya, and Samuel Hutchinson. 1999. *Lenin's Embalmers*. London: Harvill Press.

# Notes on Contributors to the
# Death of the Father Project

**John Borneman** is professor of anthropology at Princeton University in Princeton, New Jersey. He received his Ph.D. in 1989 from Harvard University, and specializes in political and legal anthropology. He has written widely on national identification in Germany and on the relation of culture to international order. He is currently working on problems of individual and group accountability.

**Tone Bringa** is senior research fellow at Chr. Michelsen Institute at the University of Bergen, Norway. She received her Ph.D. in 1991 from The London School of Economics and Political Science. She has worked on issues relating to religion, ethnicity, coexistence, and conflict in the former Yugoslavia and in Bosnia-Herzegovina since 1987. Her 1993 documentary, *We Are All Neighbors* (Grenada TV), about the effect of war on families, friendships, and neighborhoods in an ethnically mixed village in Bosnia, won several international awards. In 1995, she worked as policy analyst for United Nations peacekeeping operations in Croatia and Bosnia, and has been an expert witness to the International Criminal Tribunal for the former Yugoslavia in The Hague.

**Maria Pia Di Bella**, anthropologist at the Centre National de Recherche Social (CNRS-CRAL/EHESS) in Paris, France, received her Ph.D. in 1973 from the Ecole Pratique des Hautes Etudes, and specializes in the relation between religion and law. She has completed major projects on Pentecostalism in southern rural Italy and on the relation of justice to piety through the popular sanctification of executed criminals in Sicily, and has written widely on themes relating to the strategies of speech, the body and pain, and religious and legal practices. Her most recent project compares work on capital punishment in Europe and the United States after World War II.

**Linda Fisher** is a composer/audiovisual artist and web designer in Ithaca, New York. She has worked for many years as an independent interdisciplinary artist and videographer, with interests that embrace the interface between art, scholasticism, and technology. She has a background in software design and the construction and use of custom-designed electronic and non-electronic musical instruments and theatrical props, and has toured both the United States and Europe in performance of her solo and ensemble works. She has also taught analog and digital synthesis in the music program at Vassar College.

Kyung-Koo Han is professor of social anthropology at Kookmin University in Seoul, South Korea. He received his Ph.D. in 1991 from Harvard University, and specializes in the relations of ideology, labor relations, and political structure in postwar Japan and Korea. He has recently completed studies on structural change in Japan, the consumption of culture, and the impact of globalization on Korean society, and he is in charge of the "culture" section in a long-term joint Korea-Japan study sponsored by the Center of Asiatic Studies at Korea University and the Japan Foundation of Japan.

Baber Johansen is Directeur d'études, Ecole des Haute Etudes en Sciences Sociales, in Paris, France. He specializes in the history of Islamic law, especially the period from the ninth to the twelfth centuries, but also works on contemporary topics, including modern intellectual life and jurisprudence of twentieth-century Arab courts. He has lectured extensively at American and European universities, and his works on Islam and Islamic law have been published in many languages, including French, German, Arabic, and English. From 1972 to 1995 he was professor of Islamwissenschaft at the Free University of Berlin (Germany).

David A. Kideckel is professor of anthropology, Central Connecticut State University in New Britain, Connecticut. He received his Ph.D. in 1979 from the University of Massachusetts, Amherst, Massachusetts, and specializes in comparative political economy with a focus on rural life. He has written widely on regional and local social change during and after the socialist period in Eastern and Central Europe. His current research focuses on transformations in the physical lives and perceptions of workers in the former state socialist sector of two regions in Romania.

John S. Schoeberlein is director of the Central Asian Project and research associate of the Russian Research Center at Harvard University in Cambridge, Massachusetts. He received his Ph.D. in 1991 from Harvard University, and specializes in ethnic and cultural identity and its relation to changes in political form in the southern republics of the former Soviet Union.

Noni Korf Vidal is digital projects archivist and curator for Visual and Electronic Collections, Division of Rare Books and Manuscript Collections of Kroch Library, at Cornell University in Ithaca, New York. She designs and manages several digital projects and specializes in multimedia imaging.

# Index

Ceauşescu, Elena: as scholar, 18, 129, 130, 145n. 14; execution, 2, 26, 123–124, 134–135; grave, 2, 136–137; personality cult, 124, 131–132, 145n. 14, 144n. 7; in politics, 127, 128, 131–132, 143, 144n. 10; trial, 2, 26–27, 134–135, 137; as "wicked mother," 17

Ceauşescu, Nicolae: anecdotes and jokes about, 123, 144n. 12; as author/scholar, 18, 130–131; corpse, 2, 136; death, vi, 2, 19, 26, 123–124, 125, 133–136, 137, 142, 143; in genitor role, 20–21, 25, 127–130, 131, 142, 143; execution, 2, 19, 26, 123–124, 125, 129, 134–135, 136–137, 142; family, 129, 131–133, 144–145n. 13; grave, 2, 136–137; legacy of, 136–143, 144n. 9, 145n. 20; mourning for, 136, 137; in pater role, 17, 25, 127, 128, 131, 143; personality cult, 124, 127–131, 137, 144n. 11; policies of, 126–127, 128–129, 133, 143, 144n. 4; rehabilitation, 135, 136–137; trial, 2, 26–27, 134–135, 137

Ceauşescu, Nicu, 132, 144n. 13
Chernenko, Konstantin, 202
Chetnik movement, 150, 178, 183, 186, 188, 196n. 4
Chile, 3, 70
China, People's Republic of, 3, 20, 26, 105, 127
China, Republic of (Taiwan), 105, 113, 127
Chirot, Daniel, 28
Christian Democratic Union (CDU), 70, 72
Christianity, 5, 7, 11, 43–44, 68, 73, 75, 76, 94, 98n. 9, 100n. 19, 101n. 23, 105, 110, 132, 150, 174, 185, 188, 191, 197n. 11, 198n. 29, 199n. 48, 208–209, 212, 217
Christo and Jean-Claude, 93
Churchill, Winston, 150
Ciano, Galeazzo, 46, 47
Cioaba, Florin, 141
civil society, 141
class, 11, 14, 68, 74, 77, 79, 86–87, 92, 93, 107, 108, 111, 130, 136, 139, 154, 183, 186, 190

Coco, Francesco, 56
co-dependence, 8, 74, 76, 94, 95
Cold War, vi, 7–8, 64, 84–88, 91, 93–94, 105, 126–127, 144n. 4, 151, 169, 170, 203, 214
collectivization (of agriculture), 133, 205, 209, 210
Comaneci, Nadia, 132
Cominform, 151, 162, 197n. 14
communism, vi–viii, 1, 7, 17, 21–22, 26, 50, 58n. 13, 70, 105, 125, 127, 130, 143, 144n. 4, 144n. 9, 145n. 13, 149–150, 151, 153, 155, 158, 160–165, 169, 172, 178, 183, 190, 203, 205, 206, 209, 210, 215, 217, 218. *See also* state socialism
Communist Party: Italian, 50, 55; Romanian, 124–125, 129, 130–131, 133–134, 137, 138, 144n. 1; Serbian, 175, 181; of Soviet Union, 26, 149, 197n. 14, 201, 202, 204, 205, 206, 215; of Yugoslavia, 149, 151, 160, 162, 163, 164, 165, 167, 169, 170, 173–174, 178, 181, 182, 186, 187, 197n. 17, 198n. 22
Communist Youth League, 155, 156, 167
Confucianism, 110
conjugal couple, 8, 13, 19–20, 24, 29n. 3, 71, 75, 81, 83, 91, 107, 131
conspiracy theories, 115, 118, 134–135, 174, 214
Constantinescu, Emil, 125, 138
Constitutional Court (Germany), 71–72, 91, 93, 94, 95
Constitutional Police (West Germany), 66
consumption, 85, 94, 135, 136, 142, 144n. 8, 161, 165, 170
Corpo Volontari della Liberta, 51
corpse: of Bismark, 68; of Ceaucescu, 2, 136; exhumation: of Emperor Taisho, 117; of Frederick II, 67–67; of Hitler, 2, 63–65; of Honecker, 72; of Lenin, 2, 25, 201, 207–208, 213, 217; of Mussolini, 2, 25, 50–55, 59n. 20; of Prince Lazar, 185; of Nicholas II, 202, 214, 217–218; of Stalin, 2, 201, 202, 213–214, 217; of Strauss,

state *(cont.)*
  nation-state model, 12–13, 74–75,
    107, 148, 155, 174, 178, 185, 191,
    205; *Rechtsstaat* (state of law), 75,
    81, 84, 93; and stateless societies,
    22–23, 24; *Volksstaat* (state of peo-
    ple), 81, 84; welfare, 13, 86
Stauffenberg, Claus, Graf Schenk von, 95
Steakley, James, 78
Stepinac, Cardinal, 150
Strauss, Franz Josef, 67, 68–69
Stuckart, Wilhelm, 80
subject, modern, 3–4, 12–15, 17, 19, 24,
    28, 29n. 5, 84, 155, 209; subjectivity,
    3, 12, 13, 90
suicide, 2, 10, 25, 186, 207; of Hitler
    and Eva Braun, 2, 19, 21, 25, 63–65,
    67, 84
Sukarno, 3
Sulis, Edgardo, 42
surveillance, 7, 105, 179
Switzerland, 47, 49, 57n. 5
symbolic: form, vi–ix, 2–3, 10, 12, 23,
    65, 75, 88; identification, crisis of, 1,
    13, 24, 116; symbolic register/order,
    15–18, 23–24, 26, 71–73; symboliza-
    tion, 2, 6, 9–10, 16, 34, 38, 69, 76, 77,
    79, 81, 82–83, 89, 90, 105, 109, 111,
    114, 124, 142, 148–149, 156, 173, 176,
    181, 186, 187, 191, 201, 205, 208,
    212–213, 217 *See also* image
Syria, 3

Tajikistan, 211, 216
Taylor, Charles, 14
temporality, 12, 18, 22, 35, 107, 115,
    117–118, 184, 188–189 gengo system
    (Japan), 113, 115, 117; holidays/dates,
    12, 66, 100n. 16, 114, 118, 121n. 8,
    137, 154, 156–157, 171, 184, 185; his-
    tory, political use of, 18, 21, 94, 126,
    127, 130, 137, 153, 181, 184, 186,
    188, 212
Țepeș, Vlad, 125, 127, 134
territory, 174, 176, 185
terrorism, 55–56, 87, 149, 217
Third World, 7, 126
Thompson, Mark, 168, 197n. 17
Țiriac, Ion, 141,

Tito, Josip Broz: birthplace, 149, 155,
    178–179, 182; corpse, 183, 184, 187;
    calls for disinterment of, 183;
    death, vi, viii, 2, 22, 27, 148–149,
    152, 155, 157, 158, 160, 161,
    164–165, 166–172, 173, 174, 175,
    179–180, 186, 190, 192, 193, 198n.
    23; demythologization, 27–28, 158,
    168, 174, 178–180, 183–184, 192; fic-
    tional resurrection, 179–180;
    funeral, 2, 167–169, 185; in genitor
    role, 20, 21–22, 25, 127, 154,
    159–162; grave, 168–169, 183–184;
    legacy in different former Yugoslav
    republics, 27–28, 158, 172–174,
    178–189, 190–193, 197n. 12, 199n.
    45, 199n. 46; marriages and family,
    20, 159–161, 166; Milošević and
    Tudjman as "illegitimate sons" of,
    27, 161, 180–183, 184, 186–187;
    mourning for, 27, 167–171, 179, 180,
    192; in pater role, 21–22, 25, 27, 154,
    159–162; period as partisan, 20, 148,
    150–151, 153, 154–155, 158, 162, 164,
    168, 172, 174, 178, 181, 184, 186,
    189, 196n. 3, 198n. 32; personality
    cult of, 152–154, 156–159, 161, 162,
    166–173, 178, 182, 192, 195, 197n.
    18, 198n. 29; project of "brother-
    hood and unity," 2, 20, 22, 153–155,
    156, 163, 171, 187, 191; relationship
    to Stalin, 151, 196n. 5, 197n. 14; resi-
    dences of, 152–153, 168, 182, 188,
    196n. 7, 196–197n. 8; speech
    (dialect) of, 155, 197n. 13; Yugoslav
    model of, 162–164, 171–174,
    187–193, 198n. 33
Togliatti, Palmiro, 50
Tökes, Laszlo, 133
Tokyo War Trials, 26, 111
Tormey, Simon, 18
totalitarianism, vii, 1, 8, 29n. 1, 29n. 5,
    155, 165, 203,
trauma, 1, 10, 12–15, 25, 70, 79, 85
trial, 70, 150, 151; of Ceaușescus, 2,
    26–27, 134–135, 137; of Mussolini,
    25, 47, 49, 53; Nuremberg Trials, 26,
    84; Tokyo War Trials, 26, 111